The Name of God in

One of the most powerful traditions of the Jewish fascination with language is that of the Name. Indeed, the Jewish mystical tradition would seem a two millennia long meditation on the nature of name in relation to object, and how name mediates between subject and object. Even within the tide of the twentieth century's linguistic turn, the aspect most notable in – the almost entirely secular – Jewish philosophers is that of the personal name, here given pivotal importance in the articulation of human relationships and dialogue.

The Name of God in Jewish Thought examines the texts of Judaism pertaining to the Name of God, offering a philosophical analysis of these as a means of understanding the metaphysical role of the name generally, in terms of its relationship with identity. The book begins with the formation of rabbinic Judaism in Late Antiquity, travelling through the development of the motif into the Medieval Kabbalah, where the Name reaches its grandest and most systematic statement – and the one which has most helped to form the ideas of Jewish philosophers in the twentieth and twenty-first centuries. This investigation will highlight certain metaphysical ideas which have developed within Judaism from the Biblical sources, and which present a direct challenge to the paradigms of western philosophy. Thus a grander subtext is a criticism of the Greek metaphysics of being which the west has inherited, and which Jewish philosophers often subject to challenges of varying subtlety; it is these philosophers who often place a peculiar emphasis on the personal name, and this emphasis depends on the historical influence of the Jewish metaphysical tradition of the Name of God.

Providing a comprehensive description of historical aspects of Jewish Name-Theology, this book also offers new ways of thinking about subjectivity and ontology through its original approach to the nature of the Name, combining philosophy with text-critical analysis. As such, it is an essential resource for students and scholars of Jewish Studies, Philosophy and Religion.

Michael T. Miller is a researcher in Jewish mysticism and modern philosophy, with a focus on Jewish thought from the Second Temple period to the medieval Kabbalah. His philosophical interests cover modern Jewish philosophy as well as philosophy of language and metaphysics.

Routledge Jewish studies series
Series Editor:
Oliver Leaman
University of Kentucky

Studies, which are interpreted to cover the disciplines of history, sociology, anthropology, culture, politics, philosophy, theology, religion, as they relate to Jewish affairs. The remit includes texts which have as their primary focus issues, ideas, personalities and events of relevance to Jews, Jewish life and the concepts which have characterised Jewish culture both in the past and today. The series is interested in receiving appropriate scripts or proposals.

The Name of God in Jewish Thought

A philosophical analysis of mystical traditions from apocalyptic to Kabbalah

Michael T. Miller

Routledge
Taylor & Francis Group

LONDON AND NEW YORK

First published 2016
by Routledge

2 Park Square, Milton Park, Abingdon, Oxfordshire OX14 4RN
52 Vanderbilt Avenue, New York, NY 10017

Routledge is an imprint of the Taylor & Francis Group, an informa business

First issued in paperback 2019

British Library Cataloguing-in-Publication Data
A catalogue record for this book is available from the British Library

Library of Congress Cataloging-in-Publication Data
Miller, Michael T., author.
The name of God in Jewish thought: a philosophical analysis of mystical
traditions from apocalyptic to Kabbalah / Michael T. Miller.
    pages cm
    1. God (Judaism)–Name. 2. Rabbinical literature–History and criticism.
    I. Title.
    BM610.M57 2015
    296.3'112–dc23   2015016774

ISBN: 978-1-138-94405-3 (hbk)
ISBN: 978-0-367-87390-5 (pbk)

Typeset in Times New Roman
by Wearset Ltd, Boldon, Tyne and Wear

For one who understands, and so will understand.

Contents

Acknowledgements

This study has been several years in the making and many people have helped me along the way. First I will extend my warm gratitude and respect to Agata Bielik-Robson who provided excellent guidance and friendship, even in the difficult circumstances of living in two countries at once. The same is true of Holger Zellentin, whose expertise in Late Antiquity, positivity and enthusiasm have been enormously beneficial. I would also like to extend thanks to Oliver Leaman and all at Routledge for their support and assistance, and to Philip Goodchild and Daniel Weiss for their insightful comments.

My parents have been a source of constant encouragement as well as emotional support. This project would not have happened without them in more ways than one, and I am eternally grateful for all they have done for me.

I have benefited from a close group of friends who have provided mutual support in often trying times. I am especially thankful for the company of Gökçen Yaşayan, Benjamin Hallatt, Kasia Nurzynska, and Nuno and Nela Jorge as well as Chris, Bernie, Sarah, Ian, King and other friends in Nottingham Theology Dept., at Nottingham Animal Rights, Mutante Cinephilia, the music scene regulars and older friends outside the city. Especially from the department I must extend a special thanks to Marton Ribary, who provided accommodation and company for me at the World Congress of Jewish Studies in Jerusalem 2013, and also to Mateusz and Magda who showed me around Warsaw earlier in the year. Likewise, Eshbal Ratzon very kindly gave me a place to stay in Tel Aviv prior to travelling to the Shalem Center in 2011. A special thanks is due to Andy Green, who proved formative in bringing me back to academia and encouraging the earliest phase of my research. Thanks are also due to Dylan Sebastian Evans for help with proof-reading. Finally, I am very grateful to Matthias Reidl and Katerina Kolozova for their consistent support for my work.

This project has benefited from the papers I heard and conversations I had at the World Congress as well as at the Shalem Center's *Philosophical Investigations of the Hebrew Scriptures, Talmud and Midrash* conference in 2011, the SBL International Meeting of 2013, and the British Association for Jewish Studies conference of 2012. Finally, I am indebted to Giulio Busi of the Institut für Judaistik at the Freie Universität Berlin for providing two relevant texts from The Kabbalistic Library of Giovanni Pico della Mirandola series for my research.

Abbreviations

Abbreviations for classical texts follow *The SBL Handbook of Style* (1999). In addition the following are used:

GE	*Ginat Egoz*
HekhR	*Hekhalot Rabbati*
HekhZ	*Hekhalot Zutarti*
MMarq	*Memar Marqah*
MMerk	*Ma'aseh Merkavah*
MerkR	*Merkavah Rabbah*
ShN	*Sha'are haNiqqud*
ShQ	*Shi'ur Qomah*
SN	*Sefer haNiqqud*
SO	*Sha'are Orah*
SY	*Sefer Yetzirah*

When phonetic transliteration is not possible, the following system will be used for Hebrew letters.

א	A	ל	L
ב	B	מ	M
ג	G	נ	N
ד	D	ע	O
ה	H	ס	S
ו	W	פ	P
ז	Z	צ	Tz
ח	Ch	ק	Q
ט	T	ר	R
י	Y	ש	Sh
כ	Kh	ת	Ṭ

Introduction

> For what is it with the name? An ethic of the name would still be conceivable –
> (one's given name). Even a logic of the name – (name of a thing). But a theology
> of the name? Even when otherwise a name is not sound and smoke, yet with God
> surely it is?
>
> (Rosenzweig, 1998, 43)[1]

It is possible to divide the Jewish fascination with language into three tradition
streams: the linguistic or verbal nature of Creation; the Torah as a linguistic
blueprint or paradigm for the world; and the Name of God.

In the first instance, God creates through language: he *speaks* the world into
existence – 'through ten utterances was the world created', as the common rabbinic edict has it. In the Bible language is never created – it appears already
present and ready for God to use in the process of creation. It is thus not merely
within the created world, but transcends it as part of the divine sphere.

In the second instance, the Torah is understood (already by the time of second
century BCE sage Ben Sira) as the blueprint for reality, or the pre-existent guide
to creation which God consults – here then, reality itself is merely an aspect of
the text which allows for its existence.

And in the third instance, the Name of God is the most holy aspect of existence, the single word which cannot be spoken and sometimes seems even to
replace God as the foundation of reality. This third stream indicates a broader
tradition within Judaism on the metaphysical nature of names which, in contrast
to the Greek tradition that western philosophy has inherited, claims that a name
somehow has an essential relationship to what it represents, going straight to the
heart of its object. These three traditions are not separate but are perpetually
interwoven, always interacting and often directly depending on each other.
However, the most powerful and on-going tradition is that of the Name. The traditions of Creation and Torah have often been emptied into the Name tradition,
by identifying the generative word spoken as God's own Name, or claiming the
Torah is a concealed list of divine names. Even within the tide of the twentieth
century's linguistic turn, the aspect most notable in – the almost entirely secular
– Jewish philosophers is that of the personal name, here given pivotal importance in the articulation of human relationships and dialogue. So, we find thinkers

such as Benjamin, Rosenzweig, Kripke, Levinas and Derrida all focussing substantial parts of their thought on the role of the name.

The Jewish mystical tradition, having always displayed a bold fascination with the Name of God, may in some sense be seen as a two millennia long meditation on the nature of name in relation to object, and how name mediates between subject and object. Therefore this investigation is intended to develop a deeper understanding of the native Jewish conception of naming as displayed (or catalysed) by the idea of the Name of God, and how names relate to objects – a relationship which may appear to have crucial importance for the nature of objects themselves, and the relationship between objects and subjects.

The subject matter of this study is to be the unique role of the personal Name YHWH, the Tetragrammaton, in relation to the Jewish divinity. While in ancient times, gods were usually named, being specific to their people or their function, Judaism is unique among the Abrahamic faiths in retaining this characteristic. Christianity and Islam have extensive collections of 'names' for God, but these are never more than titles; God Himself,[2] in Himself, is essentially nameless. Judaism alone has a personally named God. However, this study will not be an investigation of the meaning or etymology of the Jewish God's Name, YHWH. Neither is it a solely historical investigation of the use (either in magic or prayer situations) or traditions surrounding the Name. Rather, I propose a philosophical study of the Tetragrammaton as the personal Name of God and the implications that this has for the metaphysics of naming within Judaism. The Name of God forms the paradigm of all names, and structures the nature and role of names in language.

However, it is still the personal Name of God that concerns us here; not naming generally. It is how the specific theological conception of YHWH as the personal Name of God has evolved within rabbinic Judaism (and especially the Jewish mystical tradition) and what this means metaphysically in terms of identity, relation and being.

In the introduction to Agata Bielik-Robson's edited issue of the journal *Bad-midbar* titled 'Jewish Nominalism?', Bielik-Robson and Adam Lipszyc suggest that such a Jewish Nominalism may be 'an overall theoretical attitude, which privileges the singular name over the general concept' (2012, 7). In posing the question of Jewish Nominalism, Bielik-Robson locates the name in three areas – ontology, creation, and messianism – thereby suggesting that the name conditions Jewish conceptions of reality from beginning to end. This singularity may then reinscribe the apparently outmoded distinction between Jerusalem and Athens, evident in 'the opposition between singular names given to things by the Biblical Adam and the general ideas that are to be known by the Platonic philosopher.'

Thus, what this investigation hopes to achieve is not a comprehensive overview of the development of the nominal tradition within Judaism. Rather, it will provide an analysis of specific exemplary texts and traditions, in accordance with the metaphysical issues raised by twentieth century Jewish philosophers, in order to extract from these a rethinking of the metaphysics of naming. This will allow us to understand how even in the twentieth century, secular Jewish philosophers emphasised the fundamental nominal aspect of its ethical philosophy where human relationships are defined in terms of 'the name'. This study will therefore be not merely a historical overview but rather a metaphysical investigation which will expose a conceptual system that can be found when the tradition is analysed as a whole, a system which we can find expressed in a variety of forms throughout history. It is worth pointing out here that this system may not necessarily be one which was intended, or consciously held by the authors of, or authorities cited in, the texts under discussion. The temporal historical nature of the emergence of the metaphysics at the core of the Jewish nominal tradition are not the concern of this study, but rather the examination of the nature of that which can be extracted from the various texts when viewed as a single tradition. In this sense, the study is a continuation of the agenda and methods of the medieval mystics who interpreted their religious source texts in the light of contemporary philosophical concerns.

There have been two seminal texts on the Name of God in Jewish mysticism:[3] Scholem's 'The Name of God and the Linguistic Theory of the Kabbalah' (1972/1973) and Joseph Dan's 'The Name of God, the Name of the Rose, and the Concept of Language in Jewish Mysticism' (1996). While Scholem offers a detailed historical overview of the development of a name and language doctrine in Jewish mysticism, Dan offers a broad, speculative essay which locates Jewish thought alongside Christian and Muslim consideration on the Name.

Scholem claims that:

> The central standpoint [is] of the name of God as the metaphysical origin of all language, and the conception of language as the explanation – by dismantling – of this name, such as it appears principally in the documents relating to Revelation, but also in all language in general. The language of God, which is crystallised in the name of God and, in the last analysis, in the one single name itself, which is its center, is the basis of all spoken language, in which it is reflected and symbolically manifest.
>
> (1972, 63)

This, when combined with: 'The conception that creation and revelation are both principally and essentially auto-representations of God himself,' and 'the further conception that language is the essence of the universe,' forms the basis of Scholem's discussion. However, Scholem affirms the primacy of the Name in historical terms because: 'Even before speculation about language really got under way among the esotericists of Judaism, the name of God was central to their area of interest' (1972, 68).

Historically, Scholem finds the crux of Judaism's language mysticism with the conceptual unification of the creative 'word' of God with the Name of God which occurred at some point during Late Antiquity. This led to a significant conceptual shift where first, as the word becomes the Name, the previous bearer of information becomes now bearer of itself, in that God's speech expresses

Himself and his Name externalises what was previously only within God; and second, as the Name becomes Word it forms the essence of God's language and therefore the crucial mediating factor between God and humanity. Scholem further articulates an important distinction in the traditions where on the one hand God has a Name 'which is only known to God himself, a name which, as one might perhaps put it, expresses his self-awareness.' And on the other, God is formally nameless, because 'All names are [merely] condensations of the energy which radiates forth from him' (1973, 175).

Scholem covers the Hebrew Bible's interest in the word and the Name of God, and the implications of a linguistic creation. He argues this tradition transposed into a *nominal* creation at some point; from Psalm 33:6's: 'By the word of YHWH were the heavens made', via the 'glorified, honoured, sublime and almighty name, which made heaven and earth and all things together,' of Jubilees 36:7, into b.Berakhot 55a's 'letters from which heaven and earth were created.' This last he relates to Sefer Yetzirah, where the letters YHW 'are affixed to the creation and ... protect it from breaking asunder' (1972, 73). Progressing to the Kabbalah, Scholem cites the 'generally accepted kabbalistic doctrine' that the Torah 'as a whole, constitutes the one and only great name of God' (1972, 78). This doctrine, most famously articulated by Nachmanides (though present before him), 'signifies that, in the Torah, God has been able to express his transcendental being, or, anyway at least that part or aspect of his being which can be revealed in and through the Creation' (1972, 79). Although discussing Gikatilla only briefly, Scholem sees in his writings a clear articulation of the theology where the Name of God is present primarily in and as the Torah. That the Torah is 'the form of the mystical world' is dictated by the fact that the language of the Torah depends directly on its locus in the Name of God (1973, 180).

The kabbalistic sefirot are discussed in terms of their depiction as 'words' (*devarim*) or 'speech' (*dibburim*) of God. Scholem notes that, of course: 'In the Hebrew word *dawar* we find concealed the double meaning of thing, subject, and word, speech' (1973, 166). In the sefirot, 'the world of the pure name as the original element of the spoken word is opened up' (1973, 168). Abulafia's transformation of the Aristotelian Active Intellect and especially the fusing of this with a linguistic potency make a meditative procedure based around *tzeruf otiot*, the combination of letters, in order to attain oneness or a 'prophetic unison' with the Divine intellect (1973, 190).

Scholem finds in the writings of the thirteenth century mystic Iyyun Circle, the doctrine of two letters which stand as the 'two opening points for all linguistic movement': these are the letters *yod* and *aleph*. The *yod* as the smallest of all letters 'is precisely the original source of language, and it is from this source that all other forms are made'. The *aleph* meanwhile, with its dual role as the first of the alphabet and the smallest *phonetic* letter, 'is the laryngeal voice input of every vocal utterance, which was here understood to be the element from which ... every articulate sound originates, in the final analysis' (1973, 170). Scholem goes on to relate these two letters to a concealed Name of God, constructed of the four Hebrew vowel letters, *aleph, heh, vav* and *yod*. In this doctrine, then, the Tetragrammaton YHWH is something of a lower or corrupt name, 'no more than an emergency aid, behind which is hidden the true original name' (1973, 173).

His conclusion is worth quoting at length:

> The name of God is the 'essential name,' which is the original source of all language. Every other name by which God can be called or invoked, is coincident with a determined activity, as is shown by the etymology of such biblical names; only this one name requires no kind of backward-looking reference to an activity. For the kabbalists, this name has no 'meaning' in the traditional understanding of the term. It has no concrete signification. The meaninglessness of the name of God indicates its situation in the very central point of the revelation, at the basis of which it lies. [...] The fact that language can be spoken is, in the opinion of the Kabbalists, owed to the name, which is present in language. What the value and worth of language will be – the language from which God will have withdrawn – is the question which must be posed by those who still believe that they can hear the echo of the vanished word of the creation in the immanence of the world.
>
> (Scholem, 1973, 193–194)

Thus Scholem's investigation writes large across the Jewish mystical tradition the fundamental association of language and ontology. The names or 'words' of God are both the words belonging to God, which God uses, but also the words which are constitutive of God in His own manifestation to humanity.

Dan at the outset agrees with Scholem that: 'The concept of the divine name, its meanings and powers, cannot be separated from the concept of the divine language' (1996, 228). However, while Scholem drew the distinction between God's secret Name and God's ultimate namelessness, Dan argues that it is the first of these, taken to its logical conclusion where the Name is indistinguishable from God Himself, which is definitively Jewish – the latter in fact typifies Greek, which is to say Christian, theological thought:

> In the [Jewish] concept of the holy name of God, language stops being a means and becomes an independent divine essence, in which language and divinity are united. The holy name of God is not an expression of the divine: it is the essence of divinity itself. It is not revelation, it is the Revealer. It is not the instrument of creation, but the Creator. This is the culmination of the process which began with the appearance of the concept of scriptures: God has become a linguistic entity, His essence incorporated within a linguistic phenomenon.
>
> (Dan, 1996, 229)

Furthermore, Dan identifies a crucial aspect of the nominal tradition when he states that 'the sanctity of the name in the mysticisms of the scriptural religions is derived from the fact that a name, in essence, is that part of language in which the semantic level is minimal or non-existent' (1996, 232). Dan's argument is that the semantic and the nominal are mutually exclusive – a name cannot communicate, it must only point:

> [W]e can define a sacred name of God as that linguistic expression of the divine which is not communicative, it just is, representing in a linguistic form the inexpressible essence of God Himself. Such a concept represents the belief that God not only inspired scriptures and communicated His truth and wisdom to man, but that He Himself actually exists in the scriptures, in those phrases which are non-communicative and essentially meaningless – אלהים, שדי, צבאות, אדני, יהוה, and all the others. They do not have any literal meaning (although, throughout history, they accumulated hundreds and thousands of interpretations). They do not convey, inform, or describe, they are the essence of God.
>
> (1996, 237)

For Dan, the mystic is persistent in her disapproval of language – which appears a mere system of signs, improbably hoping to approach divine truth.[4] The Name then must be something outside of, and untrammelled by, the linguistic structure which is contingent, finite, and human-focussed. This prompts, for the mystically inclined, the identification of the Name as the essence of divinity itself.

Thus Dan presents the philosophy of the Name as one which combines the fundamental identity of the Name as God with the ultimate meaninglessness of the Name. The Name cannot communicate because it is not different from the essence of the divine; it could signify nothing other than itself.

Apart from these two articles, three other texts provide an important base for the present investigation. The first is Jarl Fossum's seminal *The Name of God and the Angel of the Lord* (1985) which examined Samaritan and Jewish traditions regarding a personified angelic being who is often identified with the Name of God, as background to the emergence of Gnostic theology. While not a philosophical text, Fossum's has to a large degree formed the current scholarly consensus on the significance and role of the Tetragrammaton during Late Antiquity, and his arguments will inform the starting point of two chapters herein. Marshalling a huge body of evidence from the period, Fossum argues that the Name took on an ontological status in the Late Antique period, as either a personified hypostatic being, or a power which can be bestowed upon a created entity. Thus while the Name was 'an instrument used by God when he was engaged in the creation of the world', there was also 'a tradition according to which it was a hypostasis' (Fossum, 1985, 254).

Because Fossum's principle aim is to find a source for Gnostic 'demiurge' theology, his focus on the Name of God emphasises those texts and traditions which appear to provide for a binitarian or Two Powers interpretation. The hypostatic aspect of the Name is highlighted throughout Samaritan texts such as Memar Marqah and the liturgy, early Christian material, Second Temple Jewish texts of the pseudepigrapha and apocrypha, and rabbinic literature from the Talmud to Sefer Yetzirah. Fossum concludes that within Hebrew monotheism in Late Antiquity, the belief in an angelic hypostasis 'as the creator and ruler of the universe' converged with the 'well established philosophical tradition' of a demiurgic power as distinct from, yet complementary to, God (1985, 333). However:

> The idea of the distinction and yet intimate association between God and the second power was in Judaism and Samaritanism expressed through the identification of the latter as the Angel of the Lord, who shared God's own 'Name', i.e., nature or mode of being.
>
> (Fossum, 1985, 333)

At the opposite pole, a recently published study by Noah Horwitz, *Reality in the Name of God* (2012) has offered an insightful and original philosophical exploration of some kabbalistic ideas. This text examines some theological principles according to Badiou's reading of Cantorian set theory, offering a defence of a traditional monotheistic understanding of God as infinite and as creator. The Name of God is touched on explicitly only in a few passages (despite the book's title), however Horwitz succeeds in developing a detailed philosophical account of the significance of the Name.

The text is, as mentioned, principally philosophical – while offering a deep and clear-sighted analysis of the theological problems presented by modern thinkers such as Heidegger and Levinas, Horwitz's use of Kabbalah is limited to Scholem's essay, a few introductory texts, and popular translations of kabbalistic works. His reading of Kabbalah is notably without nuance, conflating doctrines several hundred years apart without historical grounding, and smudging complex doctrinal issues by merging sources as diverse as Isaac Luria and Sefer Yetzirah into a single body of doctrine. Often his references to Kabbalah are utilised in simple quotes which apparently confirm what he has already sought to demonstrate philosophically. Jewish thought is clearly secondary to the philosophical analysis which constitutes Horwitz's real interest – this is not a problem, but it does indicate the precise agenda of his text.

That said, his analysis is insightful and his use of Cantor is particularly interesting. Taking Badiou's assertion that 'mathematics is ontology' alongside Sefer Yetzirah's promotion of the number system to the principle of creation, Horwitz focuses his analysis on Set Theory, Cantor's system which redefined the way maths and number are thought about. In Badiou's analysis, Set Theory becomes the notion that every *thing* is a unity composed of multiplicity. To have being, something must always be 'counted as one'. This includes even the Empty Set – the numerical zero which is defined as a set containing nothing at all. According to Badiou and Horwitz's reading, this means that nothingness itself has been given being by its presentation in the Empty Set. Because the Empty Set is the foundation of the number system, other numbers being expressed as sets which contain the empty set (so that 1 is the set containing one member, just the Empty

Set, 2 is the set containing two members – 1 and 0, etc.), all numbers are complex articulations of nothingness. The only thing holding them together and giving them being, is their collection into sets – i.e., being *named* as a unified whole. Zero itself, the Empty Set, enters being only as such a name. Therefore:

> Every being is a set, named and numbered. Being qua being always occurs as counted as one. But to be counted means anything that is already named and numbered. And this means that being consists of names and numbers at its most fundamental level.
>
> (Horwitz, 2012, 91)

By his use of Set Theory then, Horwitz argues that being itself is conditioned by names; to be means to have been given a name.

This is all important work in the field of ontology, and the conclusions are ones which this investigation will largely support. However, the problems begin when Horwitz attempts to incorporate *God*'s Name into the theory. While he asserts that God cannot be identified with the Void, the nothing which is presented via the Empty Set: 'The name of the void is the Name of God' (2012, 128). When noting that Badiou names the void ø, Horwitz claims that this sign is meaningless, while also claiming that it graphically represents the zero and 'the barring of sense' (ibid.).[5] Finding a point of correlation between the Void and God in their transcendence of being, Horwitz argues that although they are not identical, their name is shared: 'The empty set instantiates the void and thereby forms the Name of God. The Name of God is the mark of the void. But through creation it will become the primary name of Being itself, its subsistence and matter' (2012, 131). Each is present to the world 'only in and by its Name' (2012, 129). This confusion of the void and its name is intentional: Horwitz attempts to identify the void with its own name, reasoning that: 'The void would no longer be if its name [merely] belonged to it' (ibid.). However, 'the name of the void can be included in the void, which amounts to saying that, in the situation, it equals to the void, since the unpresentable is solely presented by its name' (ibid.). This is expanded upon and supported for Horwitz, by an identification of the void/Name with the process of *tzimtzum* (2012, 140–157). God then stands as something behind the void, behind nothingness, which creates this nothingness in an act of withdrawal which is identical with the act of naming it as the Empty Set, creating a place absent of God. And from this named absence, all else comes. The Name of God then is something fundamentally separate from God, the trace (*reshimu*) of God left after His withdrawal.

From here, Horwitz enters an examination of information theory, reasoning that the cosmos' source in the Name (and especially the initial *yod*) which is identifiable as ø, means that reality is a linguistic-information system based around the alternation of 0 and 1, nothing and being. In concluding, he presents a picture of the world unified in God's Name, as a single intellect which is effectively computational; a procedure which sees all the names used of God by human beings reunified into a single name, as indicated by the oft-quoted passage of Zechariah: 'God will be King over all the world—on that day, God will be one and his name will be one' (14:9).

This use of the name of the void as the Name of God clearly has no basis in Jewish thought, and the Name given throughout Judaism's history, YHWH, is all but ignored, despite its on-going central importance for the kabbalists.

As such, Horwitz provides a detailed philosophical investigation of ontology which uses Jewish mystical speculation as a foil to prove the theological conclusions he wishes to draw. The arguments are often poorly constructed, despite their insight. Most importantly, the principle that the Name must be semantically meaningless, a claim found also in Scholem and Dan, Horwitz provides no philosophical *or* theological basis for; it is asserted with an appeal to negative theology and the sentence: 'God can be named and conceived only in the very same instant such naming is necessarily overturned' (2012, 114) but not explained; neither is any reference made to where this might be found in the kabbalistic tradition.

Bielik-Robson has, for some time, been pursuing the idea of a 'Jewish Nominalism'. Having coined the phrase, her edited volume of *Bamidbar* then presented her own ideas about the nominal philosophy unique to Jewish thinkers. It represents, in her words, 'a "true concretion" of a material singularity which could not thrive philosophically in the tradition of Western idealism and its "icy wasteland of abstraction"' (2014, 233). Placing Jewish Nominalism in contrast to the philosophical (indeed, western) tendency to reduce everything to other, simpler things, slicing all objects into their component parts, Bielik-Robson argues that the former 'all conceive the world as comprised ultimately of singularities, [yet] they do not treat names as mere *flatus voci*, i.e. arbitrary conventions which express our cognitive helplessness in face of the material chaos of things' (ibid.). Naming, then, 'opens the gate to a special relationship with reality' (ibid.). Interpreting Scholem's claim that 'God's language has no grammar' (1995, 293), Bielik-Robson concludes that at the heart of this is the absence of metaphysical mediation between God and creature: the direct relationship of creator to creation is a rejection of emanatory cosmology.

Arguing that Christian and Jewish nominalisms represent 'alternative epistemologies of the name' (2012, 17), one negative and one positive, Bielik-Robson posits the metaphysical ground of Christian nominalism in Neoplatonism and the ontological dependence of all beings on their participation in the divine. Jewish nominalism, on the other hand, 'is based on the idea of separation' (ibid.). Where the 'ontological multitude … cannot be ordered according to the modes and degrees of existence, because it exists in exactly the same way and manner as the God who created it' (2012, 17–18). So: 'Just as God is unique and singular [*echad*], bearing a distinct Name, so is his creation: equally separate, singularized, and free to express itself in the particularity of the name' (2012, 18). While the Christian nominalism ultimately fails because it places beings outside of the ordered hierarchy envisioned by a perfect language, the Jewish succeeds for the very same reason: by means of their names, beings gain an independence from the divine.

Implicit in this analysis is the association of negative (Christian-Neoplatonic) nominalism with idealism and its thoroughgoing subsumption of particulars under the general – citing anti-idealist tendencies of Rosenzweig, Benjamin and Wittgenstein, she avers that for them, 'the larger part of language is not about producing meanings but about fixing and continuing reference' (2012, 28). Thus in creating particulars 'by name', the Jewish tradition 'inaugurates a welcome emancipation of language from the tyranny of general concepts and ideas' (ibid.). This focus on 'ontologically liberated particulars' released *through* nominalism is one that Bielik-Robson finds throughout modern Jewish thought, from Spinoza to Herman Cohen, and the next generation of Rosenzweig, Scholem, Benjamin and Adorno. This rejection of totalising thought-patterns then affirms the statement of Scholem that divine language 'consists only of names' (1995, 293). Finally, the Name of God is 'the paradigmatic case of naming' (2012, 29) because I Am That I Am 'does not reveal the divine essence' but is 'a *pure name* where no auxiliary description is involved, no compromise with the order of conceptuality' (ibid.).

These five texts together provide significant grounds for an examination of the texts of Judaism in terms of the Name of God as a metaphysical concept. What we do not have so far is a philosophically grounded investigation of the sources of 'Jewish nominalism', one which reviews the historical evidence in order to provide a comprehensive picture of the metaphysics which underlies such nominalism, and therefore the unstated assumptions which pass beneath the textual radar and yet are still present within the world-views of Jewish thinkers in the twentieth and twenty-first centuries. This, I hope, is what this study will provide.

The Name of God in the Hebrew Bible and Second Temple period

I have mentioned that this study is not concerned with the historical aspects of the Name YHWH's usage, its provenance, or its meaning. However, in order to set the scene it is necessary to review what we know about the origin, meaning and significance of the name which is the Name. This historical introduction will establish some of the trends which influenced Jewish theology in Late Antiquity, and the scholarly debates which inform this study. Examining this in some detail will provide context for the developments which occur later as well as helping to demonstrate how much of the apparently modern concerns are in fact a part of ancient and biblical theology as well.

Famously, there are a great number of names and titles by which God is addressed in the Hebrew Bible. He is known variously as Adonai, Shaddai, El, Elohim, YHWH and YHWH Tzvaot. Of these, YHWH is the most common, occurring 6,828 times in the Tanakh. The name appears to have come into use during the time in which Moses may have lived (Mettinger, 1988, 21). The original pronunciation was likely 'something like' Yahweh, which over time became shortened to Iao in less formal (i.e. non-Temple) contexts (McDonough, 1999, 116–122). Debate is on-going about its meaning, although it is generally held to come from the root HYH, 'to be,' though this association with existence could be interpreted in several different ways. McDonough (1999, 31) gives 'the two most likely explanations of the Name YHWH: "He is" and "He causes to be"',[6] and *Encyclopaedia Judaica* states that:

> Like many other Hebrew names in the Bible, the name Yahweh is no doubt a shortened form of what was originally a longer name. It has been suggested that the original, full form of the name was something like *Yahweh-Asher-Yihweh*, 'He brings into existence whatever exists' or *Yahweh Ẓeva'ot* (1Sam.1:3, 11), which really means 'He brings the hosts [of heaven – or of Israel?] into existence'.
>
> (*Encyclopaedia Judaica*, 2007, 675)

The story of God's appearance to Moses in the burning bush is, of course, the supposedly crucial revelation of God's name; yet it is not YHWH that is given here. Rather, God names himself as Ehyeh Asher Ehyeh: a phrase difficult to interpret, but which would literally mean 'I will be what I will be'.[7] However, the scholarly consensus is that the name revealed at Exodus 3:14 and the name YHWH are etymologically related. In fact, many scholars believe the Exodus revelation offers an explanation of the name YHWH.[8] Mettinger (1988, 30) argues that it presents a first person conjugation, God's name for Himself: 'I am...' which Moses then switches to the third person, 'He is,' being YHWH. Thus the two crucial – and personal – names of God are semantically related.

Mettinger (1988, 33–36) gives three possible interpretations of God's self-declaration: 'I am who I am', an evasive form which is evidenced in a similar grammatical construction at other places (e.g. Exod.4:13, 1Sam.23:13, 2Ki.8:1); 'I am the one who is', the philosophically inclined meaning which we find given during the Hellenistic era in the LXX, emphasising the existence of God; and '*I Am* is who I am' or, 'my name is *I Am*, because I am'. This last, favoured by Mettinger, provides for the interesting notion of the identity of name and essence – here the name I Am describes God's ultimate nature. It is notable that the LXX takes the second meaning, although no quick conclusions can be reached from this due to the influence of philosophical models of thinking during this time and most especially among those educated in the Greek language. Some arguments have been made that a more proper Hebrew construction of this meaning would be *ani hu asher ehyeh*, though this would clearly lack the poetic quality that the extant formulation holds. It may well be that both or all three are implied within the Biblical text – given that we are unaware of how the passage was formed, we would be wise to take all the possible variations into account, especially as since that initial formulation every single reader has had to make up their own mind about it, including those readers involved in transmitting and rewriting the texts. However, it is worth bearing in mind the argument that Hebrew (language and thought) does not articulate the kind of metaphysics which we have inherited from Greece – as Thorlieff Boman (1960) has cogently argued, Hebrew is rather a language of action and relation (as opposed to the staticity of Greek, and temporal rather than Greek's spatial preference). As such, existence as an onto-logical category, which the second interpretation depends on, appears not to be a concept native to the language.

In support of this we may note that Mettinger (1988, 38) relates some findings in Ebla (northern Syria) where the verb 'to be' is used in some personal names. In these cases: 'They do not refer to the existence of the God in question versus his nonexistence; instead they point to the way the god in question "was present [and helped]", for example, by means of the birth of the child'. Mettinger posits that we may find here a reason to amend the divine 'He is' to 'He is [here and is now helping]'. He concludes that:

> At the oldest stage of the tradition, it is likely that one heard in the 'He Is' of the divine Name an assurance of God's active and aiding presence ... Thus the theological content of the divine Name comes surprisingly close to the divine promise that is so frequently uttered in the patriarchal narratives: 'I shall be with you.'
>
> (1988, 42)

This notion, of not existence but presence encoded in the Divine Name, is one that will have substantial import for the present study, and it is worth noting that it is precisely the conclusion that Rosenzweig reached regarding his attempt to translate the Name; for him the 'most important point' is 'the resonating "with you"' (Galli, 1994, 76).

We are wise anyway to note that the initial meaning of the names of God are only of a restricted importance; more relevant for us are the subsequent develop-ments in interpretation, and how these have affected the common understanding of divine nature, divine presence, and the Name's role in mediating these. While the intention behind the text remains necessarily opaque to us, we are able to observe clearly how the possible interpretations of the text have evolved and influenced the ideas of later generations of thinkers.

There are two important precedents for the importance of the Divine Name within the Torah, both of which are important for this study. First, there are fre-quent appearances of 'the angel of YHWH', an angelic being who appears as a kind of hypostatic presence of God, and who bears the Name – this is implicit through his title, but its import is made explicit in Exodus 23:20–21:

> I am going to send an angel in front of you, to guard you on the way and to bring you to the place that I have prepared. Be attentive to him and listen to his voice; do not rebel against him, for he will not pardon your transgres-sion; for my name is in him.

On the nature of this Name Angel, Elliot Wolfson writes,

> The line separating the angel and God is substantially blurred, for by bearing the name, which signifies the power of the divine nature, the angel is the

embodiment of God's personality. To possess the name is not merely to be invested with divine authority; it means that ontologically the angel is the incarnational presence of the divine manifest in the providential care over Israel.

(2000, 244)

Benjamin Sommer meanwhile, writes that in these cases, '*shem* functions ... both as a synonym for God and as a hypostasis or emanation of God that is not quite a separate deity' (2009, 59).

Second, yet more famously, Deuteronomy presents a picture of a God who is actually distinguished from his Name, which appears to be a hypostatic element present on earth, localised in the Temple. God is in heaven (4:36, 26:36), but the Name is in the temple (12:5, 11; 14:23; 16:11, etc.). In his formative work, *The Deuteronomic Name Theology* (1969), S. Dean McBride argued that the localisation of the Name was intended as a polemic to centralise the worship of YHWH, by arguing that He was *only* present through His Name as it was used in the Temple.

The notion that the Deuteronomistic reform represented a paradigm shift in Israelite theology, from a wholly immanent and anthropomorphic God to one abstract and transcendent, whose Name goes proxy in the world, has been popular in scholarly circles throughout most of the twentieth century.[9] In the last decade this view was challenged by Sandra Richter whose linguistic analysis appears to show that: 'The traditional rendering of the Deuteronomic formula as "the place in which YHWH your God will choose to cause his name to dwell" represents a substantial mistranslation of the phrase' (2002, 37). She concludes it is much more mundane, a Mesopotamian loan-idiom, 'having to do with the making and installation of inscriptions, and having transitive meaning' (2002, 216). Thus it would refer to the place where the Name was used by human beings.

Sommer rejects Richter's hypothesis, arguing that the Deuteronomic Name-Theology is in fact a polemic against both divine immanence and divine fragmentation. In this reading, the *shem* is not part of God but only a sign – God resides solely and totally in heaven, not on earth: 'So insistently do deuteronomic traditions maintain that God is not on earth that it becomes clear that for them the *shem* is only a sign of divine presence, not a manifestation of God Himself' (Sommer, 2009, 62). Solomon's speech in 1 Kings 8:14–66 presents the *shem* as 'a token of divine attention', an extension of God *into where He is not*; because God is not on earth, it is only through His Name that humans can approach Him.

According to the deuteronomic Name theology, then, the *shem* is not God, it is not a part of God, and it is not an extension of God. The *shem* is merely a name in the sense that Western thinkers regard names: a symbol, a verbal indicator that points toward something outside itself.

(Sommer, 2009, 65)

This, of course, indicates that there must have been precisely such a view (that YHWH could be immanent in location, and also locally fragmented) present in Israel for the deuteronomist to repeal. Sommer shows that this is precisely the case, with some eighth century BCE texts which refer separately to 'YHWH of Samaria' and 'YHWH of Teman' (2009, 39). This multiple embodiment of a single deity appears to be achieved through the *shem*, the name which can be utilised by different groups of people at different places and times. The deuteronomists thus are redefining the use of the term *shem* in order to deflate it from its existing hypostatic associations. Sommer argues that the *Shema* of Deuteronomy 6:4 is an argument against the kind of fragmentation we have seen with other ANE deities:

> Why does this verse use the tetragrammaton, a personal name, rather than stating what we might have expected – that there is one God? The answer lies in part in the tendency of ancient Near Eastern deities (including Yhwh...) to fragment into semi-independent geographic manifestations. Yhwh, we are told, is simply Yhwh.... Further, even the *shem* is not multiple.
>
> (2009, 67)

Not multiple, for it is only in the single Temple that the *shem* will be.

Michael Hundley (2009) has provided an alternative response to Richter's criticisms, putting the Deuteronomic use in the context of the broader ANE. He argues that in the ANE and Hebrew Bible, the Name acts to represent presence, while leaving the precise nature and question of how God is present ambiguous. In fact, in Deuteronomy the significant development precisely is its obtuseness, because the Name represents God's practical presence with his people, while shrouding the nature of this presence – and the nature of God – in mystery.

In summation, we can quote McBride, who began his study of Deuteronomy with the assertion that:

> [Š]ēm in the various formulations of Name Theology connoted a mode of divine immanence at least in part distinct from God himself ... the divine 'name' acted as an extension of God, establishing a link between his transcendent being and those who sought him in worship.
>
> (1969, 3)

Or, in the words of Exodus 20:21: 'In every place where I cause my name to be mentioned I will come to you and bless you'.

The last three decades have seen an increasing emphasis on the complex developments in belief which Judaism underwent after the biblical period and prior to the emergence of rabbinic thought.[10] Several key texts have helped to establish a general consensus on the presence of some kind of angelic vice-regency, hypostatic power or binitarian theology during the late Second Temple period. Robert Hayward's *Divine Name and Presence: The Memra* (1981) examined the targumic Memra as an articulation of the Name of God; Alan Segal's *Two Powers in Heaven* (1977) demonstrated that the Talmudic reports on the Two Powers heresy were in response to internal Jewish theological debate; Jarl Fossum's aforementioned *The Name of God and The Angel of the Lord* (1985) attested to the presence of a hypostatic Name-Angel during Second Temple times; and Larry Hurtado's *One God, One Lord* (1998) investigated several kinds of personified 'Divine Agents' as precursors to Christianity, including the 'divine attributes' of Logos and Memra, 'exalted patriarchs' such as Enoch and Moses, and of course 'principal angels' such as Michael.[11] These studies have served to demonstrate the abundance of hypostatic or virtual-binitarian imagery in late Second Temple Jewish sources.

This has been a focal point for Daniel Boyarin's recent work (2004). Focussing on the drawn-out process of differentiation between Christianity and rabbinic Judaism, his argument is that the two faiths only emerged as distinct communities with clearly-defined independent doctrines through a gradual process of boundary-drawing, and up until the fourth century there were almost no clear boundaries in place. So, we find that the roughly binitarian-hypostatic theological trend continues within what we think of as the Jewish tradition for a surprisingly long time, and 'in these early centuries there were non-Christian Jews who believed in God's Word, Wisdom, or even Son as a "second God,"' (Boyarin, 2004, 90) a second God referred to variously as 'Logos, Memra, Sophia, Metatron, or Yahoel' (Boyarin, 2004, 92).

According to this reading, the idea that any text or tradition within this milieu could be categorised as either Christian or Jewish is an error. Christianity, from its outset, drew on internal Jewish ideas and, as a movement within Judaism, influenced Jewish thought such that what was once conceived as the bleeding of the edges is better understood as a vast penumbra without partition lasting several centuries, right up until the isolation of the two was unanimous. Indeed even after this, influence still passed between them. The idea of a divine intermediator was a powerful, though far from monolithic, motif in Second Temple Judaism – and the notion that the Christian use of this formed a dogmatic rupture within a pre-existing Jewish orthodoxy is based on an anachronistic interpretation of subsequent developments. Prior to the completion of the Talmud and the solidification of rabbinic power, the diaspora – who continued to practise Judaism without the guidance of an external authority – could rely only on their collective memories of what Judaism was, thus heightening their susceptibility to the ambient influences of their pagan and Christian neighbours.[12]

That this hypostatic 'heavenly man' was identified with God's Name has been tacitly supported by three articles in the last decade: Charles Gieschen's 'The Divine Name in Ante-Nicene Christology' (2003) examines early Christian traditions, concluding that in several New Testament and Gnostic documents Jesus has or *is* the Name of God; Steven Scott's 'The Binitarian Nature of the Book of Similitudes' (2008) argues for a binitarian reading of this Enochic text[13] based around the distinction between the Lord of Spirits and His Name; and finally Robert Hall's aforementioned 'Pre-existence, Naming, and Investiture in the

Similitudes of Enoch and in Hebrews' (2011) offers an interesting – and important – reading of Enoch's investiture with the name 'Son of Man,' where his assumption of a new, messianic, nature is dependent upon his taking of the title.

We can conclude that the Second Temple period saw a development of the Biblical Name-theology, where the Name is no longer present *in* the Temple or an angel, but is on the way to becoming a personified hypostatic entity, synonymous with God's presence on earth and ultimately – in Christianity – with the Messiah.

The structure of this text

While the primary aims of this study are philosophical and theological, the ground from which this work must grow is that of textual tradition: texts and traditions which themselves have emerged from a localised historical context. Therefore the investigation will be structured in terms of specific historical and conceptual periods, so that each idea and its contribution to the whole may be given a thorough and realistic examination. The study can then be thought of as falling into several different divisions: first, there is the historical-philosophical axis, which guides individual chapters. Each chapter is given as a description of a group of texts, their theology, and the relevant scholarly debates, followed by the analysis of these texts in terms given to us by one or more modern philosophical thinkers. Although I have chosen to highlight the presence of each theme within a specific historic and cultural milieu, it is evident that each idea has been present across different times and in different contexts. Thus, I refer also to the evolution and development of each theme, while concentrating on the single most solid and thoroughly worked-through manifestation of it. In each chapter the textual data will be examined, with reference to modern scholarship, and an analysis offered which utilises modern and contemporary philosophical work in order to attempt to uncover the (often quite obscure) metaphysical principles which lie beneath the traditions.

The application of philosophical agenda to textual analysis is uncommon, but not without precedent: it is a tradition begun by Scholem (in concert, to an extent, with Benjamin, although the two stand at opposite poles of the issue – Scholem presenting a basically historical analysis with speculative overtones, Benjamin attempting a philosophical project which occasionally referenced historical material). Scholem's method of interpreting the Kabbalah principally through a philosophical rather than strictly historical method, has been continued by Moshe Idel and Elliot Wolfson, who have often sought a philosophical analysis of Jewish traditions while maintaining a historically realist approach to the texts, taking them in the context in which they were written. One of the precepts of this approach is that philosophy cannot happen in a vacuum, but is always contextualised: historical facts, in this case existing in texts preserved from centuries past, provide the solid ground from which speculation can emerge.

Second, there is the Late Antique-Medieval axis, which separates the earlier formative texts from the fully-realised expressions of the same motifs in the early Kabbalah (and its heirs). In the Late Antique period, rabbinic Judaism was taking shape and forming its ideology from the Biblical sources and traditions it inherited, often in dialogue with its younger sibling Christianity. This was a time of both crisis and reformation, due to the destruction of the Temple and the loss of Jerusalem, while the emerging rabbinate gained power and influence with their new vision of Jewish spirituality. In the Medieval period, once the Rabbinate had established their authority and their canon, speculative thinkers were emerging who were synthesizing this canon with other ideas both new and old, organically creating new ways of thinking Judaism and its theology.

Finally, there is a smaller grouping, of chapters in pairs: the first two describing what Jewish Name Theology is not, the ideas that were early on rejected by the emerging orthodoxy; the second two describing what rabbinic Judaism establishes positively during the Common Era in terms of Name Theology; the third pair deal with the beginnings of kabbalistic speculation on the Name; and the sole seventh chapter the full realisation of the Name Theology in messianic form. It is worth highlighting at this point that while the initial chapters are highly historical in nature, though with philosophical analysis and conclusions, this ratio is one which shifts as the study progresses so that the final chapter is entirely metaphysical in nature, a methodological structure which itself reflects the intention and conclusions herein. The literal-historical, while necessary to both the development and comprehension of the metaphysical conclusions, itself fades from view, ultimately to be discarded as these are identified.

It has been argued that traces of a creation doctrine involving the Name YHWH can be found in some extra-canonical and rabbinic texts, pointing to a long-standing tradition regarding the role of the Name in creation which persisted from Second Temple times. Chapter 1 will offer a new analysis of this theory and the texts on which it is based in order to disentangle the facts and discover what may stand at the heart of the notion of 'sealing with the Name' – a concept which implies the role of the name in forming identity and difference. This will be highlighted and interpreted in terms of Rosenzweig's work on the role of language in regard to manifestation and transcendence, and the utility of logic versus human language's inability to describe the being of otherness.

Chapter 2 will analyse the emergence in the late Second Temple period of the hypostatised Name, personified as an independent being, which, while finding its definitive expression in early Christian writings, is also present in several other textual groups. The common theme throughout all these areas is that the Name (the Tetragrammaton YHWH in Hebrew, or *Kyrios* in Greek) is a virtual second God, the 'firstborn' and handmaid to creation, but also that aspect of God which is present in the world and allows for human-divine relationship. This quite blunt ontological reading of nominalism however has some stark consequences for theology. Derrida's philosophical musing on apophatic theology will be used to demonstrate why this strand was ultimately rejected by the emerging Rabbinate.

As the body of rabbinic Jewish thought solidified during the centuries of the Common Era, the angel Metatron, 'whose name is like his Master's,' steadily gained prominence and although much work has been done speculating on his emergence from the available sources, the assumption remains that Metatron is a second person, who may or may not be within the godhead. Chapter 3 will argue that there is much at stake in this reading, and while the academic opinion has usually been that the three Metatron passages in the Talmud represent something of a damage-limitation exercise, using the established figure of Metatron in order to argue against the 'heretical' theological positions of Christianity, Gnosticism and even the Hekhalot literature, the texts may present a significantly more complex picture than this. With a close textual analysis of the manuscript traditions, and the interpretive system of Husserl, this chapter argues for a substantially more sophisticated theological position whereby the three passages use Metatron to demonstrate an epistemological – or *intentional* – principle central to the naming of God.

Standing between the rabbinic and non-rabbinic forms of Judaism is the literature of the Merkavah mystics. Chapter 4 will pursue the developments present in the Hekhalot literature as it persistently blurs the boundaries of the divine and created, with an amorphous flurry of angelic and heavenly beings, many of which bear the Name of God.[14] Angelic beings such as Metatron, Akatriel and Anafiel seem to form a heavenly retinue where the identity of God is fragmented into several distinct potencies. Scholars have stared aghast at the virtual polytheism of these texts and their vitiating of distinct entities. However, Saul Kripke's philosophy of naming allows for a new reading whereby the 'pleroma' is not one of variegated divine identities, but one constituted of names as subjective, relational aspects of the singular divinity.

Having established a textual and philosophical base in the rabbinic use of the Name, Chapters 5 to 7 will progress to an analysis of how these traditions were developed in kabbalistic thought. With these chapters we enter the far more speculative stage of the study. Having established a background of Late Antique thought, the following chapters will present a speculative attempt to rethink the Kabbalah in the terms of twentieth century Jewish philosophy. It is acknowledged that many modern Jewish philosophers found inspiration in the Kabbalah; from Derrida, whose entire ideology of Deconstruction may be traced back to a single quote mentioned by Gershom Scholem (Idel, 2010, 168–175), to Walter Benjamin, whose correspondence with Scholem appears to have deeply influenced the messianic and linguistic thought of them both. The three chapters in this section will focus less on text-critical matters, and more on the systematic thought of the writers, which succeed in weaving together all the previously examined threads into a single cohesive world-view. It may be useful here to offer a little in terms of theoretical basis for the investigation of the Kabbalah.

The prehistory of the Kabbalah is still a murky affair and much work remains to be done in discovering the sources and methods from which the kabbalists developed their doctrines. At this stage, it may be most convenient to describe the Kabbalah as a combination of Neoplatonic philosophy with the heritage of

Merkavah mysticism and Sefer Yetzirah in a highly speculative framework. Thus the diverse angelology of the Hekhalot texts is refined and honed down to blend neatly with the ten *middot* of Maimonidean rationalism and the ten sefirot of the Yetzirah, and the ineffable singularity of God in Neoplatonic-influenced theology of Maimonides is cast into a mythological drama whereby reality is emanated by a linguistic process from the supreme Godhead which transcends human thought.

From the earliest kabbalistic texts there is a consistent regard for the centrality of the Name. This is evidenced by Nachmanides' famous dictum that the Torah is constituted entirely of names of God, and as soon as a cursory glance is given to the early kabbalists we find that they discuss again and again the metaphysical role of the Name. It is especially evident in Isaac the Blind's commentary to Sefer Yetzirah, where, although it is not made the central topic of discussion, it is repeatedly mentioned, elaborated and alluded to. There is clearly a detailed and crucial doctrine of some kind behind the text. In fact, Abraham ibn Ezra quotes Isaac describing the mystics as 'those who meditate on His name', and in doing so 'cleave to Him' (Scholem 1987, 302), and his nephew R Asher ben David dedicated a section of his treatise *Sefer haYichud* to a commentary on the Divine Name. The fact that this tradition is not articulated as the central concern of any of the texts is not because it is not present but rather because it is so present as to be almost unworthy of being mentioned – or perhaps incapable of being articulated in any satisfactory way.

In fact, it is traditional to claim that the Kabbalah articulates into two distinct traditions – one linguistic, based on the knowledge of God via His names, and one theosophical, based on the knowledge of God via His presence in creation. This polarity of the nominal-linguistic and the sefirotic kabbalahs was first made by no less than Abraham Abulafia in the late 1280s. Chapters 5 and 6 will offer something of a rejection of this, demonstrating that the sefirotic presence of God is in fact fully integrated with the nominal.

There are three important themes which the second section will elaborate. First, the doctrine of the sefirot has, from the earliest, incorporated a central aspect of Maimonidean philosophy[15] regarding the scriptural 'names' of God, the potencies which emanate from the primal Name YHWH. Maimonides took the talmudic doctrine of the unerasable names of God[16] and blended it with the thought of Jewish philosophers.[17] For Maimonides the Tetragrammaton refers exclusively to the essential nature of God, whereas all the other titles used in scripture are derived from God's actions in the world and are thus descriptive, at least in the limited capacity that humans have to use them.[18] In a famous passage he writes that: 'It is well known that all the names of God occurring in scripture are derived from His actions, except one, namely, the Tetragrammaton' (1956, 1.61, 89). The Tetragrammaton itself is 'the distinct and exclusive designation of the Divine Being'[19] (ibid.). He claims that: 'The derivation of the name ... is not positively known, the word having no additional signification' (1956, 1.61, 90), and therefore it 'is the only name which indicates nothing but His essence' (1956, 1.61, 91). Because of this it 'undoubtedly denotes something which is

peculiar to God, and is not found in any other being' (ibid.). This lack of semantic meaning is clearly important – perhaps more important than the rationalist
Maimonides realised – we have seen already the bifurcation of sense and reference, of meaning and naming. As Michael Fagenblat reads Maimonides' doctrine, 'the Name designates the true reality of God because it empties the idea of
"God" of all semantic content' (2010, 136). Only in the absence of literal semantic meaning can God truly be referred to.

The Name in this sense, that which indicates God's essence and therefore His
primal unity, became for the kabbalists the root and seed of creation, the source
of reality. This theory is present in the thought of Abulafia as well as most early
kabbalists, but it is articulated most clearly in Gikatilla, where 'the entire universe as well as the divine names and the Torah, ontologically emanated from
the four letters (YHWH) of the Divine Name which is the principle of their
existence' (Blickstein, 1983, 68).

Second, we find the idea that the sefirot themselves are the Name, the four
letters being spread across the tree, assigned to individual sefirot. This theory is
less clearly articulated, but forms an important part of Abulafia's work as well as
many of the early kabbalists.[20]

Last, we find an interesting and original distinction between two (or more)
tetragrammata, where the names YHWH, AHYH and AHWY compete for the
highest position. This appears in several early kabbalists including Isaac the
Blind, the Iyyun Circle and Gikatilla.

It may go without saying that these three theories are densely interlinked and
often dependent on each other so that even when unspoken the influence of each
can be discerned in the others. The kabbalists were familiar with each other's
works and so the doctrines that we find in these two chapters are suggested in
the writings of all of them, even up to the Zohar; thus while I have selected
Gikatilla and Abulafia as the two exemplars respectively, this is because of their
explicit focus on the nominal themes I examine, rather than because they are the
unique carriers of the doctrines. To demonstrate this I will often attempt to highlight passages from other writers and texts which mirror or help to elucidate the
doctrines found crucially in Gikatilla and Abulafia.

Chapter 5 looks at the writings of Yosef Gikatilla, where the Name is the
primal unity – the *point* – from which all else emerges via a linguistic process
which, I argue, is strikingly akin to that logical-linguistic structure described in
Wittgenstein's *Tractatus* (and with more than a slight nod to Leibniz, who
himself absorbed a significant amount of kabbalistic material). A second theme
which emerges in this chapter is AHYH as the internal name of God, one present
in the highest sefirah and before the process of emanation has begun.

In Chapter 6, the direction is reversed with the investigation of Abraham Abulafia's linguistic-nominal cosmology. Abulafia's prophetic method of returning to
the source by breaking names into their letters will demonstrate a concealed return
to the earlier theme of hypostatic nominalism, as the nexus of concepts including
Name, Messiah, and Metatron become eschatologically unified. Interpreting his
thought in the light of Levinas and Lacan will demonstrate the essential nature of

the Name not only in identity and otherhood but in providing the gateway to a structural (metaphysical) understanding of the cosmos.

While this section will have recourse to the Zohar, and touch on the work of later figures such as Isaac Luria and Sabbatai Sevi, it is in these two thirteenth century thinkers that the most comprehensive systematisation of a Kabbalah of the Name is found. The investigation will not progress beyond the thirteenth century, not because the Kabbalah, or Jewish mystical interest in the Name ended there (it surely did not), but because these two contemporaries together articulate a clear and bold theology of the Name which afterwards, in the writings which followed them and the Zohar, only became shadowed by less clear and less systematic articulations. Likewise the movement of Hasidism which, inheriting the kabbalists' fascination with the Name, provided an innovative interpretation according to their mores, in terms of a practical and magical performance; the theoretical element in Hasidism however is based to a comprehensive degree on the earlier kabbalists, and most especially the writings of Abulafia. Rather the twentieth century shall be placed as the heir of the thirteenth, and most especially the philosopher Walter Benjamin who was privy to Scholem's own research on the Kabbalah and incorporated this into an onto-messianic doctrine both strikingly original yet strangely faithful to Abulafia's own. Chapter 7, then, will find us back in the Garden of Eden, Adam's naming of the animals offering a precognition of the Messianic Age in which all things take on their proper name. This chapter will show that Benjamin's writing forms the completion of the nominal theory given by Gikatilla and Abulafia, where language is coextensive with existence, and yet objects cannot be identified with their names.

Finally, the conclusion will draw together the findings of these chapters, offering a speculative framework which contextualises the results in terms both theological and philosophical.

As this overview makes clear, this study covers the intersection of two major fields: history and philosophy (both of which may here take the prefix 'Jewish'). While the subject matter requires a historical approach, and some historical conclusions are certainly reached, the overwhelming intent is to use history in the service of philosophy; the factual in the service of the speculative. As such, the work as a whole may constitute something of an exercise in anachronism, finding new conclusions by forcing together apparently irreconcilable outlooks such as Yosef Gikatilla and Ludwig Wittgenstein, or the hyper-rational Kripke and the strange mystical underworld of the Hekhalot literature. The apparent irreconcilability will be shown to be just that, as one of the precepts that I hope to demonstrate is exactly the consistency of modern Jewish philosophy of the Name with Jewish theology of the Name.

Thus, the outcome of this study is to be the speculative re/construction, from the historical textual materials, of a systematic philosophy of the Name of God, and how this relates to language, identity and names in general. The final philosophy of the Name which will be reached posits the Name as a phenomenal encounter: the Name is that aspect of God which emerges into the human world;

the Name, then, is the shape that God's essence takes for finite human subject-ivity. But that there is an essence yet other than this, a 'hidden' aspect of God which is God in His ipseity, means that while the Name presents God for human beings, it also serves to conceal that which cannot be known.

One aspect of this concealing role is that the Name then cannot *define* God; that is, it cannot be a semantic equivalent for the nature of God, or a statement of His essence. To be so, would be to make God contained within the world. As such, the Name forms not only the beginning point of language, but also the limit of language. Names refer to what language cannot describe. And while the creative function of language enshrined in countless Jewish texts *does* allow for an accurate linguistic description of reality, a linguistic equivalence with the world, this description is limited to only what can be broken into its constituent semantic elements; that which cannot be totalised cannot be described but only referenced.

The Name is not a being however; it is rather a mode of being. It is through the Name that God interacts with creation; this action, while positing an essence behind it, is still itself the presence of that essence as an event. This will be high-lighted in the later chapters, where the essential emptiness of that which is con-cealed by the Name will be shown. The Name posits an essence; but apart from the Name, there is no such essence, and in looking behind the Name we find nothing. There is nothing to be found (but, to paraphrase Rosenzweig, this nothing is still a nothing *of* God).

The speculative nature of this re/construction would encounter criticism from scholars of the more historical and literal perspectives. I will argue that this is still a valid, and validly *Jewish* method of textual exegesis. The Rabbinic/Jewish tradition of constant reinterpretation is embodied in the talmudic tale where a debate between R Eliezer and R Joshua is interrupted by a *bat kol* which sup-ports the reading of Eliezer. Joshua counters by quoting Deuteronomy 13:12: 'It is not in Heaven' – the interpretation of scripture is now in the hands of human beings, not decided from above.[21] In the question of Jewish philosophy, the method is arguably one of pursuing philosophy by specifically Jewish means of reading traditions. The endeavour of Jewish philosophy, then, should always begin and proceed with the midrashic analysis of Jewish texts. The argument is not historical; in fact, it is trans-historical. I am arguing for a meaning which transcends history; a systematic philosophy which may or may not have ever been held by any of the authors, sages, philosophers or mystics discussed herein, but one which is reachable from the sum of their writings; one which can be read as implicit within the tradition, and expressed throughout its development, where each moment expresses only a part of the whole. For this reason, I term it a re/construction.

A second aspect of this is that the texts as we have them are irreparably divorced from the 'intended' conscious meaning of any individual thinkers (in this case, usually rabbis) represented therein. This is not a statement about the nature of text per se, but rather about two specific and independent factors. First, the layers of redaction evidenced in the Talmud and other rabbinic writings demonstrate a constant reinterpretation where in many cases at least half a dozen different editors have been concatenated into a single sugya. The editorial process may have taken in rabbis and traditions across significant gulfs in space and time: from Palestine to Babylon, from the second century to the sixth. If each editor has their own interpretation of the meaning of a phrase, and of an interpretation of that phrase, how are we to approach finding an original meaning? If the original (biblical) material was seen as fair game for reinterpretation from its surface meaning to prove a theological point of which the interpreter was convinced, then so were the rabbinic sayings which passed to the next generation. This layering of intention is a fact of the Talmud and classical rabbinic writing in general; but still we search for a single meaning behind passages. This study offers an alternative approach to establishing meaning, and this is the second factor. Text itself transcends its author, especially when the authors are multiple and engaged in an on-going process of reinterpretation across generations. Yet, there is a logic inherent in thought. If text constitutes a tradition, regardless of any one specific intention, then the meaning of that tradition can be found within the text; certain aspects or implications which never were obvious to any one author can still be considered internal to the tradition. It is the work of philosophers often to analyse ideas and patterns of thought in order to uncover the necessary implications which do not appear on the surface; the subsequent stage of the pattern which has not yet made itself apparent in the minds of previous thinkers. For this reason, it is important to utilise philosophy to interpret text in order to reveal the concepts which lie unstated within (or above) it. At many points in the study I will argue that certain ideas of a distinctly twentieth century (or later) flavour are integral to the interpretation of material hundreds of years prior.

So while on the one hand I argue that an original meaning or intention to the traditions preserved in many of the texts (certainly those in Section A) is not only something now undiscoverable to us, epistemically obscured, but even a mirage to which there is no fundamentally real counterpart; on the other hand, I still hold that whatever the (necessarily transient, or non-objective) meanings available to us from individual texts are, we are best placed to attempt to interpret them holistically, as moments in the development of a tradition which itself may not ever have necessarily been manifest at any single point throughout its instantiations. The evolution of the tradition displays a form; that form is what this study is interested in.

A note on definitions and translations

This text will refer repeatedly to the terms Jewish mysticism and Jewish philosophy. Much ink has been spilt trying to clarify and refine the meanings of these terms, both of which are to a greater or lesser degree inaccurate in that they are Greek in origin and largely Christian (or Islamic in the case of the latter) in historical development. My own use of the terms herein is purely conventional: I accept them as pragmatic terms to define certain movements and ways of thinking within Judaism. Although precise concepts of how a mysticism can be Jewish may vary,[22] what texts fall under that concept are almost entirely agreed upon. The Hekhalot literature, the Kabbalah, the Ashkenazi Hasidim and modern Hasidism are all certain components; Late Antique apocalypticism exists on the periphery, being mostly pre-rabbinic and therefore without some basic tenets that define Judaism as we understand it, although the influence of this literature on the Merkavah mystics offers a way in.

Jewish philosophy is equally hard to define. Of those appearing in this text, some are more contentious than others. While Rosenzweig, Levinas and Benjamin all wrote extensively on Judaism, taking it as the basis for much of their thought (as did, to a lesser extent, Derrida), figures such as Husserl, Wittgenstein and Kripke offer more of a challenge: to what extent is their Jewishness substantial? Kripke of course is a practising member of the Orthodox, and although it is questionable how much this influences his philosophical thought, it has not gone unnoticed that certain aspects of his philosophy appear to draw on, for example, Maimonides' doctrine on the Name (in *Naming and Necessity*, esp. 52–53). Husserl was born of Jewish parents, but later converted age twenty-nine. Did this Jewish background influence in any way his thought? It seems impossible to judge, without indulging in circular reasoning about the nature of the effect such an influence might lead to. Wittgenstein was three quarters Jewish, although his parents had converted; while he pursued Christianity for much of his life, he returned again and again to the consideration of his Jewish identity, as is evidenced in the *Culture and Value* collection, where he terms the Jewish community 'my people' (1980, 20). Equally importantly, he had even claimed that 'my thoughts are one hundred percent Hebraic' (Drury, 1996, 175).

These are not the only philosophers I use in this study, although they are the central ones. I also refer to Hilary Putnam, Lacan and Leibniz. The former is of course Jewish and practising, but the latter two are by no means Jews. They have been used simply because their work establishes an important theoretical connection with the schema being developed at certain points, and it would be misleading not to mention them. However, it should be noted that there is also a significant influence of Judaism on both their work – Lacan's work on the Name of the Father, and Leibniz' use of kabbalistic traditions evidence, in different ways, their relevance.

The answer then can only be vague. All the central thinkers have a certain heritage, whether or not it has been expressed religiously. In fact we witness a whole spectrum of different factors and ways of understanding what 'Jewishness' may mean. It may be religious, but doesn't have to be; it may be cultural but not necessarily so; it may be ethnic but is not so essentially. The one thing which could really be said of all the central thinkers used herein is that they have, for at least much of their lives, considered themselves to be Jews. This is, I believe, a more definitive statement than I would be able to attempt.

Where not noted, translations are my own.

Notes

1 The reference 'sound and smoke' is from Goethe's *Faust*, where Mephistopheles says: 'Happiness, heart, love, God – I have no name for it – feeling is all; names are but sound and smoke dimming the glow of heaven'.

2 Throughout this study I will refer to God in the masculine, solely for the reason that this is the tradition within the Jewish texts that I am working with. Doing otherwise would make the transition from text to commentary unwieldy. The convention of capitalising nouns referring to God will also be used, as in many cases this will help to clarify the reference.

3 Two other texts deserve mention: the first chapter of A. Marmorstein, *The Old Rabbinic Doctrine of God* (1927) is given over to 'The Names of God' – however this is more to do with Biblical appellation and rabbinic synonym for God, with little discussion on the philosophy of naming which stands behind them. The seminal text of Ephraim E. Urbach, *The Sages: Their Concepts and Beliefs* (1979) covers some rabbinic material in Chapter 7, entitled 'The Power of the Divine Name,' being an investigation of the traditions surrounding the use of the Name – but again this presents individual pieces of evidence without seeking to find an underlying pattern or structure to account for their emergence. There have of course been numerous smaller studies on the Name in particular thinkers and texts. These will be examined thematically throughout the course of this study.

4 This perhaps is evident if we understand mysticism as the attempt to go beyond duality – a system of signs presumes two sides to mediate between. Therefore the search for union must begin with the attempt to transcend or go through language to get to the real on the other side.

5 Quoting Badiou (2006, 69).

6 The prefix *yod* indicating the imperfect second person masculine singular, and the *vav* being a vestigial element preserved from an early stage in the language's evolution.

7 There is no strict future tense in Biblical Hebrew, but the imperfect denotes generally action which has not been completed.

8 Mettinger (1988), McDonough (1999) and John Day (2002) to name just three. But see also Parke-Taylor (1975, 51), who claims that Exod.3:14 is a late attempt at a folk-etymology to explain the name YHWH, whose original meaning has by then become forgotten.

9 Though see the assessment of various competing views in Wilson (1995, 3–9).

10 Boccaccini (2002) divides Second Temple Judaism into three streams: Zadokite, Sapiential and Enochic – although these should not be understood as equal in presence or effect. The first stream is based on a static, perfect world-view. The Enochic was catalysed by a unique conception of evil as caused by the fallen angels, and the subsequent corruption of the created order. Thus Apocalyptic is fundamentally Enochic and not Zadokite. On the relationship between the Enochic and Mosaic traditions, see also Orlov (2004).

11 Hurtado (1998) argues however that Christianity constitutes a significant leap from these traditions, in presenting Christ as not merely an agent of the divine, but a separate person deserving of independent worship.

12 We know of oddities such as the synagogue of Dura Europos (in modern-day Syria), whose edifice displays a number of 'heretically' depicted pagan deities, the visible remnant of an inevitable fusion of Judaism with local and non-Jewish traditions.

13 Although the relationship between this text and early Christianity was for a long time contentious, the most recent research concluded that it was composed in the first century BCE, and therefore its Son of Man motifs are not drawing on Christian influence – indeed, the opposite now seems more likely – see Chapter 2, Note 6.

14 The inclusion of the Hekhalot literature in the Late Antique period may be contentious – scholarship has increasingly downdated the texts from the initial assessment of Scholem, such that much of the corpus is now seen as stemming from the Islamic

period. However, the existence of parallel traditions in the Bavli, and the undeniable body of traditions which the Hekhalot literature grew from, including those evidenced in the Aramaic incantation bowls which are still being translated and analysed, strongly implies that many of the traditions we have before us are not as late as the redaction of the texts themselves.

15 The general influence of Maimonides on the early Kabbalists has been discussed by Wolfson (2004) and Idel (2004). For Abulafia's own use of Maimonides, see Idel (1998). The kabbalists appear to thrive on a love-hate relationship with the work of Maimonides. In the single year of 1232, Jonah of the Gerona school was a leading voice for the excommunication of Maimonides' work, at precisely the same time that Nachmanides was attempting to demonstrate the theological similarity between the work of Maimonides and the kabbalists (Chavel, 1978, 399). Nachmanides appears to have won the argument though, as the Guide itself was quickly picked up by mystics and mined for secrets allegedly buried beneath its strictly rational exterior. Abulafia wrote three separate commentaries to the Guide, applying the same kind of esoteric analysis to that text which is usually reserved for the Bible, and at one point claiming that the Guide's path to redemption is its thirty-six concealed secrets, as hinted at by the word לו, which has the gematria value of thirty-six, in the sentence '*Ge'ulah tiheyeh lo*'; at another point he interprets the number of chapters (177) as identical with the gematrial value of the phrase Gan Eden. Gikatilla also wrote a kabbalistic commentary to the Guide.

16 YHWH, Adonai, El, Eloha, Elohim, Shaddai, Tzvaot, as detailed in b.Shev.35a. Although the Talmud treats the Name YHWH as the holiest name of God, requiring enormous deference and prevarication in its use, it is not held to be essentially different in its nature from the other names applied to God in scripture. As noted above, one passage requires any word used in reference to God to be treated with the same level of respect, being itself a 'holy name.' Cf.: 'There the word 'faithful' is descriptive, but here it is a name' (b.Shabb.10a).

17 The use of these names as attributes was actually developed by Saadia Gaon from SY – although the ten spheres or intellects also surely drew influence from Arabic Islamic philosophers who were busy systematising the cosmos.

18 This was not originated by Maimonides, being found already in Judah HaLevi's Kuzari (*c.*1140) as well as Abraham ibn Daud. The similar formulations of Abraham bar Hiyya (d. *c.*1136), and their dependence on Jewish philosophers such as Saadia Gaon and probably adopted into Judaism from the Islamic Mu'tazilites, as well as bar Hiyya's own influence on the early Kabbalah, is detailed in Dauber (2004). Uniquely for bar Hiyya, the attributes through which God acts in the world are also referred to as 'holy names' (ibid., 2004, 76), and it is perhaps from here that the kabbalists found their doctrine of the sefirot as names. For bar Hiyya, the identity of name and attribute is a claim to the identity of name and description:

> In each and every occasion He, may His name be blessed, is called by the name that is appropriate for the purpose of bringing that attribute upon human beings. Regarding the good things that befall the world He is called a God, merciful and gracious, slow to anger, bestowing kindness, and similar such names…
> (*Hegyon ha-Nephesch ha-Atzuvah* 126, Dauber, 2004, 77)

However, even bar Hiyya does admit that 'no created being in the world shares with him in this great name [YHWH]', while the name Elohim 'is used equivocally both for God and for adjudicators and judges' (*Hegyon ha-Nephesch ha-Atzuvah* 108, Dauber, 2004, 80).

19 This is a slight – though important – deviation from the rabbinic tradition which claims even YHWH as describing a mode of action – the attribute of mercy, as opposed to Elohim (judgement); we also find the names Sabaoth and El Shaddai assigned to war against the wicked and the suspension of judgement, respectively (see

Exod.R., Shemot 3, 6, which concludes: 'This is the meaning of the words, "I am that I am", namely, I am called according to my deeds'. Cf. Tanh., Shemot 20 f.88b). Likewise, Gen.Rab. to Gen.8:9 asserts that Elohim and YHWH are all 'mere different names for one and the same God' (cf. Midr.Ps. on L, 1 (139b)).

20 This is detailed with particular reference to the Zohar in Wald (1989).

21 b.Bab. M. 59b; also in p. Hag. 81:11; b. Hul. 44a, etc.

22 A good overview of the debate so far has been compiled in Schäfer (2009, 9–20).

Bibliography

The Babylonian Talmud (32 vols). 1990. Edited by Rabbi Dr. I. Epstein. London: The Soncino Press.

Encyclopaedia Judaica, Second edition (22 vols). 2007. Edited by Michael Berenbaum and Fred Skolnik. Detroit: Macmillan Reference USA.

Old Testament Pseudepigrapha (2 vols). 1985. Edited by James Charlesworth. New York/London: Doubleday.

The SBL Handbook of Style: For Ancient Near Eastern, Biblical, and Early Christian Studies. 1999. Edited by Patrick H. Alexander, John F. Kutsko, James D. Ernest, Shirley Decker-Lucke and David L. Petersen. Peabody: Hendrickson.

Badiou, Alain. 2006. *Being and Event.* Translated by Oliver Feltham. London: Continuum.

Bielik-Robson, Agata. 2012. The Promise of the Name: 'Jewish Nominalism' as the Critique of Idealist Tradition. *Bamidbar* 1(3), 11–35.

Bielik-Robson, Agata. 2014. *Jewish Crypto-Theologies in Late Modernity: Philosophical Marranos.* London: Routledge.

Bielik-Robson, Agata, and Adam Lipszyc. 2012. Introduction. *Bamidbar* 1(3), 1–11.

Blickstein, Shlomo. 1983. *Between Philosophy and Mysticism: A Study of the Philosophical-Qabbalistic Writings of Joseph Giqatila (1248–c.1322).* PhD diss., Jewish Theological Seminary of America.

Boccaccini, Gabriele. 2002. *Roots of Rabbinic Judaism: An Intellectual History from Ezekiel to Daniel.* Grand Rapids: Eerdmans.

Boman, Thorlief. 1960. *Hebrew Thought Compared With Greek.* London: SCM Press Ltd.

Boyarin, Daniel. 2004. *Borderlines: The Partition of Judeao-Christianity.* Philadelphia: University of Pennsylvania Press.

Chavel, D. 1978. *Ramban: Writings and Discourses, Vol. II.* New York: Shilo Press.

Dan, Joseph. 1996. The Name of God, the Name of the Rose, and the Concept of Language in Jewish Mysticism. *Medieval Encounters* 2(3), 228–248.

Dauber, Jonathan Victor. 2004. *Standing on the Heads of Philosophers: Myth and Philosophy in Early Kabbalah.* PhD diss., New York University.

Day, John. 2002. *Yahweh and the Gods and Goddesses of Canaan.* London: Sheffield Academic Press.

Drury, Maurice O'Connor. 1996. *The Danger of Words and Writings on Wittgenstein.* Edited and introduced by David Berman, Michael Fitzgerald and John Hayes. Bristol: Thoemmes Press.

Fagenblat, Michael. 2010. *A Covenant of Creatures: Levinas' Philosophy of Judaism.* Stanford: Stanford University Press.

Fossum, Jarl E. 1985. *The Name of God and the Angel of the Lord: Samaritan and Jewish Concepts of Intermediation and the Origin of Gnosticism.* Tübingen: Mohr Siebeck.

Galli, Barbara E. 1994. Rosenzweig and the Name for God. *Modern Judaism* 14(1), 63–86.

Gieschen, Charles A. 2003. The Divine Name in Ante-Nicene Christology. *Vigilae Christianae* 57(2), 115–158.

Hall, Robert G. 2011. Pre-existence, Naming, and Investiture in the *Similitudes of Enoch* and in Hebrews. *Religion & Theology* 18, 311–333.

Hayward, Robert. 1981. *Divine Name and Presence: The Memra*. Totowa: Allanheld, Osmun & Co.

Horwitz, Noah. 2012. *Reality in the Name of God, or, Divine Insistence: An Essay on Creation, Infinity, and the Ontological Implications of Kabbalah*. Brooklyn: Punctum Books.

Hundley, Michael. 2009. To Be or Not to Be: A Reexamination of Name Language in Deuteronomy and the Deuteronomistic History. *Vetus Testamentum* 59, 533–555.

Hurtado, Larry W. 1998. *One God, One Lord: Early Christian Devotion and Ancient Jewish Monotheism*. Second edition. Edinburgh: T&T Clark.

Idel, Moshe. 1998. Abulafia's Secrets of the Guide: A Linguistic Turn. *Revue de Métaphysique et de Morale* 4, 495–528.

Idel, Moshe. 2004. Maimonides' 'Guide of the Perplexed' and the Kabbalah. *Jewish History* 18(2/3), 197–226.

Idel, Moshe. 2010. *Old Worlds, New Mirrors: On Jewish Mysticism and Twentieth-Century Thought*. Philadelphia: University of Pennsylvania Press.

Jackson, David. 2004. *Enochic Judaism: Three Defining Exemplars*. London: Continuum.

Maimonides, Moses. 1956. *The Guide for the Perplexed*. Translated by M. Friedlander. New York: Dover.

Marmorstein, A. 1927. *The Old Rabbinic Doctrine of God* (2 vols). London: Oxford University Press.

McBride, Samuel Dean. 1969. *The Deuteronomic Name Theology*. PhD diss., Harvard University.

McDonough, Sean M. 1999. *YHWH at Patmos: Rev. 1:4 in its Hellenistic and Early Jewish Setting*. Tübingen: Mohr Siebeck.

Mettinger, T.N. 1988. *In Search of God: The Meaning and Message of the Everlasting Names*. Philadelphia: Fortress Press.

Orlov, Andrei. 2004. *The Enoch-Metatron Tradition*. Tübingen: Mohr-Siebeck.

Parke-Taylor, Geoffrey H. 1975. *Yahweh: The Divine Name in the Bible*. Waterloo: Wilfrid Laurier University Press.

Richter, Sandra L. 2002. *The Deuteronomistic History and the Name Theology*. Berlin/New York: Walter de Gruyter.

Rosenzweig, Franz. 1998. *God, Man, and the World: Lectures and Essays*. Edited and translated by Barbara E. Galli. Syracuse: Syracuse University Press.

Schäfer, Peter. 2009. *The Origins of Jewish Mysticism*. Tübingen: Mohr Siebeck.

Scholem, Gershom. 1972/1973, The Name of God and the Linguistic Theory of the Kabbalah. *Diogenes* 79(1972), 59–80; *Diogenes* 80(1973), 164–194.

Scholem, Gershom. 1987. *The Origins of the Kaballah*. Edited by R.J. Werblowsky, translated by Allan Arkush. Princeton: Princeton University Press.

Scholem, Gershom. 1995. *The Messianic Idea in Judaism and Other Essays on Jewish Spirituality*. New York: Schocken Books.

Scott, Steven Richard. 2008. The Binitarian Nature of the Book of Similitudes. *Journal for the Study of the Pseudepigrapha* 18(1), 55–78.

Segal, A.F. 1977. *Two Powers in Heaven: Early Rabbinic Reports About Christianity and Gnosticism*. Leiden: Brill.

Sommer, Benjamin D. 2009. *The Bodies of God and the World of Ancient Israel.* Cambridge: Cambridge University Press.

Urbach, Ephraim E. 1979. *The Sages: Their Concepts and Beliefs* (2 vols). Jerusalem: Magnes Press.

Wald, Stephen G. 1989. *The Doctrine of the Divine Name: An Introduction to Classical Kabbalistic Theology.* Atlanta: Scholars Press.

Wilson, Ian. 1995. *Out of the Midst of the Fire: Divine Presence in Deuteronomy.* Atlanta: Scholars Press.

Wittgenstein, Ludwig. 1980. *Culture and Value.* Edited by G.H. Von Wright, translated by Peter Winch. Chicago: University of Chicago Press.

Wolfson, Elliot R. 2000. Judaism and Incarnation: The Imaginal Body of God. In: Tikva Frymer-Kensky, David Novak, Peter Ochs, David Fox Sandmel and Michael A. Singer. eds. *Christianity in Jewish Terms.* Boulder: Westview Press, 239–253.

Wolfson, Elliot R. 2004. Beneath the Wings of the Great Eagle: Maimonides and Thirteenth-Century Kabbalah. In: Görge K. Hasselhoff and Otfried Fraisse. eds. *Moses Maimonides (1138–1204): His Religious, Scientific and Philosophical Wirkungsgeschichte in Different Cultural Contexts.* Würsburg: Ergon Verlag, 209–307.

1 Presence and speech

Rosenzweig's ontology and the rabbinic doctrine of creation via the Name

> He chose three simple letters and fixed them in his great name. And he sealed with them the six edges (of the universe).
>
> (Sefer Yetzirah §15)

In his contribution to the text *20th Century Jewish Thought*, Josef Stern claimed that Genesis is a commentary on the nature of language as much as creation. What was previously the 'amorphous lump' of reality emerged into discrete objects through a process which we might call *articulation*:

> [C]reation is their [objects'] emergence through separation and division. But by integrating acts of speech and naming into the sequence of creation, the Torah suggests that how the world presents itself, divided into objects and structured into kinds, is also inseparable from language.
>
> (Stern, 2009, 543)

In this reading, names are not just descriptors, applied to ontologically pre-existent objects, but are 'the expression of criteria of individuation and identity, without which there would be nothing to be named' (ibid., 544). In God's hands, words do not merely describe but determine the world.

This chapter will examine some early rabbinic traditions regarding the linguistic nature of creation and how it relates to naming and the Name of God.[1] As mentioned above, Scholem located the beginnings of Jewish language-mysticism at the point where the creative word used in Genesis became identified with God's Name. Certainly, this is a common idea found explicitly in many late rabbinic texts, in the lead up to the Kabbalah. Scholem did not specify the point at which this identification occurred, but some years later Jarl Fossum offered an answer in the form of his monograph *The Name of God and The Angel of the Lord*. Through the use of rabbinic, Samaritan and apocryphal writings, Fossum (1985) attempted to show that the tradition of the Name of God as a creative tool or agent stretched back into the Second Temple period. This claim was defended successfully in the book, and has since become a basic precept of much work done in the field of Jewish theology in Late Antiquity. That from the earliest period the rabbis held to some kind of doctrine of creation through the Name YHWH is now largely accepted.[2]

I will present a new consideration of the evidence, arguing that while some of Fossum's interpretations are flawed and should be rejected, there is in fact a persistent association of the Name with not *generation*, but *completion*. This will involve a degree of textual scholarship in order to reconstruct exactly what the rabbinic and Samaritan texts claim they believed, and what has been passed down in the texts they compiled – a process which may be tiring for those interested in more metaphysical issues, but which is important nonetheless; the source of this study, and the root of Jewish tradition is text, and so analysing text to find what traditions it contains, as opposed to those it denies, is crucial. Doing this will help to refine the question being discussed, and may even bring us more into line with Scholem's precise statement: 'it is this [God's] name which brought about the creation, or rather the creation is closely affixed to the Name – i.e., *the creation is contained within its limits by the name*' (1972, 69, my emphasis). This shift in emphasis from the initial conditions or the elements of creation to the final form those elements take and the nature of how they are bound together highlights an important philosophical principle, one which I will demonstrate using Rosenzweig's work on ontology and epistemology and the relationship between them.

The textual evidence

While there is certainly no doctrine of creation via the Name in the Hebrew Bible, we do find suggestive passages such as 'the name of YHWH who made heaven and earth' (Ps.124:8) and by the second century BCE we read in Jubilees, of 'the glorious and honoured and great and splendid and amazing and mighty name which created heaven and earth and everything together' (Jub.36:7).[3] These and several other passages have been used by scholars who claim that there is a long-standing Jewish doctrine of 'creation through the Name'.

The rabbinic texts

In several passages, the early rabbinic writings refer to the involvement of individual letters in creation. In b.Menachot 29b, R Judah the Patriarch asks R Ammi about the passage: 'Trust ye in YHWH forever; for in Yah YHWH is an everlasting rock' (Is.26:4). Ammi refers to R Judah b.R Ila'i who interprets the second part of the verse as 'for by [the letters] *yod heh*, YHWH formed the worlds'. The letters *yod-heh*, he claims 'refers to the two worlds which the Holy One, blessed be He, created; one with the letter *heh* and the other with the letter *yod*'. The two worlds, this world and the world to come, were created through the use of letters; *heh* and *yod*, respectively. This is explained via a rereading of Genesis 2:4, the word *behibbaram* being divided to read *be-H baream*: 'by *heh* He created them'.

Genesis Rabbah 12:10 begins with this reading of *behibbaram* but goes on:

> R Abbahu said in R Johanan's name: He created them with the letter *heh*.
> All letters demand an effort to pronounce them, whereas the *heh* demands
> no effort; similarly, not with labour or wearying toil did the Holy One,
> blessed be He, create His world, but *By the word of the Lord.*
>
> (Ps.33:6)

The passage then continues to parallel b.Menachot 29b. These passages should
be seen in the context of Genesis Rabbah 39:11. Here, R Abbahu states that the
letter *heh* which God added to Abram's name is from the word *hashamayimah*:
'It is not written: 'Look now *hashamayim*', but 'Look now *hashamayimah*.'
[God said:] 'with this *heh* I made the world'.

So we have three texts all citing the involvement of the letter *heh* and possibly *yod* in creation. It is logical and tempting to see in these references a suggestion of the Tetragrammaton, especially given the emphasis on the letter
heh, which has long been a rabbinic abbreviation of the Name.[4] Utilising these
three texts (b.Men.29b, Gen.Rab.12:10 and Gen.Rab.39:11), Fossum argued
that there was both a rabbinic and initial *pre-rabbinic* tradition of the Name
YHWH as 'an instrument used by God when he was engaged in the creation of
the world' (1985, 254). However, there is no indication of this in the texts
themselves – in fact they offer two different explanations for the use of that
letter, and neither mentions the Tetragrammaton. In Genesis Rabbah 12:10 creation via *heh* is understood to imply a lack of effort on God's part. Although
the Biblical passage cited in b.Menachot 29b is clearly using the Name of God,
the rabbis appear rather to be reinterpreting the text to find a method of creation using the letters *yod* and *heh*, *without themselves making any explicit reference to the Name.*[5] In Genesis Rabbah 39:11, the *heh* is not from God's
Name, but from Abraham's.

Another text frequently used in connection to the Name and creation is the
following, referencing the creation of the tabernacle in light of God's creation:
'Rab Judah said in the name of Rab: Bezalel knew how to combine the letters by
which the heavens and the earth were created' (b.Ber.55a). Again, this text does
not make any assertion that these letters are of the Name, but that has not
stopped scholars reading a nominal doctrine into the text.[6] Similarly, the story of
the creation of a calf (b.Sanh. 65b and 67b), which does not mention the Name
at all, has often been cited in this context.[7]

On the other hand, there is explicit evidence that the letters of creation are not
limited to *yod* and *heh.* In a passage from the *yerushalmi*, we read:

> R Jonah said in the name of R Levi: 'The world was created by the letter *bet*'.
> As *bet* is closed on all sides except one, so you have no right to investigate
> what is above, what below, what went before or shall happen afterward,
> only what has happened since the world [and its inhabitants were created].
>
> (p.Hag.2:1, 16a)[8]

Bet of course has no connection to the Divine Name YHWH (it is rather here a reference to the initial letter of the Torah).

So we have three separate traditions all tying into the analysis of Isaiah 26:4 and the letters YH. The three separate appearances of the passage which ana- lyses Isaiah 26:4 (in both the Bavli and the Yerushalmi) mean this latter passage is highly likely to predate the appended traditions, which offer a more refined analysis of the use of the letters *yod* and *heh*. But crucially, never do the rabbis claim the letters are from God's Name and nor are they claimed to represent it; and meanwhile, other letters with no association to the Name are also mentioned in terms of creation.

The Samaritan texts

Fossum's argument regarding the rabbis found a lot of support in contemporary Samaritan texts, which would then suggest a common tradition. The *Memar Marqah*[9] contains several interesting passages, discussing 'the great name by which our Lord brought the world into being' (VI.11), 'the name by which the world was created' (VI.11), and 'the name which brought all created things into being' (IV.2). Perhaps most suggestive, however, is the passage 'ה is the name by which all creatures arose' (IV.2).

However, there is more to these passages than the sections above, and while Fossum cites several passages from the liturgical texts in support of his argument,[10] several passages of MMarq itself point unequivocally away from that assumption – including even the passages above, as used by Fossum, once we take them in context. So, where the text mentions 'the great name by which our Lord brought the world into being', the preceding line establishes that this name cannot be the Tetragrammaton, for the speaker here is the letter *alef*, who says, 'I was made the first of the letters and the first of the great name by which our Lord brought the world into being' (VI.11). In his edition of the MMarq, Macdonald – logically – relates this as the name ALHYM of Genesis 1:1 (1963, II, 243n119). Slightly later the letter *heh*, however, claims:

> My number was made the number of the name by which the world was created. It was repeated in both great names AHYH and YHWH, and I sealed your name, O prophet; by me Abraham and Sarah were made great.
>
> (VI.11)

Again I am fully in agreement with MacDonald that the 'number of the name by which the world was created' indicates the name ALHYM, which is composed of five letters – the numerical value of *heh*. Thus we have two separate passages which explicitly cite the name Elohim as the creative name, one of them directly relating the letter *heh* to that name.

The third passage is that which contains the crucial line: '*Heh* is the name by which all creatures arose' (IV.2). Shortly before this we find the statement, 'the name which brought all created things into being sealed the whole. Therefore He said, "ALHYM finished"' (Gen.2:2). So even in the same passage which Fossum used to claim that *heh* was representative of the Tetragrammaton as agent of creation, we find the agent stated as Elohim. A few pages later, we find a discussion of several letters which claims: '*Alef* is the great name which teaches that it is one, His scripture and His name are one, just like another' (IV.4). As for *heh*: 'there is no need to examine it, for the whole is concluded by it. It is the seal of the great name' (IV.4). *Yod* 'is the beginning of the great name and represents the foundations of creation' (IV.4). While I must agree with MacDonald that in contrast to the previous symbolism, here *alef* represents ALHYM, and *heh* and *yod* are representing YHWH, this is separated from Fossum's quote by two intervening sections, and the letters are discussed in relation to one another; furthermore, the *heh* itself is interpreted here not as representing the great name YHWH, but only as its seal, i.e. the last letter which completes the name, just as it earlier claimed to be the seal of Moses' name. This therefore does not add any weight to the use of *heh* on its own to indicate the Name YHWH as a whole.

Last, Moses distinguishes between two of God's names: 'Your Name by which You created the world' and 'Your Great Name' (IV.7) the former being invested in Moses[11] and the latter revealed to him.

Thus we can conclude that the early Samaritan tradition, as evidenced in MMarq, holds the name of creation, consonant with the Biblical text, to be Elohim, whereas the Name YHWH is God's Great Name which He revealed only to Moses.

The association of the name Elohim with creation is of a wholly different kind to the later association of the Tetragrammaton which interests us. Biblically, God appears under the name Elohim during the entire process of creation; this is the 'guise' he takes. But the MMarq never separates the name Elohim into a hypostasis, or depicts it as an instrument: it is simply a name that God goes by.

So, despite Fossum's assertion that 'it is certain that the Name has a demiurgic role' (1985, 78), there is no evidence for the Samaritans doing this at any time prior to the fourteenth century; and although the Samaritan liturgy may preserve ancient material, the foregoing analysis establishes that such a belief is not a part of this ancient material. However, what we do find is an association of the name Elohim with creation,[12] and a corollary association of YHWH with completion.[13] In fact, MMarq actually claims YHWH not as the Name of creation, but as the seal. It is YHWH by which 'the world is bonded together' (I.4). This is consonant with the claim of *heh* as the 'seal [חתמת] of the great name' (IV.4), being the last letter of YHWH. We find the same when, after explaining the significance of *heh*, *shin*, *yod* and *resh*, the last *heh* is 'the seal' of the word השירה (IV.1).

Other texts

It is noteworthy that there is little other corroborating evidence for creation via the Name in the texts of the time. There is no record of the creative Name in the Qumran literature[14] or the Septuagint, although four texts from the apocrypha and pseudepigrapha are worth mentioning.[15]

First, in the second century BCE text *Jubilees*, we find a commonly cited passage which describes 'the glorious and honoured and great and splendid and amazing and mighty name which created heaven and earth and everything together' (Jub.36:7). This has been cited repeatedly as evidence for creation via the Name. However, this passage is part of a long missive which Isaac relates to Esau and Jacob, asking them to swear by an oath which will bind them into moral behaviour towards each other; the actual passage describing creation (2:1–17) makes no mention of the Name, and even within the text we find that no part of creation is explicitly described as being created verbally, the closest passage being God commanding the motion of the waters during creation (2:5–6). Jubilees then does not itself appear to depict creation occurring via the Name.

In the *Prayer of Manasseh* (3rd BCE -poss. 3rd CE) read: 'You who made heaven and earth with all their order; who shackled the sea by Your Word of Command, who confined the deep and sealed it with Your terrible and glorious Name' (1:2–3). This text, interestingly, manages to combine the verbal commandment of creation with the sealing by the Name. As it stands the text suggests an identity of the Word of Command and the terrible and glorious Name, although this is by no means certain. It should be borne in mind that this text is still of uncertain date and provenance, and may be either Jewish or Christian.[16]

Similitudes (the latest part of *1 Enoch*, now dated to roughly first century BCE[17]) describes an 'oath' which seems to contain the Name, and which founds and guarantees creation from beginning to end (1En. 69:13–25).[18] This passage has been afforded far more importance than it is due in the context, being quoted in full by both Fossum and Gieschen. Although the Name is apparently contained within the Oath, it is unequivocally the Oath which is responsible for creation, not the Name. The Name is, perhaps, the source of the Oath's power, but this does not make the Name itself the agent of creation any more than petrol is an agent of travel.

Finally, *Liber Antiquitatum Biblicarum*, a first or second century CE Latin text also known as *Pseudo-Philo*, mentions that: 'Darkness and silence were before the world was made, and silence spoke and the darkness came into sight. Then your name was pronounced in the drawing together of what had been spread out' (60:2).[19]

The last three texts evidence the role of the Name not in creating the world, but in completing or sealing what has been created; the world and its objects already exist, but require an action which will pull them together and contain them. Although this is *related* to creation, the Name is clearly not used *to* create. In this, they are roughly aligned with the statements of MMarq that the Name YHWH is the 'seal of creation'.[20] While God's Name appears in these texts, with an instrumental function, it is not the case that it is actually used to create; rather it comes into use after any initial act of creation, as an instrument to seal together the elements which God has formed. And while these four texts together can be used to give the appearance of an established tradition during the late Second Temple period, the foregoing analysis shows that the Name as creator is explicitly evidenced in only one pseudepigraphic text: *Jubilees*. And herein, we find only this single passing reference to suggest that creation was accomplished through God's Name along with much that contradicts it. This cannot realistically be taken as a tradition; it could be a scribal slip or even a later gloss by, perhaps, a Christian editor. It could even be the case that the word 'Name' was a placeholder where the copyist didn't want to record the name itself for some reason (as has been evidenced in other contemporary sources).[21] Then, the text would originally have read 'the glorious and honoured and great and splendid and amazing and mighty YHWH who created heaven and earth and everything together' – itself a reading which is entirely uncontroversial.

So, it seems fairly safe to say that there is almost no evidence of the Name as creative tool in Second Temple Judaism, with only one mention of actual creation via the Name in the non-canonical literature, and none in the protonormative writings of the rabbis during the formative period, i.e. between the destruction of the Temple in 67 CE and the completion of the Talmud in the sixth century CE.[22]

There is of course undeniable and abundant evidence of the tradition in later times – it is found in *Targum Pseudo-Jonathan*,[23] the Hekhalot literature,[24] and several Medieval texts.[25] The question of what happened between these groups of texts is one that requires investigation beyond the scope of this study, but I will suggest that the rabbis were aware of the Samaritan tradition and this should be taken as the background to their own analysis. Further, the early Christian identification of Christ as the manifest Name of God (to be discussed in Chapter 2), often appears alongside an assertion that creation occurred through Christ.[26] It is entirely plausible to imagine that between these Christian and Samaritan doctrines, which associate a logos-like second god, or a name known by the letter *heh*, with the event of creation, the rabbis felt the need to combat what was becoming a dangerously potent doctrine. Some groups may have even merged the two doctrines, forming an outright Two Powers theology where creation was effected by the god Elohim but was ruled by the god YHWH. Thus, their argument that creation was the result of letter-manipulation by God manages to incorporate certain aspects of textual interpretation used by other groups, while maintaining the sole authority of God.[27]

Sealing with the Name

In the analysis of the various texts above, a frequent motif of not *creating* via the Tetragrammaton, but *sealing* with it has been apparent. This motif is not limited to just those texts, and suggests a more deeply embedded tradition than that of creation via the Name. I will now take a look at some other examples of this tradition in order to demonstrate its claims regarding the nature of the Name's role in sealing. This will lead into an analysis which will demonstrate the important differences for ontology between the doctrines of creation via the Name and sealing via the Name.

The tradition of sealing with the Name is perhaps most famously found in SY. Here, God is said to seal the six spatial directions with combinations of the three letters YHW. At another point, due to the binary combinations of the twenty-two letters: 'The result is that all creation and all speech go out by one name.' (§19; cf. §22, where 'he makes all creation and all speech one name'[28]). While creation here is clearly an alphabetic or linguistic process, the Name is not the generative aspect, but is used to form a seal, or a boundary. Peter Hayman believes this sealing is a protective process, limiting the threat of that unformed *prima materia* which, in the earlier ANE stories, had to be overcome, and which, without the binding power of the mighty Name, could still threaten to break through and spill into the now ordered cosmos which humanity inhabits. So, 'in rabbinic Judaism the Torah suppresses the chaos of the world outside Judaism, whereas in SY God the Magician did it at the time of creation' (Hayman, 1989, 229).

In numerous passages we find this use of the Name as a kind of seal or constraint, to limit that which threatens; this is often expressed as the primordial watery chaos,[29] a force which in the ANE the gods had to conquer before order could be asserted.[30] This tradition dates well back into Second Temple times, being evidenced in several pseudepigraphic as well as Gnostic texts.[31] In the aforementioned *Prayer of Mannasseh*, God 'shackled the sea by Your Word of Command, [...] confined the deep and sealed it with Your terrible and glorious Name' (1:2–3), and it is through *Similitudes'* Name-containing 'oath' that 'the earth was founded ... the sea was created ... the [pillars of the] deep were made firm ... the sun and the moon complete their course ... the stars complete their courses'[32] (1En.69:15–25). At other points, the foundation stone of the world was engraved with the Name in order to seal the mouth of the oceans (Tg.Ps.-J. to Exod.28:30), and David is said to write the Name upon a potsherd, and throw it into the deep in order to subdue the waves (b.Sukk.53a-b).[33]

Throughout these passages we find a consistent association of the Name with the power to contain, constrain, and provide protection from, chaotic forces. The Name has a power to protect the good (the formed) from the evil (the unformed).

The emphasis on completion rather than generation implies that the crucial point, the point at which a thing can be said to substantially 'be', is when it is sealed into a unity, rather than when the elements that constitute it are created; existence as such is thus a holistic rather than reductionist quality. It is integrity which grants the power to resist dissolution or overpowerment by chaos.

While the Greek conception of existence or creation is a binary one of existence – non-existence, and is conceptualised spatially, the Hebrew is gradual, admitting of degree, and conceptualised temporally (Boman, 1960). Creation, then, is not a matter of popping into existence from nothing, but is a matter of emerging into presence. There is no early Jewish doctrine of creation *ex nihilo*[34] (Wolfson, 1947, I, 302–3; Goldstein, 1983, 307–11; May, 1994[35]).

What then is creation for the rabbis? At this point, the Jewish concept of creation is not based on clearly-defined ontological states of being and non-being, but rather is related to emergence from mere potentiality into actuality; objects which subsist in potentiality are awaiting the calling of their names, the act which brings them into the presence of the namer, and therefore into reality. This would explain why God's own Name does not figure in creation – rather, it is the individual objects' names which are spoken in order to instigate them.[36]

This view of creation is supported by several ANE texts. The *Enuma Elish* describes the initial pre-formation state of the cosmos described as: 'When above the heaven had not (yet) been named, And below the earth had not (yet) been called by a name' (1–2);[37] this relationship of naming to being is further highlighted in terms of the gods' own existence:

> When none of the (other) gods had been brought into being, (When) they had not (yet) been called by (their) name(s, and their) destinies had not (yet) been fixed. (At that time) were the gods created within them. Lahmu and Lahamu came into being; they were called by (their) names.
>
> (7–10)

These two passages suggest that to exist is to be named: a name cannot be applied to something not present, something not within the manifest realm. Something's name cannot be called when it is not yet there to be referred to. Or, vice versa, to be named is to exist: once a name is spoken, an object is given form and presence. The last sentence implicitly conveys the latter, relating the coming into existence of the gods Lahmu and Lahamu to their being named. This is to say that once they were referred to by their proper names, they had existence of a kind. They had been conjured into the presence of the namer, whoever that namer was.[38]

Several other examples can be produced: one Babylonian creation story tells that Marduk 'created the Tigris and Euphrates and set (them) in place; Their name(s) he appropriately proclaimed' (23–24). In a Memphite Egyptian myth, Ptah created everything that exists by calling its name.[39] In the introduction to the Sumerian *Gilgamesh, Enkidu and the Underworld*, the qualification of the post-creation world includes: 'When the name of man had been fixed' (10). The prologue to the *Rulers of Lagesh* describes the time after creation, as the time when: 'The name of mankind having been called'.[40] Here we see the implied identification of the use of humanity's name with their existence. Finally the Memphite Theology describes 'the teeth and the lips in his mouth, which proclaimed the name of everything', and the demiurge 'who created names' (col. 55).[41]

We find in these examples a consistent association of naming with creation – though the gods never use their *own* names to create. To use something's name, to name it, is to cause it to be. For something to have a name makes it a part of reality, present in the world. Really what the calling of the name seems to imply, is a calling forth from the abyss – a calling into presence, the absence of which may be identical with non-existence. Here we have some possible indication of the different ontology of the ANE – an ontology of presence (requiring relation) rather than abstract existence.[42]

Analysis

So far we have established that, while there was no Second Temple-era tradition of God creating through His Name, and no rabbinic use of this motif until well into the Islamic period, there is a persistent notion that the Name YHWH forms a seal to the world, conferring integrity and protection against the chaotic undercurrents only once the world has been created. There is a deeper idea here, that a name, while not generating an object, can be used to bind the unformed into a unity, into a cohesive thing. A seal is like a surface, the name as that which holds a scroll together and identifies it. I have discussed the ANE metaphysics, and I argued that in those texts 'being' must be conditioned by presence – so that coming into existence is not a matter of a quantum leap from absolute nothingness into substantial actuality, but rather the emergence from absence into presence; a coming-into-view out of the hidden recesses. Franz Rosenzweig similarly called into question the western philosophical tradition regarding being, preferring to think reality in terms of relation, in this case between the three substances of his philosophy – the elements God, Man, World.

In articulating reality into three mutually transcendent substances, Rosenzweig argued for both a material and an epistemological separation: the knowledge of each to the others is available only via an asymptotic process whereby *relative* being can be perceived, but not essential being – which is unconditioned by subjectivity. The absence of knowledge, however, is always a specific absence, one tied to the being of the element in question; as he writes in the opening passage of his magnum opus, *The Star of Redemption:* 'Of God we know nothing. But this ignorance is ignorance *of God'* (Rosenzweig, 1971, 23, my emphasis). In this way, the absence of knowledge is itself an affirmation, an affirmation of being which is concealed behind the lack of appearance. Beginning from an absolute absence of knowledge, the elements emerge into knowability through a process which is fundamentally linguistic (and admits of a strict grammar) – the access of objects to each other happens via language, which is to say that to the extent that they are knowable, they are speakable; they are rationalisable, and translatable into some kind of language. In relating to each other, they speak together, but this is not to reduce their internal being to what is speakable or knowable of them, for the speakable is always something of a misrepresentation, being located necessarily in a subjective stance, derivative of a contingent relationship (of the specific terms of a language, we might say). The objects themselves always remain concealed, inaccessible and indescribable.[43] But whereas the three elements 'exist' (to whatever degree we can use this term without prejudice) in hiddenness, their real coming-to-be is in their presence to the others and the interaction between them. So their own essential nature is concealed from knowledge, awaiting their emergence into the field of one of the other two. In their isolation they are effectively non-existent, but in interaction they come to be.

In blurring the ontological and epistemological phases of being, Rosenzweig echoes the idea of creation which we have found in the ANE texts. Non-existence is always non-existence-*to* a specific subject. For Rosenzweig, language as surface allows for the manifestation in consciousness of the objects which transcend each other. It is language – which in this case we might read as *names* – which allows the emergence of Elements from the dark hiddenness into relationship with each other. It is the conjunction of the basic 'no' and 'yes' of relative non-being and being which 'is the keystone of the arch of the substructure over which the edifice of the *logos* of linguistic sense is erected' (1971, 33).

In his analysis of Rosenzweigian apophaticism, W. Franke writes that while logic requires 'determinate objects' before it can make statements, language appropriates everything it touches:

> [T]here are no givens entirely outside its scope: whatever it touches becomes, in some sense, language, and to this extent it conjures its elements out of nothing but itself. In language the original presentation of the elementary terms is itself a linguistic production: a named object, as opposed to a logical object, already has a contour that is inextricably linguistic. Without its name, this element is ... nothing.
>
> (2005, 169)

Language, then, presents by reforming; in providing access to objects via their names, language also restates them as part of itself, which is to say, restates them in terms which are accessible to the subject.

For Rosenzweig, beginning from subjectivity means accepting the assumptions given in experience, rather than attempting to think beyond them into a rational a priori realm which anyway is always doomed to be a posterior – a post-experiential attempt to begin anew. Likewise, we can understand objects not through attempting to rationalise back into the point before their existence, when they were nothing, but rather analysing them now, as they are to us. And before their presence-to-us, they were merely not-present: the 'nothing' we find when inspecting the pre-beginning of our knowledge is not a nothing-of-them, but a nothing-to-us. Franke provides some interesting analysis here, arguing that what is unsayable 'neither is nor *is not*' (2005, 172, emphasis in original), because even applying the word 'is' (or verb 'to be') to it is to place it in the context of language, and to reduce it to a symbol; to speak it.

Language exists *as* the function of interaction between elements – it is not merely a communication, but is the actuality of revelation because language defines the relative properties of each element. The surface of each object is made linguistically and objects exist in relation to each other only via language. Language then is not a tool of mediation, but is relationship itself. The possibility of unfolding into external properties is provided *by* language, and happens *as* language. This is the reason for Rosenzweig's cryptic comment that 'language is rooted in the subterranean foundations of being' (1971, 145).

Rosenzweig's, then, is an ontology of surface: objects exist to the extent that they are manifest, in that their qualities and their actuality only unfold in relation to an other. The surface which glides against the other is the reality of that object, for that other.

But there is something more here. In naming, we represent yet also misrepresent an object; we create it as an other. To word something, to enword it, makes it something immediately that the word itself is not. As well as bringing the thing to us, the word becomes a screen which prevents access to the thing itself so that language both presents and masks being. A name states and yet distances irredeemably the object from the subject. Rosenzweig does not state this point explicitly, but it is present *in nuce* in his argument that the elements do not – cannot – know each other aside from their subjective manifestation as language. The dark ground of the elements in-themselves occurs prior to language and so is unknowable; unmanifest. At this point they are only the shadow of a being, but this shadow is still cast behind the linguistic presence perceived within subjectivity. He explains in the Urzelle to the Star that 'there "is" a God before all relation, whether to the world or to Himself, and this being of God, which is wholly unhypothetical, is the seed-point of the actuality of God' (Rosenzweig, 2000, 56). This is God's dark ground, 'an interiorization of God, which precedes not merely His self-externalization, but rather even His self' (ibid., 2000, 57). This comes with no mention of a prior epistemic framework through which we must understand the statement, leading Benjamin Pollock to write that: 'Rosenzweig wavers back and forth … between viewing the 'nothing' of God as God's nothing and viewing it as the 'nothing' of our knowledge of God' (Pollock, 2009, 160). The reading as solely an ontological statement would fall into the fallacy of proclaiming definitive knowledge via subjectivity, precisely the claim which Rosenzweig wants to refuse; rather, the emergence of God into ontological being is identical with the epistemological being of relation, while the corollary of this is not that God does not exist beyond relation, but that the formative absence of knowledge of God's internality is identical with a formal absence which *is* God.[44] What is concealed behind the language of a thing? Precisely the *nothing* which we would know without language; precisely its lack of being, a lack which yet still is specific to that thing. It may be wrong to call this an essence; it is not the root or core of the thing, but it is still there as that which identifies the substance and links the different instantiations of it as the same thing. This 'essence', then, is hidden only in a sense; in another sense there is nothing to be hidden, because hiddenness suggests something which could be brought to view whereas here it is precisely the opposite: the perception has created the possibility of something which transcends it.

Now, if language is an action, rather than a stasis, then names will have a pivotal function in identifying entities. The relationship between a name and its object is not that of signifier and signified. A name designates otherhood, but it is much more than merely a tag for us to identify that other: A person's name identifies her among others, but also her as a unity. In direct correspondence to Rosenzweig's claim that the objective must be approached – can only be approached – subjectively, he also believes that language is not a mask which conceals or distorts meaning but is the beginning of allowing access to that meaning. Just as language is the essential characteristic of humanity because it is 'the only visible witness to his soul' (1971, 147), so the visible witness to the inner nature of anything is its language. This is true especially for the Name of God. Barbara Galli writes,

> God's name ... as revelation, will by no means be a mere humanly devised label attached to a datum, nor can it become a name associated with magical powers for coercing God. As revelation, the name will nevertheless say something about God. But that saying will demonstrate 'the submission of subjectivity to an outside authority.' The humanly spoken name for God, in its submissive saying, then conveys both something of the divine, and something about revelation to a listener of that saying. This limitation, this 'something' of the divine and of revelation, means that the name by which we call God will be restricted to that which God reveals, but can contain, and convey, no less than that.
>
> (1994, 66)

Stéphane Moses talks about the distinction between God's transcendental essence and the Name as revealed:

> ... [T]he speakable Name, the one that Jewish tradition substitutes for the revealed Name considered unspeakable. For [Rosenzweig], the apparently paradoxical nature of this prohibition, which pertains to the revealed Name, disappears when one understands that the prohibition aims at making man conscious of the fact that this Name is not a substitute, that it sends back, beyond the world of speech, to an unnameable essence.
>
> (1992, 268)

In Moses' reading of Rosenzweig the essence is concealed behind the Name, because of the very fact that it is expressed *by* it. The Nothing has become Something, in the Name.

In Rosenzweig and Buber's Bible, the revealed name Ehyeh Asher Ehyeh is not translated in an ontological sense, but rather in an ethical one – as the One Who will be there with His people – and here, Rosenzweig's statement that: 'The name of God is only a special case of the problem of names in general' (1999, 89) is crucial, in that naming holds a power: it calls into presence, it does more than just point and refer, it brings the other before us. It identifies them to us, as an individual existing thing. So, Rosenzweig says:

> With the proper name, the rigid wall of objectness has been breached. That which has a name of its own can no longer be a thing, no longer an

everyman's affair. It is incapable of utter absorption into the category for there can be no category for it to belong to; it is its own category.

(1971, 186–7)

Naming admits of an identity which is more than the sum of its parts, and is too individual to allow subsumption under general categorical definitions – it refuses to be part of a totalised framework. Naming thus functions both to differentiate an object from the subject, by giving it an integrity, but also serves to bring that nature before us. The object, previously unknown in its separation from us, is now presented as a separate with an irreducible unity in itself. Although this essential object cannot be dissolved within the subject, it is now real to us in some sense; the essence is not knowable and the object is not totalisable, but we can recognise that it is indeed an object, and therefore does have an essence.

And it is here, finally, that we may be able to offer a different reading of the rabbinic discourse on creation; the *heh* through which God creates is not the *heh* which stands in for His Name; it is not merely a letter of the alphabet; rather it is a word, the prefix definite article *ha-* which connotes specific individuality. The being of individual things outside of any categorical definition (what Bielik-Robson [2012] defined as emanation) is the outcome of creation, and this creation is accomplished not by the generation 'in the beginning' of the material which constitutes them, but by the specification of their unique substantial identity, by their naming.[45]

Rosenzweig in fact argues that God's creation of the world neither negates, nor predates, the world's own existence: 'God spoke. That came second. It is not the beginning. It is already the audible fulfilment of the silent beginning' (1971, 112). The nothing of the world inheres without this relation to God. The world in-itself still is, though at this point awaiting the verbalising which will materialise it. In one telling passage, he claims: 'That God created the world is unlimited truth only for the subject.... Without involving the subject, no mere analysis of this sentence can elicit a true statement about the object alone.' (1971, 119). Creation is thus not a physical process, but a metaphysical one. The world takes its nature as creature in 'being created, not of having been created' (ibid.), creation being an on-going process of manifestation via the speaking of names.

Notes

1 Depending on one's priorities, the aspects of linguistic creation can be divided differently. Idel (2002) makes creation via the Name one of four linguistic creation motifs, the others being Studying Torah, combining letters, and speaking things into existence. Tzahi Weiss (2007) describes only two more: creation via the alphabet, and creation of the upper world via the alphabet. More recently, Weiss has argued that the mythical role of language or letters in creation is not uniquely Jewish but rather is a frequent motif representing the powerful fascination which language holds for human beings. So:

   [I]n several cultural contexts of Late Antiquity, there was no doubt that the world had been created from letters ... [furthermore] in ancient Greece, independent of

Semitic conceptions concerning the importance of alphabetic signs, the word *sto-icheion* (στοιχεῖον) was used both to refer to letters and to signify the physical foundations of the world.

(2009, 102)

In fact it is the Greek word *stoicheion* which demonstrates the shared 'atomic' nature of both reality and language.

2 Elliot Wolfson writes of:

[T]he archaic belief that heaven and earth were created by means of the name of God, an idea attested in apocryphal, rabbinic and mystical sources as well, specifically in terms of *yod* and *he*, the first two letters of the Tetragrammaton used to signify the complete name.

(2000, 255)

For similar references see also Janowitz (1989, 26 and 85–86), Endo (2002), and McDonough (1999, 128–130).

3 Two other non-canonical texts make use of the Name in reference to creation, these being *Liber Antiquitatum Biblicarum* and the *Prayer of Manasseh*. However there is a clear difference in type between these traditions and Jubilees, which I will return to in the second section of this chapter.

4 Fossum writes: 'The letter *He*, occurring twice in the Tetragrammaton, is here obviously representing the full Name of God' (1985, 253, cf. 246–247). This is highly uncertain though. *Heh* is often used as an abbreviation of the Name YHWH – but only in obvious contexts in order to prevent the Name being pronounced or written out in full; it's a scribal convention, not a standard of symbolism. Lauterbach, in his classical analysis of rabbinic abbreviations and substitutes for the Name of God, writes that although a word is often abbreviated to its initial letter: 'Another method of abbreviating a word in talmudic times was to represent it by its last letter or one of its middle letters. Accordingly, the letter He was used as an abbreviation for the Tetragrammaton' (1931, 41). But this must surely not be taken to apply to every time the letter is used, especially if an alternative meaning is provided in the text itself.

5 In fact, a more obvious interpretation of the passage would be the creative word, *yehi* – also constituted of the letters *yod* and *heh*. This is argued by McDonough (1999, 130). It is clear that there is room for speculation on the relationship between the creative word YHY and the Tetragrammaton YHWH: aside from the likely etymological similarity (discussed above), *yehi* of course contains the letters יה, a common shortening of the Tetragrammaton used throughout the Bible. It is easily possible then to perceive a relationship between God's own Name and the process of creation. A wealth of evidence supports this from the time of the Kabbalah onward: the Samaritan liturgy reads: 'It was created by a word, [namely by] יהי' (Fossum, 1985, 78). The Zohar's *Book of Concealment* relates *yehi* to YHWH, in articulating the distinction between the *yod* which is of Chokhmah and the *yod* which is of Tiferet, 'with the H between serving as a symbol of completeness' (Rosenberg, 1973, 19). The (slightly earlier) Unique Cherub Circle interpreted the phrase *Yehi Shemo* as indicating that the Name of God was *Yehi* (Dan, 1999, 80). However, as this study shows, there is no explicit evidence within the texts themselves that this was done at any point prior to the thirteenth century CE.

6 See, e.g. Scholem (1972, 71), and Wolfson (2000, 249). In fact Scholem, writing that: 'One can presume that among these letters those of the divine name are to be understood, although it might also be conceivable that in an extended sense a combination of the alphabet is intended, thus a broader notion', is much closer to the evidence than Wolfson, who appears to read back into Late Antiquity a kabbalistic doctrine of the ontological primacy of the Name as the cause not only of matter but also of the rest of the alphabet and language.

7 E.g. Scholem (1996, 166ff.); Fossum (1985, 246).

8 This passage goes on, as with Ber.Rab.12:10, to parallel b.Men.29b.

9 This text was at the time of Fossum's writing dated to the second to the fourth century CE (Macdonald, 1963, xvii–xx). It has now been redated such that only the first two books date from this period, the later ones – from which comes Fossum's evidence – seem to originate in the sixth century or later: see the detailed analysis of Ben Hayyim (1988). The current dating makes Fossum's conclusions regarding its importance less tenable, but it remains important to address the material due to its centrality in his argument and the strength of the doctrine's apparent presence within the text. All translations are based on Macdonald's, with minor alterations (and noting the valid criticisms in the review of Ben-Hayyim [1996]).

10 The liturgy, although in part dating from the fourth century, contains material from right up until its redaction in the fourteenth century.

11 It is evident that, while much is made of the fact that Moses (משה) is an anagram of *HaShem* (השם, or equally the Aramaic *Shemah*, שמה) which has since become an equivocation for the Tetragrammaton, Exod.7:1 does record God telling Moses: 'See, I make you a god (*Elohim*) to Pharaoh'. Thus we have a biblical basis for the investment of Moses with the name of God, where this name is not the 'Great Name' YHWH but the creative name Elohim. Fossum (1985, 89) discusses W.A. Meeks' argument around this passage and its use in MMarq, but ultimately defers to his own, flawed, conclusion that *heh* must represent the Tetragrammaton. Fossum's claim that 'when Moses is said to have been vested with the name of Elohim, this is obviously a secondary notion, derived from the original idea of his investiture with the Tetragrammaton' (1985, 90) thus seems precisely backward: rather, it is investiture with the Tetragrammaton which has later been assumed from the earlier sources which talk both explicitly and suggestively about investiture with the name which is Elohim.

12 Confusingly, one passage inverts the usual associations: 'Heh for the Creation, Alef for the Day of Vengeance; Heh began and Alef ended!' (IV.7). I am unsure how to reconcile this.

13 In fact there is a surprisingly similar pattern discernible in the Unique Cherub Circle some thousand years later, who appear to hold the highest divine power Elohim as responsible for creation, while the emanated potency of the Kavod, which bears the name YHWH, comes into full being only at the completion of creation (Dan, 1999, 142–160).

14 We find some references to the creative word in *Songs of the Sabbath Sacrifice* (4Q400) 33–36, 4Q381 and 4Q422 but these are never related to the Name. On creation in Qumran, see esp. Gordley (2008) and Nitzan (2002). 4Q381 and 4Q422 are analysed in Endo (2002).

15 The isolation of these four texts is based on a thorough analysis of the texts collected in *Old Testament Pseudepigrapha* (1985), as well as the readings offered by Endo (2002). Creation via the word is a repeated motif of these texts, but this does not indicate a doctrine on the nature of the word or language; the word is only one divine attribute utilised in descriptions of creation, others include God's wisdom and his hands, often within the same texts. I concur with Endo that these divine attributes are utilised in order to highlight the fact that no one else but God was responsible for or involved in creation; even His tools are aspects of His own being. Rubin (1998) on the other hand has provided a well-constructed argument for the presence of a strongly nationalistic vision of Hebrew as the sacred language of creation and revelation from the second century BCE onwards, which may contribute to the highlighting of creation via words.

16 'The recent recovery of a Hebrew version in a medieval manuscript from the Cairo Geniza does not seem to provide evidence to help resolve the debate' (Davila, 2007, 76).

17 See Chapter 2, Note 6.

18 There is still much debate about the nature of the oath in *Similitudes*, as well as the perhaps related terms *biqa* and *akae*. For the most recent in depth discussion see Nickeslburg and VanderKam (2012, 304–310). Ben Dov and Ratzon (2015) have offered a clear-headed reappraisal of the issues, arguing in part that the powerful name of 69:13–14 was originally in the possession of Kasbe'el, Michael being a later interpolation. The name then may not even be that of God at all. Olson (2004, 271) points to a remarkable parallel in Zohar *Shemot* 9a–9b, which claims that בך is a divine name, related (by its gematria value) to the name of twenty-two letters. However, this certainly says more about the Zohar and its possible knowledge of *Similitudes* than it does about *Similitudes'* own intention.

19 This text was noted by Fossum (1985) but apparently without spotting this passage, which was first noticed by Endo (2002, 139).

20 And in fact, this is closer to what Scholem himself asserted, 'it is this name which brought about the creation, or rather the creation is closely affixed to the Name – i.e. the creation is contained within its limits by the name' (1972, 68).

21 Some LXX manuscripts from the same period do not write the Name of God in any transliteration or equivocation, but rather render it in Paleo-Hebrew. This suggests that originally the scribe may have left a space in the text where the Name would be inserted later. This is notably the case in Papyrus Fouad 266, a first century BCE manuscript, and Papyrus Rylands 458, a second century BCE manuscript – both of which have a blank space where the Tetragrammaton would (presumably) later be inserted. This finds further support in Ben Dov and Ratzon (2015), who argue that the mysterious 'number' of Kasbe'el in 1En.69:4–14 was in fact a later scribe's explanation of the lacuna left for the number to be written in with a different script or pen, which has since become integrated as a part of the text.

22 In fact creation via the Torah is much more prominent – see e.g. m.Avot3:14, Ber. Rab.1:1, Sifre Deut.48, Midr.Tanh.1:5, Ag.Ber.24. It is entirely plausible that this tradition was highlighted by the rabbis in order to counter the tradition of creation via the Name which had morphed into binitarian doctrine (see Chapter 2). In an interesting inversion of the earlier tradition that the Name is inscribed on humans or angels, Idel (2002, 43) notes a late midrash, *Aseret ha-Dibberot*, which has the Torah inscribed on God: 'Before the creation of the world, skins for parchments were not in existence, that the Torah might be written on them, because the animals did not yet exist. So, on what was the Torah written? On the arm of the Holy One, blessed be He, by a black fire on [the surface of] a white fire'.

23 On the Urim and Thummim 'is clearly inscribed the great and holy Name through which the three hundred and ten worlds were created' (Tg.Ps.-J. to Exod.28:30). Tg.Ps.-J. is dated, at the earliest, to the fourth century CE (Mortensen, 2006), but may be much later.

24 MMerk appears to equate the creative speech of Genesis with God's Name, claiming within a few lines that: 'You spoke and the world existed, By the breath of your lips you established the firmament' (§587) and the one who spoke was: 'Creator of the world by his one Name, fashioner of all by one word' (§596). Likewise in HekhZ, God 'established the irrefutable name, with which to design the entire universe' (§348, following Morray-Jones (2009, 278). In *3 Enoch* God writes on Metatron's crown:

> [T]he letters by which heaven and earth were created … seas and rivers were created … mountains and hills were created … stars and constellations, lightning and wind, thunder and thunderclaps, snow and hail, hurricane and tempest were created; the letters by which all the necessities of the world and all the orders of creation were created.
>
> (13:1)

Later, a near identical passage has these letters 'engraved with a pen of flame upon the throne of glory' (41:1–3). That these creative letters would be those of the Name is confirmed when 'all the sacred names *engraved with a pen of flame on the throne of glory* fly off like eagles' (39:1, on the motif of God's crown inscribed with His Name, see Green, 1997, 42–48). At other points Metatron is said to be written with the letter (singular) by which heaven and earth were created (e.g. §389 in manuscripts N8128 and M40) – a letter we may presume to be *heh*, in light of the early traditions discussed above.

25 The ninth century *Pesiqta Rabbati* records R Judah b.Simon stating that, 'the name of God creates and destroys worlds' and 'even one letter of His name is capable of creating hosts as the whole of His name' (104A, Marmorstein 1927, 43). Likewise the tenth century *Alphabet of R Akiva* states that 'יה is none other than the Ineffable Name by which the world was created.' (Urbach, 1979, 198) Also in the tenth century, R Solomon ben Isaac Rashi of Troyes states that: 'They used to combine the letters of the Name, by which the universe was created. This is not to be considered forbidden magic, for the works of God were brought into being through His holy Name' (Fossum, 1985, 246).

26 Texts such as 'your name, the source of all creation' (1Clem.59:2), and: 'The Name of the Son of God is great and infinite, and sustains the whole world' (Shepherd of Hermas 9.14.5) provide an association of the Name with creation stronger than we have seen in any other Jewish literature of the time. Stroumsa (2003, 237) has noted that the Didache invokes God's Holy Name, for whose sake all things were created (10.2), and is apparently glossed by Col.1:15–16, which claims of Jesus, 'all things have been created through him and for him'.

27 This may be supported by Barry (1999, 105–125), who locates the initial emergence of a nominal creation myth in the Gnostics Marcus and Marsanes and the text Pistis Sophia.

28 All translations are from Hayman (2004).

29 The chaotic is sometimes personified as a demon or monster. Yahoel – who famously bears 'the ineffable Name within me', – has the authority 'to restrain Leviathan ... [and] to loosen Hades' (Apoc.Ab.10:10–11). Solomon uses chains inscribed with the Name to trap the demon Ashmedai (b.Git.68a); Moses fights off Sammael, who has come to take his soul, with a staff inscribed with the Name (Urbach, 1979, 176), and in another passage attempts to fend off death by praying a prayer 'like the Ineffable Name, which he had learnt from Zagza'el, his teacher, the scribe of all the heavenly beings' (Deut.Rab.9:9). Frequently in the Hekhalot literature, the Name is an apotropaic seal, conferring protection upon the rabbis from the threatening angels. In a Greek magical papyrus 'the dragon of chaos moved and rocked the creation, whereupon God brought it to rest and made the world stable again by proclaiming "IAO!" ' (PGM XIII.539, Betz 1986, 186). Fossum (1985, 249) relates this and SY to the Gnostic *Pistis Sophia* 4.136 (third–fourth century), where Jesus calls out IAO to the four corners of the world.

30 In Psalm 104:5–9 God confines and bounds the waters, but without recourse to the Name.

31 Scholem (1972, 70) claims it is also found HekhR Ch.23, but I am unable to locate it there.

32 See Chapter 1, Note 18.

33 Cf. b.Mak.11a; and p.Sanh.29a, where David finds the potsherd which suppresses the deep – but without reference to the Name. We also find a talmudic sugya tells that sailors use a club with the names 'Ehyeh Asher Ehyeh, Yah, YHWH Tzvaot' to beat the sea and calm it (b.Bat.73a, suggestive of Jesus' calming of the waters and statement of 'I am' in John 6:20). In *3 Enoch*, R Ishmael witnesses 'water suspended in the height of the heaven of Arabot, through the power of the name Yah, Ehyeh Asher Ehyeh' (42:2) and lists a number of heavenly miracles accomplished or sustained through the power of the various divine names: fire, snow and hailstones which do not consume one another; lightning and snow which do not quench one another; thunder

and voices sustained within flames; rivers of fire and water which coexisted. Here the power of the Name to separate is evident.

34 In Gen.Rab.1:9 Torah, Throne of Glory; Patriarchs, Israel, the Temple, the name of the Messiah, and Repentance were all created prior to the world. The speaker doesn't know whether Torah or Throne was first, but R Kahana claims it was the Torah. Cf. b. Pes.54a:

> Seven things were created before the world was created, and these are they: The Torah, repentance, the Garden of Eden, Gehenna, the Throne of Glory, the Temple, and the name of the Messiah. The Torah, for it is written, *The Lord made me as the beginning of his way* [Prov.8:22].... The name of the Messiah, as it is written, *His name shall endure for ever, and has existed before the sun!*
>
> (Ps.72:17, cf. b.Ned.39b)

35 May concludes that: 'Only with Christian theologians of the second century did the traditional saying, that God created the world out of nothing, take on a principled ontological sense' (1994, 22). Winston concurs, in that 'there is no evidence that the rabbis were especially attached to a doctrine of creation *ex nihilo*' (1971, 202). In fact it is not even present in Sefer Yetzirah; Hayman writes: 'The predominant image in SY of God as creator is that of the artist working on pre-existent materials' (2004, 35). Those passages which do suggest creation *ex nihilo* appear to be corrective glosses.

36 Some kabbalists also refuted creation from nothing – R Ezra of Gerona argues against creation ex nihilo – citing Pirq. R El.3: That God does not create something from nothing should not be considered a diminution of His power, just as there is no diminution in His inability to create logically impossible entities.... For this too is included in the general category of impossibility (Commentary to Song of Songs 3:9, Brody 1991, 70). However, R Bahya b. Asher of Saragossa seems to disagree with Ezra – 'heaven and earth and all of their generations were created on the first day from complete nothingness and absolute non-existence, as is denoted by the verb "created" [*bara*], which refers to the creation of being from nought' (*Commentary on Genesis* 1:1–2, Brody 1991, 211). For many of the early kabbalists however, the doctrine of existence [*yesh*] from nothing [*ayin*] represents the emergence of Chokhmah from Keter – a more complex emanatory creation from the transcendent non-being of God (see Chapter 6).

37 Heidel elucidates: 'i.e., did not yet exist as such' (1951, 18). All translations are from his text.

38 Heidel (1951, 18) elucidates that: This line shows that forms or beings can exist before they have been named' by which I presume he means, exist in principle prior to emerging into reality. We see much the same in a liturgical poem by Isaac Girondi which states 'God created light from the light of His garment; before it existed, He gave it a name (*Yah 'or mi-sut 'or bera'o*, Langermann 2004, 214).

39 Hasenfratz (2002, 176).

40 Clifford (1994, 48) also remarks that this formula refers to the creation of human beings.

41 It is also present in the Gnostic *Gospel of Truth* which, among other passages, announces that God 'reveals anyone whom he desires by giving him a form and by giving him a name; and he does give him a name and cause him to come into being'.

42 Admittedly this motif is not ubiquitous in the creation myths of the ANE – other methods including sexual procreation and violent battle are if anything more common – but it serves to illustrate the nature of the power which names held within the culture that Ancient Judaism emerged from, and interacted with.

43 It is worth noting at this point that Rosenzweig does claim that objects in themselves are describable in a sense – but only via the abstract symbolism of philosophical or

mathematical logic, that 'language of the world which is prior to the world' (1971, 125). In an articulation whose import will become clear in Chapter 6, he defines God's inner nature as 'A=A', where the first term states the subject and the second the predicate. His point is that this can articulate abstract actuality, yet without making any meaningful statement that we as humans could consider informative. Meaning can only be articulated in human language, language which can only represent how things are *to-humans.*

44 It should be emphasised here that there is not, for Rosenzweig, any ontological distinction between the essential 'nothing' which pre-exists relative being, and the stated 'something' of relative being; the latter is the former in articulation, apparent to subjectivity. See esp. Rosenzweig (1999, 148). This relationship itself will be further investigated in Chapter 3.

45 Daniel Weiss (2012) has argued that precisely this is also what Rosenzweig perceived as the deliberate strategy of the Bible: to never describe God in Godself, only ever in relation to human beings, and thus avoiding any definite assertions about God. Weiss argues that for Rosenzweig there is no clearer restatement of the Biblical message as regards God's corporeality or incorporeality, because the vagueness is not an accidental affect veiling a concrete truth.

Bibliography

The Babylonian Talmud (32 vols). 1990. Edited by Rabbi Dr. I. Epstein. London: The Soncino Press.

Midrash Rabbah (10 vols). 1939. Translated by R Dr. H. Freedman and Maurice Simon. London: The Soncino Press.

The Nag Hammadi Library in English. 1990. Edited by James M. Robinson. Third edition. New York: HarperCollins.

Old Testament Pseudepigrapha (2 vols). 1985. Edited by James Charlesworth. New York/London: Doubleday.

The Talmud of the Land of Israel (35 vols). 1983. Translated by Jacob Nuesner. London: University of Chicago Press.

Targum Neofiti 1 and Pseudo-Jonathan: Exodus. 1994. Translated by Martin McNamara and Michael Maher. Edinburgh: T&T Clark.

Barry, Kieran. 1999. *The Greek Qabalah: Alphabetical Mysticism and Numerology in the Ancient World.* York Beach: Weiser.

Ben Dov, Jonathan and Eshbal Ratzon. 2015. The Oath and the Name in 1 Enoch 69, *Journal of Semitic Studies* 60(1), 19–51.

Ben Hayyim, Ze'ev. 1988. *Tibat Marqe: A Collection of Samaritan Midrashim.* (Hebrew). Jerusalem: Israel Academy of Sciences and Humanities.

Ben-Hayyim, Z. 1996. Review of John MacDonald, *Memar Marqah: The Teaching of Marqah.'* *Bibliotheca Orientalis* 23, 185–191.

Betz, Hans Dieter. 1986. *The Greek Magical Papyrae in Translation.* London: University of Chicago Press.

Bielik-Robson, Agata. 2012. The Promise of the Name: 'Jewish Nominalism' as the Critique of Idealist Tradition. *Bamidbar* 1(3), 11–35.

Boman, Thorlief. 1960. *Hebrew Thought Compared With Greek.* London: SCM Press Ltd.

Brody, Seth Lance. 1991. *Human Hands Dwell in Heavenly Heights: Worship and Mystical Experience in Thirteenth Century Kabbalah.* PhD diss., University of Pennsylvania.

Clifford, Richard J. 1994. *Creation Accounts in the Ancient Near East and in the Bible.* Washington: Catholic Bible Association of America.

Dan, Joseph. 1999. *The 'Unique Cherub' Circle: A School of Mystics and Esoterics in Medieval Germany.* Tübingen: Mohr Siebeck.

Davila, James R. 2007. Is the Prayer of Manasseh a Jewish Work? In: Lynn LiDonnici and Andrea Lieber. eds. *Heavenly Tablets: Interpretation, Identity and Tradition in Ancient Judaism.* Leiden: Brill, 75–86.

Endo, Masanobu. 2002. *Creation and Christology: A Study on the Johannine Prologue in the Light of Early Jewish Creation Accounts.* Tübingen: Mohr Siebeck.

Fossum, Jarl E. 1985. *The Name of God and the Angel of the Lord: Samaritan and Jewish Concepts of Intermediation and the Origin of Gnosticism.* Tübingen: Mohr Siebeck.

Franke, W. 2005. Rosenzweig and the Emergence of a Postsecular Philosophy of the Unsayable. *International Journal for Philosophy of Religion* 58, 161–180.

Galli, Barbara E. 1994. Rosenzweig and the Name for God. *Modern Judaism* 14(1), 63–86.

Jonathan Goldstein. 1983. *II Maccabees* (Anchor Bible vol. 41A). Garden City, NY: Doubleday.

Gordley, Matthew. 2008. Creation Imagery in Qumran Hymns and Prayers. *Journal of Jewish Studies* 59(2), 252–272.

Green, Arthur. 1997. *Keter: The Crown of God in Early Jewish Mysticism.* Princeton: Princeton University Press.

Hasenfratz, Hans-Peter. 2002. Patterns of Creation in Ancient Egypt. In: Henning Grant Reventlow and Yair Hoffman. eds. *Creation in Jewish and Christian Thought.* London: Sheffield Academic Press, 174–178.

Hayman, Peter. 1989. Was God a Magician? Sefer Yesira and Jewish Magic. *Journal of Jewish Studies* 41(2), 225–237.

Hayman, A. Peter. 2004. *Sefer Yesira: Edition, Translation and Text-Critical Commentary.* Tübingen: Mohr Siebeck.

Heidel, Alexander. 1951. *The Babylonian Genesis: The Story of Creation.* London: University of Chicago Press.

Idel, Moshe. 2002. *Absorbing Perfections: Kabbalah and Interpretation.* New York: Yale University Press.

Janowitz, Naomi. 1989. *The Poetics of Ascent: Theories of Language in a Rabbinic Ascent Text.* Albany: State University of New York Press.

Langermann, Y. Tzvi. 2004. Cosmology and Cosmogony in *Doresh Reshumoth,* a Thirteenth-Century Commentary on the Torah. *Harvard Theological Review* 97(2), 199–227.

Lauterbach, Jacob Z. 1931. Substitutes for the Tetragrammaton. *Proceedings of the American Academy for Jewish Research* 2, 39–67.

Macdonald, John, ed. and trans. 1963. *Memar Marqah: The Teaching of Marqah* (2 vols). Berlin: Verlag Alfred Topelmann.

Marmorstein, A. 1927. *The Old Rabbinic Doctrine of God* (2 vols). London: Oxford University Press.

May, Gerhard. 1994. *Creatio Ex Nihilo: The Doctrine of 'Creation out of Nothing' in Early Christian Thought.* Edinburgh: T&T Clark.

McDonough, Sean M. 1999. *YHWH at Patmos: Rev. 1:4 in its Hellenistic and Early Jewish Setting.* Tübingen: Mohr Siebeck.

Mortensen, Beverly P. 2006. *The Priesthood in Targum Pseudo-Jonathan: Renewing the Profession* (2 vols). Leiden: Brill.

Mosès, Stéphane. 1992. *System and Revelation.* Translated by Catherine Tihanyi. Detroit: Wayne State University Press.

Nickelsburg, George W.E. and James C. VanderKam. 2012. *1 Enoch 2: A Commentary on the Book of 1 Enoch Chapters 37–82.* Minneapolis: Fortress Press.

Nitzan, Bilha. 2002. The Idea of Creation and Its Implications in Qumran Literature. In: H.G. Reventlow and Y. Hoffman. eds. *Creation in Jewish and Christian Tradition.* Sheffield: Sheffield Academic Press, 240–265.

Olson, Daniel C. 2004. *Enoch: A New Translation.* In consultation with Archbishop Melkesedek Workeneh. North Richland Hills: Bibal Press.

Pollock, Benjamin. 2009. *Franz Rosenzweig and the Systematic Task of Philosophy.* Cambridge: Cambridge University Press.

Rosenberg, Roy A. trans. 1973. *The Anatomy of God: The Book of Concealment, The Greater Holy Assembly and The Lesser Holy Assembly of the Zohar with The Assembly of the Tabernacle.* New York: Ktav.

Rosenzweig, Franz. 1971. *The Star of Redemption.* Translated by William W. Hallo. London: Routledge & Kegan Paul.

Rosenzweig, Franz. 1999. *The New Thinking.* Translated by Alan Udoff and Barbara Galli. Syracuse: Syracuse University Press.

Rosenzweig, Franz. 2000. 'Urzelle' to the Star of Redemption. In: Paul W. Franks and Michael L. Morgan. eds and trans. *Franz Rosenzweig: Philosophical and Theological Writings.* Indianapolis: Hackett Publishing.

Rowland, Christopher and Christopher R.A. Morray-Jones. 2009. *The Mystery of God: Early Jewish Mysticism and the New Testament.* Leiden: Brill.

Rubin, Milka. 1998. The Language of Creation of the Primordial Language: A Case of Cultural Polemics in Antiquity. *Journal of Jewish Studies* 49(2), 306–333.

Schäfer, Peter, Margarete Schlüter and Hans Georg von Mutius. eds. 1981. *Synopse zur Hekhalot-Literatur.* Tübingen: Mohr Siebeck.

Scholem, Gershom. 1972/1973. 'The Name of God and the Linguistic Theory of the Kabbalah. *Diogenes* 79 (1972), 59–80; *Diogenes* 80 (1973), 164–194.

Scholem, Gershom. 1996 [1965]. *On the Kabbalah and its Symbolism.* New York: Schocken.

Stern, Josef. 2009. Language. In: Arthur A. Cohen and Paul Mendes-Flohr. eds. *20th Century Jewish Religious Thought.* Philadelphia: Jewish Publication Society, 543–551.

Stroumsa, Guy G. 2003. A Nameless God: Judaeo-Christian and Gnostic 'Theologies of the Name'. In: Peter J. Tomson and Doris Lambers-Petry. eds. *The Image of the Judaeo-Christians in Ancient Jewish and Christian Literature.* Tübingen: Mohr Siebeck, 230–244.

Urbach, Ephraim E. 1979. *The Sages – Their Concepts and Beliefs* (2 vols). Jerusalem: Magnes Press.

Weiss, Daniel. 2012. Rosenzweig and Divine Attributes. Paper presented at the University of Nottingham, 4 March.

Weiss, Tzahi. 2007. Three Traditions of the Creation of the World from Letters. (Hebrew). *Kabbalah* 17, 169–200.

Weiss, Tzahi. 2009. On the Matter of Language: The Creation of the World from Letters and Jacques Lacan's Perception of Letters as Real. *Journal of Jewish Thought and Philosophy* 17(1), 101–115.

Winston, David. 1971. The Book of Wisdom's Theory of Cosmogony. *History of Religions* 11(2), 185–202.

Wolfson, Elliot R. 2000. Judaism and Incarnation: The Imaginal Body of God. In: Tikva Frymer-Kensky, David Novak, Peter Ochs, David Fox Sandmel and Michael A. Singer. eds. *Christianity in Jewish Terms.* Boulder: Westview Press, 239–253.

Wolfson, H.A. 1947. *Philo: Foundations of Religious Philosophy in Judaism, Christianity and Islam.* Cambridge: Harvard University Press.

2   Losing the Name
Derrida's rejection of Logos theology

This chapter will offer an analysis of some early (Jewish-)Christian traditions which associate the Name of God with Christ. There has been a growing consensus in recent years' research regarding the linear development of early Christology from Second Temple Jewish speculation on the Principal Angel, who bore or embodied the Name. Herein I will present early Christianity, prior to the separation of the faiths several centuries later, as the logical conclusion of a certain onto-hypostatic interpretation of these traditions; one which was ultimately rejected by the rabbinic movement in its reformation of Judaism. The possible reasons for this rejection will then be explicated with the help of Derrida's *Sauf le Nom*, a textual play on *via negativa*, the possibility of naming God, and the theological implications we fall into when making too blunt statements about God's Name, if the Name is a word like any other then what it points to is an object like any other and the Name as an attempt to *incarnate* God in the world leads into some problematic territory which confuses the identity and nature of text and world.

The textual evidence

The nominal tradition is found in several documents of the New Testament, most clearly in John's Gospel, the letters of Paul, and the Revelation of St. John.[1] Outside the New Testament there is supporting evidence in several sources, including Justin Martyr and the Nag Hammadi corpus.

There appear to be three separate aspects of this nominal tradition in the early Christian documents. Jesus is appellated with the Name as a means of identifying him with God; he (and the faithful) are inscribed with the Name; and most importantly for this study, in some passages Jesus is identified *as* the Name of God.[2]

Appellation with the Name

Often in the New Testament we find statements that Jesus has been given some kind of special name. It is written that God 'highly exalted him and gave him the name that is above every name' (Phil.2:9); likewise Christ is 'above every name that is named, not only in this age but in the age to come' (Eph.1:21). Christ is the Son through whom God created the worlds, who 'sustains all things by his powerful word', and who is superior to the angels because 'the name he has inherited is more excellent than theirs' (Heb.1:1–4). It is generally accepted by scholars that 'the name that is above every name' refers to the Tetragrammaton (Peerbolte, 2006, 201).

In John, Jesus claims to 'have made your [God's] name known' in the world (17:6, cf. 17:25), but also beseeches God: 'Holy Father, protect them in your name that you have given me' (John 17:11). The conjunction of these verses implies that the name Jesus has been given is God's own, which he is now responsible for manifesting or providing to the world.[3]

That the Messiah shares the Name of God is not an exclusively New Testament construction. b.Bava Bathra 75b records R Samuel b.Nahmani claiming, in the name of R Johanan:

> Three were called by the name of the Holy One, blessed be He, and they are the following: The righteous, the Messiah, and Jerusalem.... [As regards] the Messiah, it is written: 'And this is the name whereby he shall be called: "YHWH our righteousness".' (Jer.23:6)
>
> (b.Bab.Bat.75b)[4]

The proof-text used here, Jeremiah 23:6, is not utilised explicitly in the New Testament, yet makes an unequivocal statement that the Messiah's name includes the Name YHWH.

There is also the curious rabbinic tradition which misreads Psalm 72:17 'before the sun may his name increase (יִנּוֹן)' as 'before the sun, his [i.e., the Messiah's] name is Yinnon' (b.Sanh.98b). Although the original text provides יָנִין (*yanin*; a Hiphil of the root נִין, *nin*), the *qere* (marginal reading) assumes יִנּוֹן (*yinnon*; a Niphal form), which in displaying the form YNWN is highly suggestive of the Tetragrammaton, YHWH.[5]

A strikingly similar passage to the above appears in *Similitudes* (1En.37–71):[6]

> And in that hour that son of man was named in the presence of the Lord of the Spirits, and his name, before the Head of days. Even before the sun and the constellations were created, before the stars of heaven were made, his name was named before the Lord of Spirits.
>
> (48:1–3)

Scott (2008) has argued for a binitarian reading of this text, which appears to differentiate between the Lord of Spirits and the Name of the Lord of Spirits, the latter of which is identified with the 'Chosen One'. It is fairly clear that here, the 'name' given to the Son of Man, a name which existed 'before the sun and the constellations were created, before the stars of heaven were made', must be God's own Name.[7] The Son himself 'was chosen and hidden in his presence before the world was created forever' (48.6). Further, this text itself is paralleled in John's gospel, when Jesus asks: 'Father, glorify me in your own presence with the glory that I had in your presence before the world existed' (17:5).[8]

Therefore we have both prior to and after the New Testament, similar Jewish traditions which claim that a messianic figure shares in the Name of God. This ascription of the Divine Name to the Messiah is likely a means of identifying him with God; of asserting an ontological continuity between God and His Redeemer.

Inscription with the Name

The inscription of the Name is a motif found repeatedly in Revelation, where it is obviously part of a well-developed tradition, though one we have little other evidence of. The physical inscription of a name, either God's or Satan's, is the reward of human beings for their behaviour – and the specific inscription denotes ownership by the power named. Thus, the servants of God are to be marked 'with a seal on their foreheads' (7:3); the locusts are commanded to damage 'only those people who do not have the seal of God on their foreheads' (9:4). With the lamb are 'one hundred forty-four thousand who had his name and his father's name written on their foreheads' (14:1).[9] Here, as discussed in Chapter 1, the 'seal' of the Name confers protection from evil. At the outset however, Jesus promises: 'If you conquer ... I will write on you the name of my God, and the name of the city of my God, the new Jerusalem ... and my own new name'[10] (3:12), meaning that the seal is the holy Name of God that Jesus also shares, as is made clear in some following passages – all humans will be 'marked on the right hand or the forehead, so that no one can buy or sell who does not have the mark, that is, the name of the beast or the number of its name'[11] (13:16–17). The righteous, however, 'had not received its [the beast's] mark on their foreheads or their hands' (20:4). Instead, 'his [God's] name will be on their foreheads' (22:4).

This description of a time when the righteous bear the Name of God and the wicked bear the name of the Beast seems to depend on Ezekiel 9:4, where God commands a mark to be placed on the forehead of those Israelites to be protected/saved, in order to separate them from those who will be slain.[12] In the Hebrew text the noun 'mark' is of course the spelled-out letter *Tau*, the final letter of the alphabet, whose paleo-Hebrew form was that of an X. Gieschen (2003, 134) claims that this letter was shorthand for the Name and notes that Revelation often uses *Alpha* and *Omega*, the first and last letters, to mean God and Christ. The implication of this inscription in Revelation is thus a kind of ownership – by either God or the Beast.[13] It is clear, however, that there is only one name to be inscribed on the righteous: that the names of Jesus and of God (and the new Jerusalem) are the same is implied in 3:12 and 14:1 but is stated unequivocally at 19:13, where 'his [Jesus'] name is the Logos of God'. It is clear that here the word Logos refers to the Name, so at this point we have a clear statement that Jesus' secret name is YHWH. The conjunction of the Messiah, the Righteous, and Jerusalem all sharing the Name of God is identical to b.Bava Bathra 75b (discussed above), and surely depends on a pre-existing exegesis of Jeremiah 23:6.

Identification with the Name

In John's Gospel we find two verses which together appear to identify Jesus as the Name: 'The hour has come for the Son of Man to be glorified', (12:23) and shortly after, 'Father, glorify your Name' (12:28). The Son of Man thus appears to *be* the Name of God. Likewise in 3 John 7 we read that the disciples 'began their journey for the sake of the name'.[14] Several more passages from the NT and early Christian writings make similar implications: as the apostles left the Sanhedrin: 'they rejoiced that they were considered worthy to suffer dishonour for the sake of the Name' (Acts 5:41); Paul 'is an instrument I have chosen to bring my name before Gentiles and kings and before the people of Israel' (Acts 9:15), the 'name' here presumably being Paul's protagonist, Jesus: 'Let us, therefore, obey His [the Father's] most holy and glorious Name' (1Clem.58:1).[15]

In addition to the aforementioned passage of Revelation 19:13 and the famous prologue to John's Gospel, Christ is frequently identified as the Logos, the divine 'word'. Given the importance of God's Name in the Hebrew Bible it has not been uncommon to identify this 'word' as YHWH.[16] The Greek term *logos* means simply 'word' but also carries connotations of rationality and order, being the term used by the Stoics to describe their belief in a cosmic ordering principle immanent in the universe. During the Second Temple period Jewish tradition personified this force as a hypostasis, leading to the kind of figure we find in Philo, where the Logos is a virtual 'second god' (QG2:62) and also the 'Name of God' (Conf.146).[17]

There may be a relationship between John's Logos and the Memra of the Targums. Hayward concluded that 'St John ... depicts Jesus as the *Memra*, who is God's Name, manifesting God's glory, full of the grace and truth of the covenant, dwelling *with us* in the flesh' (1978–1979, 30).[18] The Memra itself should be understood as 'neither an hypostasis, nor a simple replacement for the name YHWH, but an exegetical term representing a theology of the Name AHYH' (Hayward, 1981, xii). Further it represents not just 'saying' but 'includes as well the idea of *being with*, in that it ultimately means I AM THERE' (ibid.).

That these traditions were well known during the early centuries of the Common Era is evidenced in Justin Martyr's *Dialogue with Trypho*, most notably 64–65. In this text, the second century Samaritan convert Justin utilises biblical passages in an attempt to convert the Jew Trypho, including, again, Psalm 72:17–19, and Isaiah 42:8, both of which he interprets as differentiating between God and His Name, the latter of which is, he argues, Christ.[19]

Riemer Roukema (2006) argues that while on the one hand John's Gospel identifies Jesus with the *Kyrios*, the term that the LXX uses to translate the Biblical YHWH, on the other hand it makes an implicit distinction between the *Kyrios* and God the Father.[20] This distinction between *Kyrios*/YHWH, and God the Father would seem to indicate the same distinction as between a name and the one named. Indeed, Roukema concludes that 'according to the Fourth Gospel Jesus manifested the divine name, since he himself was not only the incarnate Logos and the Son of God, but even the incarnate *Kyrios* or YHWH himself'

(2006, 223). In this case, just as in the Hebrew Bible God's Name indicates His presence, via either the Name Angel or as the Name in the Temple of Deuteronomy, Christ in these New Testament texts represents God's presence on earth, as the manifestation of His Name, the Name of the otherwise nameless God – something ontologically related, but yet distinct. God the Father, then, is not identified with His Name YHWH, but is known *through* it – and it is Christ who manifests this Name, as 'the Word made flesh' (John 1:14).

We find this nominal Christology also in non-normative Christian writings such as the Nag Hammadi corpus. The *Gospel of Truth* introduces a long and complex theological discussion with the (deceptively) simple statement: 'Now the name of the Father is the Son'. The Name here is transcendent of the world, but it is manifest through the Son – it is invisible and cannot be spoken because it:

> [I]s not from (mere) words, nor does his name consist of appellations.... But the one who exists exists also with his name, and he alone knows it, and alone (knows how) to give him a name. It is the Father. The Son is his name.
>
> (I.3, XII.2, 1990, 49)

The passage then enters a defence of the nameability of God: whereas some may claim that God could not be named because there was no one prior to confer the name, the *Gospel* asserts that the Name of the Father is not like our names which are only 'loaned' and thus not linked to our nature or essence, but is immediately at one with Him – however because it is not of words, it could only be speakable metaphorically. To 'pronounce' the Name then is only possible for the Son: God 'is unnameable, indescribable, until the time when he who is perfect spoke of him'.

Christ in early Christian writings then, appears at least some of the time to represent the emergence of God's Name into creation. Christ himself takes up the role of the hypostatic Name which has been articulated in the other traditions. Fossum writes that:

> It is in accordance with the theology of the Old Testament that the 'Name' denotes God as he reveals himself, but the 'gospel' goes beyond the Old Testament in representing the Name as a distinctly personified entity, even the Son of God. Since the Son is the Name, there is no distinction in nature or mode of being between the Father and the Son. We have here the doctrine of the consubstantiality of God and Christ expressed about two hundred years before the production of the Nicene Creed by means of the Semitic concept of the 'Name', which, however, primarily is ontic, while the Greek concept of 'Nature' used in the Creed is ontological.
>
> (1985, 107–108)

While the Messiah as bearing God's Name implies a likeness of essence, a kind of ontological continuity between God and Christ such that the same Name points to them both, yet without positing formal identity between them, the Messiah *as* God's Name implies a sophisticated theological development of the manifest Name of a God who is formally nameless. In this case, then, the Name becomes an autonomous being who exists in the world in order to indicate the essential Being which is beyond the world – Christ is the speaking of God as it takes shape in human or finite reality. This should not be taken as a wholly Christian innovation – it is a new doctrine descended in large part from *logos* theology present during the Second Temple period and evident also in Philo and the Targums. Last, even the rabbinic literature knows the tradition that the Messiah shares God's Name – and the Bavli articulates an understanding almost identical to that found in Revelation, that the Messiah, the Righteous, and Jerusalem carry the Name of God. The early Jewish-Christian doctrine is one which could only come from the pre-Christian, Jewish, sources.

Analysis

In the foregoing I have presented Christianity as the most clear and definitive articulation of the various traditions which could be collected under the term 'hypostatic nominalism'. I have tried to establish a Christian doctrine of Jesus as the sole correct name of God, as the manifest description of God in the world, that is effectively, God made literal. As words are, in the Greek conception, not transcendent but located within the human sphere, within human consciousness, then Christ is, according to this theory, God *emptied* into His Name – Jesus the manifest Logos who walks the earth and represents the presence of God to human beings. Whereas in the Tanakh the Name designates presence which *can* be embodied in an angelic being, during Second Temple times the Name becomes a kind of hypostatised entity which is somehow intimated in creation. As the doctrines separated into Christian and rabbinic Judaism (a process which took several hundred years), we find the hypostasis concretised in Christ, and the rabbinic emphasis on the Name evolving into a metaphysics of language generally, where God's Name is the exemplar of language, and language is the exemplar of reality. Our question now must be, what are the implications of this theology and why, from a purely theological standpoint, would it not have captured the heart of Hebrew monotheism, going on instead to emerge into a radically new and different religious system? In answering this question I will draw on Derrida's *On The Name* (1995) and its analysis of negative theology, that most Christian of mystical theologies which precisely refuses the possibility of naming God, as well as the discussion provided by Susan Handelman's *The Slayers of Moses* (1982) in terms of the effects of the respective Rabbinic and Christian understandings of text and word on the relationship between God and humanity.

My analysis of this hypostatic nominalism will again use Christianity as the exemplar of these traditions, but should not be mistaken for a discussion solely of Christian religion or doctrine – and certainly not for an attack on Christian doxa. Rather, it is an elucidation of some of the possible criticisms, from a rabbinic point of view, of a theology, nascent within Second Temple Judaism, which posits the emergence of God into the world in hypostatic form as the Name; this will allow an exposition of some of the fundamental distinctions between rabbinic Jewish thought and Christian thought which this doctrinal dispute may be based on, or have led to. It seems clear at this stage that rabbinic Judaism and Christianity represent the eventual concretisations of two distinct but intertwined currents within Second Temple Judaism and, because this study is an investigation of the former, it is important to attempt the understanding of how and why the (apparently) only two currents to survive the turn of the eras distinguished and differentiated themselves from each other.

Presenting Christ as the solidification of the word in contrast to the rabbinic multiplicity of dialogue, Susan Handelman argues that Christianity distorts Hebrew theology[21] with Greek philosophy, and therefore, Christian thought unintentionally incorporates an ideological corruption: 'The central doctrine of the Church – incarnation – celebrates not the exaltation of the word, but its transformation from the linguistic order into the material realm, its conversion into the flesh'[22] (1982, 4). As Christ is the material manifestation of Logos, the word becomes static, embodied in particularity and dead to interpretation – in contrast to the rabbinic emphasis on debate and multiplicity of opinion. There is no longer the difference (of text and interpreter) which gives rise to meaning and diversity, but only the single solid fact.

Likewise, Boyarin writes that the rabbis' relocation of all Sophia/Logos talk to solely the Torah, was a mechanism of 'protecting one version of monotheistic thinking from the problematic of division within the godhead' – a move which radically enforces a kind of transcendence, and: 'It is this supersession of the Logos by Writing that arguably gives birth to rabbinic Judaism and its characteristic forms of textuality' (2004, 129).

According to this reading, the hypostatised Name kills the power of the nominal because it ossifies it, making it singular. The play of interpretation, of dispute and debate and the rabbinic experience of the 'living text' of the Torah (which we might regard here as the multiple values of the Name) is cancelled by the ontologising of Name (and Law) in the Messiah. Ironically, the manifestation of the Name kills the word in flesh, by making it physical. The word here is not alive via manifestation but dead because of it. The Name now, because of its concrete presence, no longer can designate relation because it takes an ontological status of being, adopting the static Greek metaphysics and beginning a trajectory into a very different conception of reality. The rabbinic, on the other hand, emphasises the multivalent metaphysics of relation, allowing for the play of interpretation which alone can protect the integrity of the individual engendered by a relationist nominalism.

In fact, by reducing *davar* to *logos*, Christian doctrine translates Hebrew speech into the mathematical perfection of Greek logic – Christ signifies the *silencing* of the word.[23] Whereas in Judaism language is always active, performative, in Greek thought it is just descriptive; it aligns or not with the world and therefore is never anything more than a second element, a mirror to reflect rather than participate in reality. A singular manifestation of *the* Name of God would mean that God were no longer accessible via subjectivity, and no longer multifarious, named according to His action in relation to individuals, but accessible *only* via the Messiah – in those famous words: 'No one comes to the Father except through me' (John 14:6).

So Derrida says that 'being' is the graven image of philosophy: Being which dictates an essentialism, an emphasis on substance rather than value. Binitarian nominalism might then lead necessarily to *propositional* religion, to a faith which seeks to state, to *make static*, God; to state God as a being (or indeed as Being) rather than seeking dialogue with Him. The manifest Name which we find in the New Testament represents the complete unification of God and human, which is to say of object and subject. But that which speaks only to one listener may as well be silent: for there is only one truth, the truth of identity. Speaker and listener form a system, and when there is only one such system the speaker and listener approach – achieve – identification. Then, there is the silence of identity. A self-contained truth, a system with no remainder. At once an object without a subject and a subject without an object.

In stating so loudly then the vast gulf between word and object, 'negative theology is one of the most remarkable manifestations of … self-difference' (Derrida, 1995, 71). A self-difference that seems contrary to Christian identity-theology; what Derrida characterises as '*the one* metaphysics, *the one* onto-theology, *the one* phenomenology, *the one* Christian revelation, *the one* history itself, *the one* history of being, *the one* epoch, *the one* tradition, self-identity in general, the one, etc.' (ibid.).

Can the Name enter the world? These concepts relate naturally to apophaticism, because they automatically prompt the examination of the relationship between the Name and the essence. Derrida writes that 'if we formalize to the extreme the procedures of this [negative] theology … Then nothing remains for you, not even a name or a reference' (1995, 49). How can a name point to something unimaginable, completely beyond? How can something *in* the world point outside it? The name then must surely either be of the world or of God, which is to say a mere label or equally ineffable, unpronounceable (as, in rabbinic tradition, the Tetragrammaton is); even unwriteable … how is it possible for it to stand between, for it to mediate? How can the Name connect us to the transcendent? We will find this question most effectively answered by the later rabbinic traditions of Metatron, and the Hekhalot literature, but the rabbis' answer is clear: not through Christ.

Negative theology 'powerfully contribute[s] to calling into question' the 'traditional disjunction between concept and metaphor, between logic, rhetoric and poetics, between sense and language' (ibid.). The question of the Name is then one of reference – of symbolism. How can language refer to that which is non-linguistic? What is the relationship between the Word and God? This of course is the same question provoked by Scott's reading of *Similitudes*, where God and His Name appear next to each other, placed on apparent equal ontological footing.

Derrida understands then 'negative theology as a "critique" ... of the proposition, of the verb "be" ... briefly, a critique of ontology' (1995, 49–50). Thus its emergence within Christianity is no accident, for it is the heir of hypostatic nominalism which provokes the question of ontology. Perhaps it is no coincidence then that the title *Sauf le Nom* can be rendered equally as Save the Name, or Salvation of the Name (Safe, the Name) with its hints of salvation *in* the Name, *via* the Name. But he does not seem aware of the irony when he says that erasing the word 'God' may be 'a way, perhaps, to save the name of God, to shield it from all onto-theological idolatry: God without Being [*Dieu sans l'etre*, also understandable as 'God without being God' and hearable as 'God without letter']' (ibid., 1995, 62–63) – this after all is what the rabbis appear to have done; they erased the traditions, removed the Logos of Christianity in their attempt to save the Hebrew God from this incarnate idolatry. They erased the *logos* to save the *davar, hashem*; 'as if it was necessary to lose the name in order to save what bears the name, or that toward which one goes through the name' (ibid., 1995, 58). But 'to lose the name is quite simply to respect it: as name'. I.e., not as object, but to pronounce it and use it as a means of finding *that to which it refers*. Not to lose oneself *in* the name. Not to worship instead the Name, (the principal innovation that Hurtado claims Christianity made to Judean theology[24]). To lose the Name of God then is the first step in finding God. This itself seems a fundamentally non-Hebraic or non-Jewish theology (despite vigorous attempts at several points to place the Name YHWH outside of normal profane usage), but in terms of de-ontologising the name it is valuable and in fact we will find exactly this understanding in later Kabbalah. In fact we can see in the ontological nominalism pursued by some Christian traditions the danger of going too far in the opposite direction, or valuing the Name so much that it becomes an object in-itself. The rabbinic proscription against the speaking or writing of the Name may be intended to have the same effect: to lose the Name in order to save it.[25]

Derrida claims that: 'To say 'what is called 'negative theology' ... is a language' is then to say little, almost nothing, perhaps less than nothing' (1995, 50). As little as to say that the Name (*shem*) is the Word (*logos*)? As little as to say that YHWH is *Kyrios*? Or as little as to say, with Jesus, that I am He (*ani hu/Ego Eimi*)? In fact: 'Negative theology means to say very little, almost nothing, perhaps something other than something' (ibid.), as what the Name indicates is not some*thing*, and it certainly communicates nothing at all, in factual terms.

Naming, rather, is always an act of transference, reference, difference:

> They name God, speak of him, speak *him*, speak *to him, let him speak in them*, let themselves be carried by him, make themselves a reference to just what the name supposes to name beyond itself, the unnameable beyond the name, the unnameable nameable.
>
> (Derrida, 1995, 58)

And 'by the way, is the name, the proper name or the name par excellence *in* language and what would this inclusion mean?' (ibid.). Language itself 'says the inadequation of the reference ... its incompetence as to what it is said to be the knowing of' (1995, 59). Probably, by admitting that there is always more than what is spoken, by highlighting that which cannot be spoken. This is why 'the extreme and most consequent forms of declared atheism will always have testified to the most intense desire of God' (1995, 36) – atheism as the refusal to accept the mere idea of God – relinquishing perhaps even the name – but instead to pursue the Absolute itself.

Derrida claims that apophatic or negative theology is intrinsically related to the willingness to go beyond the limits. It represents the 'crossing' of the boundary between name and object – to cross, so that the cross is itself symbol of the symbolic. The conjunction of the cross and the *Tau* are curious, little commented on. In Paleo-Hebrew the letter is cruciform, written as an X. The *Tau* is the final letter of the Hebrew alphabet, and thus exists at the limit of linguistic representation. b.Shabbat 104a claims that it represents truth, being the final letter of *emet* – but it is also the final letter of *mot*, death.[26] It implies marking, wounding – giving it an appearance of relationship to the word tattoo (*tau-tau*). There is a powerful symbolical relationship between the cross, as the functional representation of the crux of Christianity – Christ's death – and the existing symbolism of the Name as God's presence in the world; a relationship made apparent in the conjunction of Revelation and Ezekiel, where the cross-shaped 'mark' (*tau*), meaning Name, of God is inscribed on the bodies of the faithful. God's most dramatic emergence into reality then happens in the act of his material death; his assumption out of the world.

So when Paul claims that: 'The letter kills, but the spirit gives life' (2Cor.3:16), it is Jesus as the creative nominal letters YH, that kills the multiplicity of interpretation, transforming it into stasis, into the nail (*vav*), the final nail in the coffin: the letter *Tau*, the cross, the Mark, the mark of his Name upon the heads of the saved. Eleven or four hundred, not the twenty-sixth letter and certainly not the *aleph* but the twenty-second, the final letter, the last Word.

Handelman writes: 'The word of God was more than the act of saying; it was a creative force, an instrument capable of enacting realities, a concentration of power' (1982, 32). Likewise the Name of God in rabbinic Judaism is more than a substance, more than an ontological hypostasis – it becomes a manner of relation. In clearly divorcing the Greek-influenced traditions which had accumulated during the Hellenistic era and culminated in what was for the rabbis the tragedy of Christianity, they developed a highly sophisticated onomatology of their own. And perhaps it is precisely this rabbinic refusal of the static word, of the frozen eternal which leads to the destructive unity of the transcendent and the immanent, which typifies Judaism – its constant reinterpretation, its constant evolution and rewriting. Rather than reject the developments and returning to the original source, to the Bible, Judaism has preferred to reinterpret, to go forward, to continue evolving – the 'conversation between generations' which Saul Lieberman apparently learnt, paradoxically from a gentile (Riemer, 2011).

Notes

1 Longenecker (1970, 43) notes that '[i]n the Gospel of Matthew there is an emphasis on the name of Jesus such as is not found in the other synoptists'. While Mark and Luke describe the circumstances of naming Jesus but only Matthew describes the significance of the name (1:21–25); any gathering meets 'in my name' (18:20); the followers must leave everything 'for my name's sake' (18:29); 'You will be hated of all men because of my name' (10:22); pseudo-Christians are accused of preaching in Jesus' name (7:21–23); the nations will be baptised in the names of the trinity (28:18–20). Mostly these passages hinge on the name Jesus rather than the Name of God, however – and betray little in way of a nominal theory. I will return to the significance of Matt.7:21–23 shortly.

2 Many of the following have been discussed in Gieschen (2003), as well as Fossum (1985) and Hurtado (2007). Morray-Jones (1992) has also discussed many traditions and their relevance to contemporary Jewish mystical traditions.

3 Tangentially, in the *Odes of Solomon* we find the statement: 'I [Christ] was named the Light, the Son of God.' (36:3) – I suspect that this evidences the *phōs* tradition, the LXX's term for light which Fossum (1995) has demonstrated was also used to mean 'man' or person, thus instigating a myth regarding the primal Light-Man, the initial creation of God. Charlesworth (*OTP* 2, 726) claims it is 'probable' that the original language was Syriac or Aramaic, but even if originally composed in a tongue other than Greek, they would not necessarily have been unaware of the connotations in the concept of light – or even privy to the myth, without understanding the etymological roots of it. Opposingly, Charlesworth himself relates the passage tentatively to *Similitudes'* mention of the Son of Man being named in the presence of the Lord (ibid., 732).

4 Cf. Lam.Rab.1:16.

5 Other rabbinic texts mention the pre-existence of the Messiah's name, something which itself may hint at an identity with God's Name. See Chapter 1, Note 34.

6 The weight of scholarly opinion now regards *Similitudes* as essentially pre-Christian, with the corollary claim that New Testament usage of concepts such as the Son of Man draw in some way on innovations in the former. Nickelsburg and VanderKam (2012, 62) argues that while the text must be post-Daniel (as 46:1–3, 47:3 and 71:9–17 are influenced by it), 'the New Testament's use of Son of Man traditions that presuppose the interpretation of Dan.7:13 that is attested in the Parables (and 4 Ezra 11–13)' indicates the priority of *Similitudes*. Revelation too 'may well reflect knowledge of [*Similitudes*]', sharing a saviour who is Son of Man, Servant and Messiah (2012, 70). Based on very different reasoning, Charlesworth (2007) has also concluded the *Similitudes* were likely composed in the latter half of the first century BCE. In this case it also prefigures the Christian tradition of the pre-existent hypostatic Name.

7 Gieschen likewise concludes that 'the references to the "name" of the Son of Man in 1En.37–71 indicate that he shares the Divine Name of the Ancient of Days, the Tetragrammaton' (2007, 238).

8 Cf. 17:24, where Jesus again claims to have been given the 'glory' before the foundation of the world. The description of the Son of Man as hidden 'from the beginning' before creation (48:6, 62:7) is resonant of several other streams of tradition: John's Logos and the Name of Pirq. R El. ch.3; in 4Ezra 13:26, 52, the Messiah (God's 'son') is hidden in God's presence; Nickelsburg (2012, 170–1) remarks that the Son in both passages reflects Wisdom in Prov.8:22–31 and Sir.24:1–3; Gieschen (2007, 131) notes several texts that describe the divine Name as secret or concealed (Gen.32:29, Judges13:17; 1En.69:14; Jos.Asen.15:12; Pr.Jos.; Gos.Thom.13; Gos. Truth38.7–40.29; Gos.Phil.54.5 – cf. Rev.19:12–13, discussed below). The Egyptian *Pyramid Texts* also mention 'the One-whose-name-is-hidden' (Leprohon 2013, 32).

Finally, in b.Kidd.71a, it is indicated by a play of words that God wanted to keep his name hidden: 'For *shmi le 'olam* read *shmi le 'allem*. [Exod.3:15].'

9   Cf. 7:2 where an angel 'having the seal of the living God' rises from the sun.

10 Christ meanwhile 'has a name inscribed that no one knows but himself. He is clothed in a robe dipped in blood and his name is called the Logos of God.' (19:12–13) This powerful image may well derive from the vengeful warrior-Logos of Wis.18:14–25: 'Thy all-powerful Logos from heaven, from the royal throne, A stern warrior leapt into the midst of the doomed land.'

11 The whore of Babylon likewise, 'on her forehead was written a name, a mystery: "Babylon the great, mother of whores and of earth's abominations".' (17:5).

12 Also it should also be noted that Tg.Ps.-J. to Deut.28:10 has the Name 'inscribed on the phylacteries' that the people of Israel wear.

13 The Name has been used similarly as a physical mark in a few other places: Odes 8:13, God set the seal upon the face of the elect before their existence. Also 39:8 ('Put on, therefore, the Name of the Most High and know Him, and you shall cross without danger and the rivers shall be obedient to you') and 42:20. Clement in Exc.Ex. Theod.22:4 writes that 'the faithful bear through Christ the Name of God as if it were an inscription' intimating ownership (Fossum 1985, 98ff). There is a saying, attributed to R Levi, that the angels all have the name of God engraved on plates over their hearts: Midr.Tehillim to Ps.17:3, cf. Pesiq.Rab.21:10. These are both very late texts: eleventh and ninth centuries respectively. R Eleazar of Worms must have known these for his interpretation the dictum: 'My Name is in him' of Metatron, to mean that: 'The great name is inscribed on his heart' (MS Paris-BN 850, fol. 83b). Finally, Num.Rab.16:24 relates that the Israelites were engraved with the Ineffable Name.

14 The NRSV in fact opts for the translation 'for the sake of Christ.'

15 Stroumsa (2003, 237) notes also that Col.1:15–16, 'all things have been created through him and for him', appears to intentionally mirror the Didache's invocation of God's Holy Name, for whose sake all things were created (10:2). Stroumsa notes that in his role as bearer of the Name, 'he appears to be the hypostasis of the Nameless God, carrying and revealing the Name. In a way, Jesus Christ IS the Name of God, i.e., the Name that can be uttered' (ibid.).

16 See, e.g., Fossum (1985, 108–109).

17 It is curious that apart from this passage, Philo plays little on the nominal implication of the Logos. It is stated once – but never again. If the Logos were understood by Philo to be identified with the Name of God in the sense which we are searching for it, we would expect more than one casual remark in the whole of his corpus. The reason for this conceptual omission may be found in Philo's typically Greek onomatology: it is made clear in Conf. that he believes names are essentially descriptions, and thus not attachable to God (on this see *Mut.* and Runia [1988]). Philo's apparent lack of Hebrew may also be a factor – for him the Tetragrammaton has been replaced by the much less obviously potent *kyrios*. That Philo's Logos has absorbed certain Principal or Name-Angel traditions from the Second Temple Period is demonstrated by his identification of Logos with the angel of Exod.23:21, yet it appears that the Logos is less of a *name* of God than a tacit *description* of the world, *in utero*. Philo's God is irrefutably nameless, so this identification of Logos as Name must indicate some different conception: 'He has no proper name, and ... whatever name anyone may use of Him he will use by licence of language; for it is not the nature of Him that is to be spoken of, but simply to be' (*Somn.*1.230). I will suggest that this contradiction highlights the *ontological* (rather than linguistic) nature that 'the Name of God' had assumed for philosophically inclined Jews by the time of the first century. Also, Moses' ascent into heaven left behind the world of speech (Fug.92; Her.71).

18 Likewise Boyarin (2004, 103), although his reassessment of the Memra as a hypostasis (2004, 110–147) is difficult to accept, and appears to be founded on a very blunt reading of ontology. I will deal with this issue at length in Chapter 3.

19 The conjunction of this passage with b.Sanh.98b and 1En.48:1–3 strongly suggests a relationship between them. The fact that Justin was a Samaritan means he would not be expected to know the Enoch literature (unless he learnt of it as a Christian), suggesting that *Similitudes* takes this motif from an existing usage of Ps.72:17 in a Messianic setting; one which Justin and R Yannai were also aware of.

20 Of course, the jury is still out on whether *Kyrios* is indeed an original reading in LXX or a Christian interpolation (see Chapter 1, Note 21). But even if it is a Christian ideological gloss, the argument here is unaffected.

21 It is worth noting that theology is of course a Greek word – and concept. I am impressed by Harold Bloom's argument (2005), that the Biblical YHWH is an all-too human literary character, not a systematically postulated deity, precisely because theology itself is an endeavour which could only be undertaken within the intellectual milieu of Christianity. My own use of the term 'theology' here is therefore purely conventional.

22 It is worth being clear here, that this is only one possible understanding of incarnation. My intention is not to offer a general approach to Christian doctrine, but to present the probable conclusions of incarnation viewed through the *nominal* traditions of Second Temple Judaism and the New Testament.

23 The significance of this silence will become clearer during the later discussions of Rosenzweig and Wittgenstein (see Chapter 5).

24 See Introduction, Note 11.

25 'To give a name' is worrying because it 'also risks to bind, to enslave or to engage the other ... to call him-her to respond even before any decision or deliberation, even before any freedom' (Derrida, 1995, 84).

26 *Aletheia* (truth) is unveiling in Greek; in Hebrew *emet* appears related to death, and in the traditions of the Golem confers the opposite of death: life.

Bibliography

The Babylonian Talmud (32 vols). 1990. Edited by Rabbi Dr. I. Epstein. London: The Soncino Press.

Midrash Rabbah (10 vols). 1939. Translated by R Dr. H. Freedman, and Maurice Simon. London: The Soncino Press.

The Nag Hammadi Library in English. 1990. Edited by James M. Robinson. Third edition. New York: HarperCollins.

Old Testament Pseudepigrapha (2 vols). 1985. Edited by James Charlesworth. New York/London: Doubleday.

Pirkê de Rabbi Eliezer: (The Chapters of Rabbi Eliezer the Great) According to the Text of the Manuscript Belonging to Abraham Epstein of Vienna. 1916. Translated by Gerald Friedlander. London: Kegan Paul.

St. Justin Martyr: Dialogue With Trypho. 2003. Translated by Thomas B. Falls, edited by Michael Slusser. Washington: Catholic University of America Press.

Targum Pseudo-Jonathan: Deuteronomy. 1998. Translated by Ernest G. Clarke. Edinburgh: T&T Clark.

The Works of Philo: Complete and Unabridged. 1993. New Updated Edition. Translated by C.D. Yonge. Peabody: Hendrickson,.

Bloom, Harold. 2005. *Jesus and Yahweh: The Names Divine.* London: Penguin.

Boyarin, Daniel. 2004. *Borderlines: The Partition of Judeao-Christianity.* Philadelphia: University of Pennsylvania Press.

Charlesworth, James H. 2007. Can We Discern the Composition Date of the Parables of Enoch? In: Gabriele Boccaccini. ed. *Enoch and the Messiah Son of Man: Revisiting the Book of Parables.* Cambridge: Eerdmans, 450–468.

Derrida, Jacques. 1995. *On the Name.* Edited by Thomas Dutoit, translated by David Wood, John P. Leavey Jr., and Ian McLeod. Stanford: Stanford University Press.

Fossum, Jarl E. 1985. *The Name of God and the Angel of the Lord: Samaritan and Jewish Concepts of Intermediation and the Origin of Gnosticism.* Tübingen: Mohr Siebeck.

Fossum, Jarl E. 1995. *The Image of the Invisible God: Essays on the Influence of Jewish Mysticism on Early Christology.* Göttingen: Universitatsverlag Freiburg Schweiz and Van-denhoeck & Ruprecht.

Gieschen, Charles A. 2003. The Divine Name in Ante-Nicene Christology. *Vigilae Christianae* 57(2), 115–158.

Gieschen, Charles A. 2007. The Name of the Son of Man in the Parables of Enoch. In: Gabriele Boccaccini. ed. *Enoch and the Messiah Son of Man: Revisiting the Book of Parables.* Cambridge: Eerdmans, 238–249.

Handelman, Susan A. 1982. *The Slayers of Moses: The Emergence of Rabbinic Interpretation in Modern Literary Theory.* Albany: State University of New York Press.

Hayward, C.T.R. 1978–1979. The Holy Name of the God of Moses and the Prologue of St. John's Gospel. *New Testament Studies* 25, 16–32.

Hayward, Robert. 1981. *Divine Name and Presence: The Memra.* Totowa: Allanheld, Osmun & Co.

Hurtado, Larry W. 2007. 'Jesus' as God's Name, and Jesus as God's Embodied Name in Justin Martyr. In: Sara Purvis and Paul Foster. eds. *Justin Martyr and His Worlds.* Minneapolis: Fortress Press, 128–136.

Leprohon, Ronald J. 2013. *The Great Name: Ancient Egyptian Royal Titulary.* Edited by Denise M. Doxey. Atlanta: Society of Biblical Literature.

Longenecker, Richard N. 1970. *The Christology of Early Jewish Christianity.* London: SCM Press.

Morray-Jones, C.R.A. 1992. Transformational Mysticism in the Apocalyptic-Merkabah Tradition. *Journal of Jewish Studies* 43(1), 1–31.

Nickelsburg, George W.E. and James C. VanderKam. 2012. *1 Enoch 2: A Commentary on the Book of 1 Enoch Chapters 37–82.* Minneapolis: Fortress Press.

Peerbolte, Bert Jan Lietaert. 2006. The Name Above All Names (Philippians 2:9). In: George H. van Kooten. ed. *The Revelation of the Name YHWH to Moses: Perspectives from Judaism, the Pagan Graeco-Roman World, and Early Christianity.* Leiden: Brill, 187–206.

Riemer, Rabbi Jack. 2011. 100 Great Jewish Books Presented in One Volume. *Florida Jewish Journal*, 20 December. Accessed 28 October 2013. www.sun-sentinel.com/florida-jewish-journal/lchaim/fl-jjps-riemer-1221-20111220,0,3345574.story.

Roukema, Riemer. 2006. Jesus and the Divine Name in the Gospel of John. In George H. van Kooten. ed. *The Revelation of the Name YHWH to Moses: Perspectives from Judaism, the Pagan Graeco-Roman World, and Early Christianity.* Leiden: Brill, 207–223.

Runia, David T. 1988. Naming and Knowing: Themes in Philonic Theology. In: R. Van den Broek, T. Baarda and J. Mansfeld. eds. *Knowledge of God in the Graeco-Roman World.* Leiden: Brill, 69–91.

Scott, Steven Richard. 2008. The Binitarian Nature of the Book of Similitudes. *Journal for the Study of the Pseudepigrapha* 18(1), 55–78.

Stroumsa, Guy G. 2003. A Nameless God: Judaeo-Christian and Gnostic 'Theologies of the Name'. In: Peter J. Tomson and Doris Lambers-Petry. eds. *The Image of the Judaeo-Christians in Ancient Jewish and Christian Literature.* Tübingen: Mohr Siebeck, 230–244.

3   The intentional Name

Husserl and the Talmud on Metatron as a phenomenal object

In Chapter 2, I discussed some of the historical precedents and philosophical implications of a hypostatic nominalism, as it found its definitive statement in early Christology. While many scholars perceive some kind of relationship between Metatron and Christ, the nature of this is far from clear, and the debate over the origin and development of Metatron will not be settled any time soon.[1] However, if it is now established that there was an identification of Christ with the Name YHWH in some Christian circles, we do not have far to look for a similar tradition in rabbinic Judaism. This chapter will focus on Metatron, the angel who is most often claimed to bear the Name of God. I will argue that while Metatron draws on some of the traditions which formed the figure of Christ, the rabbinic figure of Metatron can be understood via a Husserlian phenomenological lens as an attempt to avoid the philosophical pitfalls which I have highlighted in early Christological nominalism. This discussion will then help to resolve exactly how we might understand an apparently personified nominalism, by rethinking what the nature of such a name-named relationship might be.

The two earliest datable references to Metatron, apparently from the fourth century, both associate Metatron with the Divine Name. First *The Visions of Ezekiel*[2] lists several names for a mysterious 'Heavenly Prince', giving the fifth name as: 'Metatron, *like the name of the Power*. Those who make use of the name say: SLNS is his name, QS BS BS QBS is his name, *like the name of the creator of the world*' (my emphasis). Second, in b.Sanhedrin 38b, a *min* (heretic) challenges R Idi (a fourth century sage) to explain Exodus 24:1, where God seems to use the name YHWH of another; Idi replies that the name in this instance refers to Metatron 'whose name is like that of his master', utilising Exodus 23:21's claim that the Divine Name is 'in' the Angel of the Lord.

This divine name-sharing is so often repeated as to be an integral part of Metatron's characterisation and possibly even his defining feature.[3] It is found throughout the Hekhalot literature (as will be shown in Chapter 4), and by the time of the medieval mystics it is cited by almost everyone who mentions Metatron, including R Asher ben David, who quotes his grandfather Abraham ben David, calling Metatron 'the Prince of the Countenance whose name is like the name of his master' (*Otzar Nehmad* 4:37, Scholem, 1987a, 212), and by R Eleazar of Worms, who gematrially equates 'that is Metatron' and 'for my Name is in him', both summing 332 (Wolfson, 1995, 71). In fact Metatron is more commonly referred to as the angel who shares in God's Name than as the Prince of the Presence, or any other qualification.

Metatron, I would like to suggest, then, forms rabbinic Judaism's attempt to personify the Divine Name – to articulate its presence in an angelic or hypostatic being. However, this is not all Metatron is – he functions in many different capacities throughout the texts in which he appears. In this chapter I will investigate the most normative of passages, those in the Talmud, with the assumption that Metatron, even at this point, is known to be the Angel of the Name. After examining the evidence, I will provide an analysis based on Husserlian phenomenology to provide some suggestions as to why the Name Angel might fill these roles.

The textual evidence

I will confine my analysis here to the three direct talmudic references. For clarity, I will state again that here the reading I offer should not necessarily be taken as a historical one; it is rather an attempt to present the material in the abstract, a method which will prepare the way for the following phenomenological analysis. This is to say, I am *not* attempting to reconstruct the opinions of the rabbis in question; rather I am engaging in an exegesis which will place this textual group in conversation with the other texts I analyse, in order to isolate the meaning which can be found through the traditions embodied in the texts as a whole.

Sanhedrin 38b

This is the famous passage which associates Metatron with the Divine Name:

> Once a heretic said to R Idi: 'It is written, and unto Moses He said, *Come up to the Lord.* But surely it should have stated, *Come up unto me!*' – 'It was Metatron [who said that],' he replied, 'whose name is similar to that of his Master, for it is written, *For my name is in him.*' 'But if so we should worship him!' 'The same passage, however' – replied R Idi – 'says: *Be not rebellious against him,* i.e. exchange Me not for him.' 'But if so, why is it stated: *He will not pardon your transgression?*' He answered: 'By our troth we would not accept him even as a messenger, for it is written, *And he said unto Him, If Thy presence go not*', etc.

The academic consensus here is that Idi is rejecting any substantial role for Metatron – he is merely an angel, a powerless agent of God's without any independent authority. Boyarin sums up the usual interpretation when he writes: 'What this amounts to is the Rabbi proclaiming that there are not two divine powers in heaven but only God and an angel whom God Godself has named God as well' (2010, 331).

However, it is difficult to see any real sense to this interpretation: just why would God name an angel 'God', especially one as irrelevant as Idi seems to claim Metatron is? The investment of the Divine Name must indicate some kind of either functional or essential quality. Traditions identifying the principal angel with the Divine Name are far and wide, but everywhere there is an implication of a very real presence of God, even though it is not simply a metaphor, another way of speaking about God without actually speaking about him.

Therefore, we should not read Idi as saying: 'Metatron is called by my name, but that is all'. This kind of dismissive statement regarding the investment of the Name would simply be impossible. However, Idi does clearly distinguish the Name from God: the Name of God is not to be identified *as* God. So while Idi allows the investiture of Metatron with the Divine Name, the crux of this passage is that this investiture binds Metatron into God, while still not equating Metatron with God.[4]

Rather, what is being warned against here is the confusion of a name with its object. While the Name, to quote Michael Hundley, 'is part of the complex nexus that constitutes a person' (2009, 550), and specifically denotes presence, it is not the totality of that in which it partakes. Further, one should not direct worship to God's Name alone because the Name cannot forgive sins – only God Himself can do this.

This final aspect of the passage perhaps gives us a clue as to the intention here – R Idi is in debate with some kind of binitarian theologian who argues that there is a special being or angel who is identified as the Name, is worshipped independently of God, and has the special ability to forgive sins. We have seen that in early Christian circles, Christ was identified by or as the Name YHWH; he was worshipped from the outset;[5] and he is able to forgive sins. Therefore this passage may be understood as an attempt to reject the identification of Christ as this being, arguing instead that the Angel who bears the Name is Metatron, one who should not be worshipped and cannot forgive sins.

Hagiga 15a

In this passage Aher witnesses Metatron in Heaven and commits the sin of blasphemy by announcing that there may be Two Powers. The general consensus regarding this text is that Aher was punished for mistaking the angel Metatron for a second god. Often, the emphasis is placed on Metatron's seated posture, which may have misled Aher into perceiving Metatron as divine (it is rabbinic tradition that angels have no knee joints[6]). However, there are some problems with this interpretation. My analysis will be based on the list of Heaven's proscribed activities which Aher appeals to.

Most scholarly treatments of Hagiga 15a have utilised a single manuscript tradition, that of the Vilna. Philip Alexander (1987) sought to redress this by analysing three different manuscript variations (Bomberg, which is here identical with Vilna, Vaticanus 134, Munich 95), and I will utilise some of his results here. The Bomberg and Vilna, as used almost universally by scholars analysing the Metatron tradition, present the pivotal section as follows:

> Aher cut the shoots. Of him scripture says: 'Do not allow your mouth to bring your flesh into guilt.' [Eccles.5:6] What does this mean? He saw Metatron to whom power was given to sit and write down the merits of Israel. He said: 'It is taught that on high there is no sitting, no rivalry, no neck and no weariness. Perhaps – God forbid! – there are two powers'. They led forth Metatron and whipped him with sixty lashes of fire. They said to him: 'Why did you not stand up when you saw him [Aher]?'

Clearly in this recension, it is Metatron's sitting which is the cause of Aher's crime. However Munich 95, the manuscript which Alexander identifies as the most original tradition, provides:

> Aher cut the shoots. Of him scripture says: 'Do not allow your mouth to bring your flesh into guilt, nor say before the angel that it was a mistake.' [Eccles.5:6] What did he see? Metatron, to whom power was given to write down the merits of Israel. He said: 'It was taught that on high there is no standing and no sitting, no jealousy and no rivalry, no neck and no weariness. Perhaps – God Forbid! – there are two powers.' They led forth Metatron and whipped him with sixty lashes of fire.

This recension not only removes both references to Metatron's seated posture, but provides an extended list of the activities not present in heaven such that sitting is no longer the crux, but only one element of six. Alexander argues that Munich 95 must represent the original due to both its internal consistency and its obscurity – the other manuscripts represent attempts to explain the story, by focussing on the element of sitting in Heaven. The list of proscribed activities as it appears in Munich 95, is also reproduced in four other manuscripts with very minor cosmetic variations, thus constituting the most attested variation and close to an absolute majority (see Appendix for table of all manuscript variations). Clearly this does not indicate priority, but it does add weight to Alexander's conclusion. The full list then, as preserved in these manuscripts:

לא עמידה ולא ישיבה
לא קנאה ולא תחרות
לא עורף ולא עיפוי

This list is obviously a crucial element of the story. However, the intention behind it is not at all clear. Alexander claims that the list was originally intended to assert 'that God and the angels are without body parts or passions'[7] (1987, 60). Segal has explained the fourfold list as intended 'to refute the whole idea of heavenly enthronement by stating that such things as "sitting" and other anthropomorphic activities are unthinkable in heaven' (1977, 61) and meanwhile Schäfer offers the following detailed analysis:

> [A]ngels are supposed to have no knee joints and therefore cannot sit; more-over, there is no competition among the angels in heaven; the angels do not turn their backs to each other (because they have faces in all directions and do not need to turn around); and they certainly do not suffer from physical weariness.
>
> (2009, 234–235)[8]

These kinds of readings remain the academic consensus: the list is either denying corporeality in Heaven, or is specifying sitting as God's right alone. It appears not to matter that reading the list as a polemic against corporeality flies directly in the face of the narrative in which it is found, which has unequivocally pre-sented a heavenly being of some description as engaged in the physical activity of writing. Schäfer's explanation is even less congruous, simply providing four individual statements which are not at all related, either to each other, or to the matter at hand in the narrative.

Based on Alexander's arguments for the priority of the long list, I would propose a different and more holistic reading of the text. It can be observed that the list is paired in conceptual couplets. In the first two this is obvious: 'no stand-ing and no sitting'. In the second two it is less clear but still perceivable: 'no jealousy/envy/emulation and no rivalry' are both negative opinions, but whereas the former is a resentment based on love or desire for another's qualities, the second is an outright wish to defeat another. They are thus opposites. The third pair is initially quite opaque, which has led to the failure to understand the couplet structure of the passage at all. Scholars translate the word עורף as neck or back, and interpret it to mean that there is no unseen, or perhaps no rear in heaven. However, the word עורף is often used biblically in conjunction with קשה to mean stiff-necked or stubborn. It is entirely plausible that this conjunc-tion was so familiar to the authors or editors that, for rhythmic neatness, the adjective קשה could be omitted. If the term עורף is used here as shorthand for stubbornness, the refusal to renege, give ground or rescind, then it is clearly the opposing principle to weariness, which is the desire to do just that. Thus the full list presents us with three pairs of opposing principles (concerning posture, passion and perseverance) and tells us these are not possible in heaven.[9]

What could this couplet-structure of opposites mean for the narrative? I contend that the passage demonstrates not that Heaven is incorporeal and pas-sionless, but that it is without duality. The passage is utilised here in order to establish that Heaven is a place without division in any sense. And why would this point need to be made here? The most obvious conclusion is that Abuya's mistake was not in fact elevating the angel Metatron to godhood, but was the separation of Metatron from God; the creation of divisions within the Godhead so that it is two and not one: the heretical pronouncement that Abuya makes is: 'Perhaps – heaven forefend! – there are two powers in heaven!'. It is not the claim that Metatron is divine which is incorrect here, but the claim that Metatron is a second god separate from Yahweh.[10]

Avoda Zarah 3b

> What then does God do in the fourth quarter? – He sits and instructs the school children, as it is said, 'Whom shall one teach knowledge, and whom shall one make to understand the message? Them that are weaned from the milk.' [Is.28:9] Who instructed them theretofore? – If you like, you may say Metatron, or it may be said that God did this as well as other things.

There is an interesting anomaly in this text which is little commented on (in fact this passage is the least discussed of all the Talmud's three references). The tradition states 'if you like, you may say Metatron, or it may be said that God did this as well as other things'. Why would the rabbis make such a muddy statement? The text does not say it is either or both of them, but that we could name the agent as one or the other and it would make no difference. The logical conclusion is that Metatron is just another way of talking about God, or to use the name of Metatron is to use one of the names of God, albeit one that specifies a particular function.[11] This may be further supported by the context of the quote taken from Isaiah, which is during a lament for the people of Ephraim who mockingly accuse the prophet, saying he should teach his wisdom to babies rather than grown adults. The rabbis may be providing a way of avoiding saying that God Himself 'lowers' Himself to teaching infants, and say it may truthfully be said that Metatron does it; alternatively it can be counted as one of God's many, many activities.

Analysis

In this reading, we find initially that Metatron is the Name Angel (Sanh.38b) – he bears the Name of God, it is 'in him', but this Name does not confer the qualities of the Divine: the Name itself is not God and should not be treated as such. However, while Metatron is a name that can be used of God (Av.Z.3b), Metatron should not be separated from God, as an ontologically distinct being (Hag.15a).

In these three passages then we have a clear statement of the nature of Metatron and, by implication, of the nature of the Name in rabbinic tradition. The Name is an aspect of God – at least, the aspect of God in relation to human beings; it is not identified fully as the essence of God, of God in Himself, and yet it cannot be separated from God into an independent essence.

The notion that the Name Angel is not an independent being but an element of the single godhead helps to make sense of several mysterious qualities found in conjunction with this figure, including his enthroned position, and the common confusion of the angel with God. This places the principal angel in line with Philo's Logos as an emanation or articulation of God which is, to quote David Winston, 'the face of God turned toward creation' (1985, 49).[12]

We can see here the rejection of a kind of nominalism which posits a name as unrelated to its object – a name in fact shares in the identity of that named. Further, this placement of Metatron both within and outside the godhead elicits some important theological points about the role of the Name of God.

I will suggest here that the rabbinic Metatron constitutes an account of the problem of epistemology; that thought is somehow able to grasp that which is beyond thought. It is not difficult to imagine the rabbis approaching philosophical questions not in dry academic debate, but in the theological terms familiar to them. The theological debate around the transcendence and immanence of God mirrors the problem of ontology-epistemology because God in some sense can be viewed as the ultimate 'object' – that which exists separately from human subjectivity yet is still able to be known. In fact, Metatron bears some interesting parallels to the 'intentional object', a concept originated by Husserl, and lately picked up by Graham Harman. The following analysis will serve to highlight the subtle and complex nature of this relationship, where Metatron does not constitute an *angel* as such, and certainly is not a *mediator* (both determining a created being who exists in its own right, and serves God's purposes); rather Metatron *is* God; inseparable from Him, yet not identical with Him; the subjective appearance *of* God which should not be taken for the whole, lest we reduce God to the knowledge humans have of Him. It *is* God who appears when we see Metatron; yet Metatron is nothing more than the *appearance* of God.

Husserl famously worked on the problem of how objects and the awareness of them are related. Approaching the problematic isolation of 'pure consciousness' or 'transcendental subjectivity' within itself, he argued that consciousness is always intentional – it intends and points toward something outside of it; it is directed toward something which is not contained in consciousness. Therefore, the manifestation of things in consciousness are not mere representations, which is to say that although signifying something – a transcendent – they are not divorced from this thing. He argues that simple 'representation' may be used for a person and their portrait, but this is possible only because both actually exist on the same ontological level: they can exist side-by-side, and so the accuracy of the representation can be assessed (Husserl, 1970, 593ff.). Each is phenomenally available for the subject in the same way, and so although there is a relationship between them, each is ontologically distinct; they are their own thing. But the relation between appearance and object is not like this, because appearance depends directly on its object, being caused by it, and is an aspect of the object. These two then exist on different planes and have a more complex relationship. Rather, it is the object itself which is presented, and it is this object *as-given* that constitutes the phenomenal.[13]

Husserl's theory is thus two-pronged: the object is neither absolutely divorced from consciousness, being only 'represented' by a conscious-object, nor is the object itself in consciousness, because the object and the intention toward it must exist on different ontological levels. This last preserves the object as a single unity, which can be experienced differently at different times while still *itself* being one. This means that an object can be perceived by different individuals and groups, and at different times, each of which find only an aspect of that object: it appears under a given perspective. The object is not given as a whole, and there is always more to the object than what we see, or even could see, as the object itself is more even than the sum of all possible perceptions of it. The object cannot be totalised and retains its integrity, while yet being the actual object of conscious intention.

The status of the intentional object is a difficult one, and Husserl spent much ink trying to refine the term. Part of this was his utilisation of a tripartite terminology, where *noesis* is the act of intending, *noema* is the object intended, and *hyletic data* is the raw sense data. In this schema we can see how the raw sense data is constituted, by consciousness in the process of *noesis*, into an object – the *noema* – which itself is not in consciousness. However, this intentional object is still somehow different from the *intended* object, being instead 'the object *as* it is intended' (ibid., 1970, 113). In this sense, there *appear* to be two things, and yet this is certainly not correct – as he avers 'only one [object] is found to be present and even possible' (Husserl, 1931, I, §90, 219). And 'the intentional object of a presentation is the same as its actual object … it is absurd to distinguish between them. The transcendent object would not be the object of *this* presentation, if it was not *its* intentional object.' (Husserl, 1970, 172). The difficulty which Husserl finds in articulating the meaning of the intentional object and its relation to the actual object echoes the difficulties the rabbis and, later, the kabbalists found in correctly relating Metatron to God. They are not two things; the Name is not something different from God, as Christian doctrine might appear to suggest. And yet it is Metatron who appears, and is not wholly identical with God. So when we speak of Metatron, or the Name-Angel, we are speaking of God … and yet there is something more to God, of whom Metatron is but an aspect. As Husserl writes:

> I perceive the physical thing, the Object belonging to Nature, the tree there in the garden; that and nothing else is the actual Object of the perceptual 'intention'. A second immanent tree, or even an 'internal image' of the actual tree standing out there before me, is in no way given, and to suppose that hypothetically leads to an absurdity.
>
> (Ibid.)

To talk of two things is to make a category error – to conflate levels of reality, as if they could exist side-by-side. And yet to wholly identify them would collapse the levels into a flat plane of phenomenal idealism.[14]

A useful way of thinking about this may be found in a modification of Walter Benjamin, who talked of the 'mental being' of objects.[15] The mental being of something is that aspect of it which is accessible to the mind. While not constituting the whole of the object in question, the mental being is still an aspect of it, and is inherently graspable intellectually. This then is not an incorrect thought, or a mere 'representation' of the thing, but is an accurate conception of the thing as it presents itself to the mind. There is not a real rose and an immanent mental rose, rather the rose which is present to the mind is the mental presence of the actual rose. Here, we find that the ostensibly different vectors of a mental being which emanates from an object, and the intentionality which human beings project in their reaching for the object, coincide: the mental being of the object is identical with that which is conditioned by the striations of human consciousness; our reaching for the object in the attempt to understand it meets its reaching out to our minds. This implication has been worked on in particular by Graham Harman, who proposes that two objects which exist in relation form a third, 'intentional object' which figures as the medium of interaction between them. Harman's intentional object allows the qualities of, for example, a tree, to be made into a caricature which I perceive and which I can interact with. Likewise, the real tree does not interact with the real me but with a reduced caricature: with the aspects of me which are accessible to the tree's faculties, or are translatable into the language of the tree. This dual relationship, the unified object which these two units, in relating, form, then constitutes the intentional object.[16] The intentional object is not merely the accidental properties of perception, and neither is it solely what the object provides of itself, but is an essential aspect of the relationship between the object and I, conditioning both for the other and as that aspect of interaction through which two mutually transcendent objects may truly interact.

This theory helps to soften and add nuance to the debate which has sprung up recently regarding the relationship between phenomenal consciousness and reality. Under the banner of Speculative Realism,[17] accusations are levelled against 'correlationism', a Kantian-derived implication that because consciousness can only sense that which is conditioned by consciousness and therefore part of consciousness, the mind never gets outside of itself, to the objective thing-in-itself. This leads to the unhappy conclusion that the human is forever isolated in the phenomenal, i.e. that which is determined by human nature. This problem itself is based on a fundamental misreading, provoked by the formulation of the question of epistemology to imply that *things-in-themselves* are necessarily unconnected to the phenomenal, because the phenomenal is mere subjective illusion. In fact the phenomenal should be just as much part of the thing-in-itself as it is part of subjectivity.[18] The Jewish mystical tradition, (as we will see with different emphasis later in the Kabbalah), argues passionately against both polarities of this reading: either that there is only the noumenal and the mental is illusory, or that there is only the phenomenal and the objective is unsupported. Rather, the two are united ('His name is like his master's'; '*he* is His power and His power is *him*'[19]), neither reducible to the other ('Do not exchange me for him'), and without polarisation ('no sitting and no standing', rather instead just one thing with an apparent aspect and a concealed aspect). This in fact is an insight writ large across the Jewish tradition, and one picked up by Rosenzweig when he asserts that the distant God and the near God are the same God, just appearing in different ways (1999, 148); and when the rabbis argue that the young man at sea and the old man are the same God.[20]

The same insight is present in Theodore Adorno's deconstruction of idealism; allowing objects to transcend the conceptual while still being *reachable* from the concept, we find that the appearance is still rooted in essence:

> In truth, all concepts, even philosophical ones, refer to nonconceptualities, because concepts on their part are moments of the reality that requires their formation.... What conceptualization appears to be from within, to one engaged in it – the predominance of its sphere, without which nothing is known – must not be mistaken for what is in itself.
>
> (Adorno, 1973, 12)

Thus the conceptual is always 'entwined with a nonconceptual whole. Its only insulation from that whole is its reification – that which establishes it as a concept' (ibid.).

These phenomenological ideas work to proscribe the mistake that Abuya and others may have been making about Metatron: God, like any object of contemplation, should not be reduced to the appearance alone, because there is an independent ground which transcends human understanding. Metatron now appears as the phenomenal aspect of God, the form which God takes in his relation to human beings. Or we could say, a symbol – one with deep roots into or towards the object itself, but not identical with that object. Metatron may be thought of as the shape that human minds compress God into, making his awe-inspiring potency palatable for the fragile human psyche.

That Metatron functions in this capacity is due to his foundational condition of bearing the Name of God. Metatron, by manifesting God's Name, acts as the presence of God and as the phenomenal projection of God into human consciousness. While the association of 'face' and 'name' has already been stated by some scholars,[21] this is most clear in Metatron as the *Sar haPannim*, the angel who is the presence or face of God, and is such because of his carrying of the Name.[22]

The Name or the linguistic being of God represents the interface between others which cannot be totalised and yet are not divorced. They retain integrity, yet allow for true interaction and knowing which is not just mediated by words, but happens as words: the name is that which identifies and isolates an object as a unity and allows us to interact with it as a whole. Yet the name is *not* the object. It is rooted into the object, and provides a route to it, defining its nature for us (in our terms) so that we can perceive it.

So we see Metatron as the Name of God presenting a picture where the Name is not divorced from the essence, but is a phenomenological projection of God into the human sphere; Metatron is that angelic presence through which we can think of God acting. Metatron, as the Name of God, presents God in corporeal form, as a skin which gives the essential shapelessness of God a definition. As the presence of God in human reality, Metatron allows for direct interaction while acknowledging that there is much more than can meet the eye.

In much the same vein as Philo's Logos, Metatron is the apparent-form that the formless God, the God who cannot be seen, takes in human perception. Refracted through the lens of humanity, the presence, or being-there, of God, takes a human shape, enthroned in Heaven. His confusing similarity with God is not because of an error on the human's part, nor because he is such a mighty angel, but precisely because he is the perceivable form of God, manifesting those qualities which make God God. The error which the rabbis are warning against is both the separation and the identification of this form-bearing symbol with the unknowable essence of God. Metatron is not independent because he is the meta-object: God-for-man, the form that God appears as when reduced by the human mind to conceivability.

Having reassessed the Talmudic evidence through the lens of Husserlian phenomenology, I believe a strong case can be made for this interpretation. The rabbinic 'doctrine' of Metatron found in the Talmud can be reread as an attempt to argue against some common conceptions of the intermediator, and refining any speculation which postulates some powerful second figure into a sophisticated theology wherein the 'second power' is neither independent divinity nor angel but only an aspect of God. That this reading was indeed taken up, in a hyper-evolved form, by the kabbalists, will become apparent in the second section of this study.

Segal confirms that this would be the goal of the later tradition:

> The final stage in the rabbinic argument against angelic mediation may be found in Ex. R 32:9 where it is recorded that wherever an angel of YHWH is mentioned one should understand that the Shekhina (i.e., God's presence) was manifested. The effect is *to remove any doubt that the manifestation of divine force can be separate from God.*
>
> (1977, 71, my emphasis)

We remember Rosenzweig's statement that naming has the power to call into presence, bringing the other before us. This action of calling which is a calling *to* the caller, functions to confer identity, as we saw in Chapter 1. To name something postulates it in relation to us and makes it knowable. But, a corollary of identity is separation: that which is identified – named – must admit of a transcendence or an autonomy in not being consumed by the subject. The name, then, also *distances* the object. By it the named is differentiated from the namer. The object, previously unknown in its separation from us, is now presented as a separate with an irreducible unity in itself. Although this essential object is not subsumable – i.e. cannot be dissolved within the subject – it is now knowable from the outside, for its reality nestles against ours. Derrida writes that:

> The name hidden in its potency possesses a power of manifestation and occultation, of revelation and encrypting. What does it hide? Precisely the abyss that is enclosed within it. To open a name is to find in it not something but rather something like an abyss, the abyss as the thing in itself.
>
> (2002, 214)

This abyss is the internal nature of the object, that which is not knowable from the outside, and not knowable precisely because it is not *something*. It has not emerged into the ontology of knowledge which prescribes identity; it is projected behind it, hidden from the linguistic gaze of subjectivity. This unknowable essence is precisely what protects the object from being totalised by others who attempt to know it. What allows us to recognise it as an object is its name; and therefore it is by the action of naming, by the calling of the name, that we know it does have an essence. Thus a name confers not just identity but also integrity. A name then, is like a surface; once we have named something we are able to perceive it via its surface, seeing it as a unity, and intuiting an identity extended behind it to which we have no access. Therefore, an object can only be known via a name: the epistemological surface which the name forms posits and allows for the non-being of the essence which lies hidden beyond it.

Notes

1 On the possibility of a direct relationship between the figures of Metatron and Christ, see particularly Boyarin (2010), as well as Stroumsa (1983). In a separate study Stroumsa writes that: 'Even if the Rabbinic evidence is later than the earliest Christian texts, it is rather hard to imagine that the Rabbis felt the need to invent a divine person which would play a role similar to that of Jesus. Rather, it stands to reason to claim that the figure of Metatron reflects an earlier Jewish archangel figure, which would come to be identified to Jesus among the first Christians' (2003, 238).

2 Scholem (1987b, 379, cf. 1996, 44–45) and Alexander (1977, 164), agree on this as the earliest text. On the dating of *Visions*, see Halperin (1988).

3 Odeberg writes that:

> The most important element or complex of elements which gave life and endurance to the conception [of Metatron] was the notion of the 'angel of YHUH, who bears the Divine Name' and the 'angel of the Face, the Divine Presence'
>
> (1928, 144)

While it is unclear why this tradition historically became associated so strongly with Metatron in particular, my 'Folk Etymology and Its Influence on Metatron Traditions,' suggests the possibility that this is dependent upon an etymological interpretation of the name Metatron as containing the divine name *Tetra.* Scholem of course believed that this was a quality Metatron absorbed as he integrated the figure of Yahoel (1987b, 89; cf. 1987a, 187); likewise Fossum writes that: 'It is obvious that Yahoel is the prototype of Metatron' (1985, 321).

4 As Idel puts it in his analysis of this passage, 'there is an ontological linkage between God and his angel rendering it a theological mistake to separate between them' (2009, 120).

5 Hurtado (1998, 81ff.) argues that this is the defining innovation of Christian thought which distinguishes its theology from 'intermediator'-type precursors in Second Temple Judaism.

6 R Hanina bar-André quotes R Shmu'el bar-Soter as saying 'the angels have no joints' (p.Ber.1:1) – perhaps based on Ezekiel's vision, where it is claimed 'Their leg was a straight leg' [Ez.1:7].

7 I am slightly dubious about Alexander's claim that the section is a quote taken wholesale from another source – there is simply no evidence for this. In the absence of any prior appearances of that text, we are wise to allow the possibility that it is originally a part of the narrative. Even if it is not, however, my argument would be unaffected.

8 Cf. 2012, 127–8, where he also suggests that 'standing' is corrupt because 'the logical conclusion would be that, if there is no standing *and* no sitting, the angels can only fly'.

9 Interestingly, Gikatilla's *Sefer ha-Niqqud*, from the thirteenth century, preserves 'the saying of our sages, peace be upon them, that "on high there is no sitting and no standing, and no ascending and no descending (ולא עליה ולא ירידה), and no back and no weariness"' (Martini, 2010, 52). The switching of jealousy-rivalry for ascending-descending here works in favour of a dualistic couplet format – Gikatilla, however, goes on to interpret it as confirmation that the upper world is incorporeal, of form and not matter.

10 The lashing of Metatron at the end of this passage clearly works against this reading; if Metatron were indeed an aspect of God, then why would he be punished? I would suggest that this final element is a later insertion to the crucial part of the passage, already discussed. This is supported by the following sentence where God asks of Metatron: 'Why did you not stand when you saw him [Aher]?' This itself makes little sense, given that the passage has already stated there is no standing in heaven. This addition to the association of the three couplets with Metatron, then appears to be intended to defame Metatron and make him in no uncertain terms subordinate to God (and to Aher). This explanation may or may not be correct, but it is ultimately not of concern.

11 It should be noted that Philip Alexander has repeatedly made this assertion. He suggests that on some of the Aramaic incantation bowls which often address Metatron: 'Metatron may be a secret name of God' (1977, 167); and in the Visions of Ezekiel: 'The natural sense of the words is quite simply that *Metatron* was also a name of God' (1977, 164). However, he has neither investigated the theological implications of these claims, nor followed the theme of Metatron's identification with God through into the other literature.

12 In fact, it is not difficult to now place one of Philo's statements in this context: in Leg.3:207 he claims that the Logos 'must be God for us the imperfect folk, but, as for the wise and perfect, the Primal Being is their God'. We can see a striking resemblance here to the rabbinic judgement of Abuyah, his heresy being not the divinisation of Metatron, but the separation of the visible Metatron from his identity in the invisible God. To isolate the principal angel as a being in its own right is thus to lack the theological insight to understand it as an articulation of the transcendent God's presence.

13 Michael Heiser (2004), presents nicely the difference between this reading and that given in Chapter 2. In reading binitarianism back into Israelite theology he makes a distinctly Christological manoeuvre in ontologising the Name, ascribing personhood to it. This paragraph illustrates clearly the inconsistencies:

> First, it is the Old Testament, not the New, where the idea of different *deity-persons*, sharing one essential *nature*, and who function in a *godhead* is first introduced. Second, since the God of Israel is uncreated and distinct from all things physical, he is by nature invisible, disembodied, and incomprehensible as he is to human beings. Consequently, he often chooses to interact with human beings in ways that humans can visually process, such as a flame or a cloud, but at other times in human appearance (e.g., the Angel). Third, the disembodied Yahweh and the visible, detectable Yahweh may be present at the same time.
>
> (2004, 131)

Here God is one nature, by nature invisible, but articulated into two persons, one of whom is visible and the other invisible, who can be next to each other (implying that at others they may not be) – even though the visible is actually just the invisible in a visible shape. Hence the apparently meaningful statement that God can be one essence and two persons – which dissolves as soon as it is analysed. Also the strange idea that both the visible and invisible Yahwehs can be next to each other – a notion which makes absurd the whole theology and destroys even the meaning of the invisible aspect; he identifies the name as the essence, and identical with Yahweh and yet still claims that they can be together or separate.

14 Metatron, the intentional object, seems then to be a conjugation of God; the verb to God's noun.

15 Benjamin will be examined in more detail in Chapter 7.

16 The reason Harman claims this is a new object is because, drawing on Bruno Latour, his philosophy accepts the term 'object' for anything which is not constituted entirely by its relations but has an autonomy, 'the only criterion for a real object is that it be a unified thing with specific qualities, reducible neither to a bundle of qualities nor to its relation to us' (2010a, 10). A relationship between two objects also has its own autonomous identity, so can be considered itself an object, just as the tree, although constituted of relations between atoms, takes on its own identity.

17 A good introduction to the school is given in Harman (2010b).

18 Of course, Husserl disputed that it was rational to talk of a thing-in-itself at all, because such a thing was, paradoxically, posited by consciousness only as a result of phenomenal perception. See, e.g. Husserl (1970, §90, 261ff.).

19 See Chapter 4.

20 E.g., Mekh.R Simeon b.Yochai, Bashalah 15 and Mekh. R Ishmael Bahodesh 5, Shirta 4.

21 Seow comments that:

> In quite a number of biblical texts the *panim* of YHWH is YHWH's hypostatic Presence. Thus it serves the same function as *shem* (Name) in the Dtr theology, *kavod* (Glory) in the Priestly tradition. and *Shekinah* in later Jewish writings.
>
> (1999, 322)

He goes on to compare Tannit as the *pane ba'al* and Ashtart as the *shem ba'al* and claims that in the ANE, 'One may surmise that 'name' and 'face' mean the same thing essentially, inasmuch as each is representative of its subject' (1999, 322). Levinas' interchange of the two will be discussed in Chapter 6.

22 It is noteworthy that Boman translates *shem* in Is.30:27 as appearance (1960, 105). Further, in Exod.33:18, God responds to Moses' request to be shown the Glory with the offer to 'proclaim before you my Name YHWH'.

Bibliography

The Babylonian Talmud (32 vols). 1990. Edited by Rabbi Dr. I. Epstein. London: The Soncino Press.

The Talmud of the Land of Israel (35 vols). 1983. Translated by Jacob Nuesner. London: University of Chicago Press.

The Works of Philo: Complete and Unabridged. 1993. New Updated Edition. Translated by C.D. Yonge. Peabody: Hendrickson.

Adorno, Theodore. 1973. *Negative Dialectics.* Translated by E.B. Ashton. London: Routledge.

Alexander, Philip S. 1977. The Historical Setting of the Hebrew Book of Enoch. *Journal of Jewish Studies* 28, 156–180.

Alexander, Philip S. 1987. 3 Enoch and the Talmud. *Journal for the Study of Judaism* 18, 40–68.

Boman, Thorlief. 1960. *Hebrew Thought Compared With Greek.* London: SCM Press Ltd.

Boyarin, Daniel. 2010. Beyond Judaisms: Metatron and the Divine Polymorphy of Ancient Judaism. *Journal for the Study of Judaism* 41, 323–365.

Derrida, Jacques. 2002. *Acts of Religion.* Translated by Gil Anidjar. New York: Routledge,.

Fossum, Jarl E. 1985. *The Name of God and the Angel of the Lord: Samaritan and Jewish Concepts of Intermediation and the Origin of Gnosticism.* Tübingen: Mohr Siebeck.

Halperin, David J. 1988. *The Faces of the Chariot: Early Jewish Responses to Ezekiel's Vision.* Tubingen: Mohr Siebeck.

Harman, Graham. 2010a. Time, Space, Essence and Eidos: A New Theory of Causation. *Cosmos and History: The Journal of Natural and Social Philosophy* 6(1), 1–17.

Harman, Graham. 2010b. *Towards Speculative Realism: Essays and Lectures.* Ropley: Zero Books.

Heiser, Michael S. 2004. *The Divine Council in Late Canonical and Non-Canonical Second Temple Jewish Literature.* PhD diss., University of Wisconsin-Madison.

Hundley, Michael. 2009. To Be or Not to Be: A Reexamination of Name Language in Deuteronomy and the Deuteronomistic History. *Vetus Testamentum* 59, 533–555.

Hurtado, Larry W. 1998. *One God, One Lord: Early Christian Devotion and Ancient Jewish Monotheism.* Second edition. Edinburgh: T&T Clark.

Husserl, Edmund. 1931. *Ideas: General Introduction to Pure Phenomenology.* Translated by W. R. Boyce Gibson. London: George Allen & Unwin Ltd.

Husserl, Edmund. 1970. *Logical Investigations,* Vol. II. Translated by J.N. Findlay. London: Routledge.

Idel, Moshe. 2009. *Ben: Sonship and Jewish Mysticism.* London/New York: Continuum.

Martini, Annett, ed. 2010. *Yosef Giqatilla The Book of Punctuation: Flavius Mithridates' Latin Translation, The Hebrew Text, and an English Version.* Torino: Nino Aragno Editore.

Miller, Michael T. 2013. Folk Etymology and its Influence on Metatron Traditions. *Journal for the Study of Judaism* 44(3), 339–355.

Odeberg, Hugo. 1928. *3 Enoch or The Hebrew Book of Enoch.* Cambridge: Cambridge University Press.

Rosenzweig, Franz. 1999. *The New Thinking.* Translated by Alan Udoff and Barbara Galli. Syracuse: Syracuse University Press.

Schäfer, Peter. 2009. *The Origins of Jewish Mysticism.* Tübingen: Mohr Siebeck.

Schäfer, Peter. 2012. *The Jewish Jesus: How Judaism and Christianity Shaped Each Other.* Oxford: Princeton University Press.

Scholem, Gershom. 1987a. *The Origins of the Kaballah.* Edited by R.J. Werblowsky, translated by Allan Arkush. Princeton: Princeton University Press.

Scholem, Gershom. 1987b. *Kabbalah.* New York: Dorset Press.

Scholem, Gershom. 1996 [1965]. *On the Kabbalah and its Symbolism.* New York: Schocken.

Segal, A.F. 1977. *Two Powers in Heaven: Early Rabbinic Reports About Christianity and Gnosticism.* Leiden: Brill.

Seow, C.L. 1999. Face. In: Karel van der Toorn, Bob Becking, Pieter W. van der Horst. eds. *Dictionary of Deities and Demons in the Bible.* Second edition. Leiden/Cambridge: Brill/Eerdmans, 322.

Stroumsa, Gedaliahu G. 1983. Forms of God: Some Notes on Metatron and Christ. *Harvard Theological Review* 76(3), 269–288.

Stroumsa, Guy G. 2003. A Nameless God: Judaeo-Christian and Gnostic 'Theologies of the Name'. In: Peter J. Tomson and Doris Lambers-Petry. eds. *The Image of the Judaeo-Christians in Ancient Jewish and Christian Literature.* Tubingen: Mohr Siebeck, 230–244.

Winston, David. 1985. *Logos and Mystical Theology in Philo of Alexandria*. Cincinnati: Hebrew Union College Press.

Wolfson, Elliot R. 1995. Metatron and Shi'ur Qomah in the Writings of the Haside Ashkenaz. In Karl Erich Grözinger and Joseph Dan. eds. *Mysticism, Magic and Kabbalah in Ashkenazi Judaism: International Symposium Held in Frankfurt a.M. 1991*. Berlin: Walter de Gruyter, 60–92.

4   The seventy faces of God

Kripke on names, identity and the angels of the Hekhalot

> He who sees this one says: 'This one is that one', and he who sees that one says: 'That one is this one', for the appearance of this one is like the appearance of that one; and the appearance of that one is like the appearance of this one.
>
> (HekhR§160)[1]

Having analysed the role of Metatron in the Talmud, this chapter will investigate the development of these Name-Angel traditions in the Hekhalot literature. I hope to establish that the multiple angelic stratifications which some scholars have seen as representing a severely compromised monotheism, may also be read as a sophisticated onomatology.[2]

The majority of the Hekhalot literature dates from between the fourth and tenth centuries CE[3] and comprises several major texts as well as some other tertiary pieces. The main texts are *Hekhalot Zutarti* (The Lesser Palaces), *Hekhalot Rabbati* (The Greater Palaces), *Ma'aseh Merkavah* (The Work of the Chariot), *Merkavah Rabbah* (The Great Chariot) and *3 Enoch* (also known as *Sefer Hekhalot*, the Book of Palaces). Spread throughout the corpus is material relating to the traditions of Shi'ur Qomah (Measurement of the Divine Body) and the Sar Torah (Prince of the Torah).[4] However, we are wise to take note of the caveats regarding the rigid stratification of material into individual units, and of the acknowledged diversity of provenance and theology. Joseph Dan has concluded that the literature 'should not be viewed as a product of one school of mystics moved by a common theology' (1998, 233). Bearing these in mind, I will endeavour to treat the Hekhalot literature as a body of textual tradition, in order to find the conclusions that exist within it.

The basic themes of the texts are the methodical ascent of a rabbi, often either Akiva or Ishmael, their procession through the various heavens, past the angelic guardians, and finally their joining in the angelic liturgy in praise of God. In these texts, we encounter many different angelic figures who have individual names, who have general titles, and who incorporate the Name of God, the Tetragrammaton. In the literature, the angels are often described as bearing the Name of God. This is done in a variety of ways: the letters are appellated after their own name, as in cases like Akatriel YHWH; they are integrated into the angel's name, as in SQDHWZYH;[5] or the letters are worn on a cloak, ring or crown.[6]

The question of identity is persistently provoked by the scores of new names used in the texts – often it is difficult to understand whether they signify God or his angels, and it is routinely impossible to determine where God begins and the angels end. Many scholars have claimed that this complex heavenly world represents a polytheistic corruption of the godhead; Rachel Elior writes that the Hekhalot literature 'seems to replace the monotheistic tradition with a polytheistic visionary myth ... nullifying the uniqueness of the single divine entity' (1993, 34) and Joseph Dan describes a 'pleroma – of divine powers surrounding the supreme God' (1998, 54). I will present a new reading which provides a different answer to this question, drawing on the work of Saul Kripke on the personal name as a 'rigid designator' of individuality and identity. This will initially require a large amount of text-critical analysis in order to untangle what may be the actual doctrines encoded in texts which have become extremely corrupt over centuries of copying. The process will be tiring to those uninterested in historical and textual details, but it has been necessary to do this work in order to reach the conclusion upon which the philosophical analysis, and developments in later chapters, are based.

The textual evidence

The two strata

A curious feature of some Hekhalot texts (most notably MMerk), are lists of descriptions or attributes of God which are repeated and inverted, often including reference to 'his name', such as 'he is his name and his name is he'. It is usual to interpret these as being circular descriptions of God, but this is not the only possibility. I will suggest that there is reason to understand this as describing some quality of the relationship between the angels and God, and the fluidity between them. Throughout the texts we find two separate strata in heaven. Beings appellated with the Tetragrammaton such as Zoharriel YHWH God of Israel (used throughout HekhR) and Totrosiai YHWH God of Israel (throughout HekhR as well as in HekhZ and MMerk[7]) seem to be cognates representing God,[8] whereas the second strata is populated by beings such as Metatron, Suryah and the other 'princes.' This is often articulated in terms of master and servant, the second strata being conditioned as the servant(s) of YHWH – for example, 'Suryah, Prince of the Presence, the servant of Totrakhiel YHWH' (§198, cf. §200).

One of the most often quoted passages is from MMerk§557, which reads: 'His name is like His power, and His power is like His Name. He is His power, and His power is He, and His Name is like His Name'. The manuscript variations of §557 are particularly difficult to reconcile into a sensible meaning, and opinions vary on the correct parsing of the prior passage, which seems to read: '...and He will not banish His companion'. Swarz makes it part of the previous sentence so that his translation reads:

Rabbi Akiba said: Happy is the man who stands with all his strength and presents song before BRWKYY YWY God of Israel and gazes at the Merkavah and sees all that is done before the Throne of Glory on which BRWKYY YHWH God of Israel is seated, and sees to commandment and to power, to the laws and good decrees, that stern decrees may be cancelled from the world, and that no one may spurn his fellow; in {the name of} ShNYT'N TRWGG YWY God of Israel, whose name is like his power...

(1992, 233)[9]

However Janowitz prefers to connect the passage with that following it so that her translation reads: '...from the world and he will not excommunicate his companion in the name of T'NTRGB Adonai God of Israel because his name is like his power...' (1989, 40).

This latter is also the interpretation preferred by Fossum, who comments that here 'God has a "companion" who shares his Name: his Name is like the divine Name; he even is God's Name' (1995, 120). A second aspect which has found little agreement is the meaning of ברוכיי (BRWKYY). While Janowitz suggests it may be related to 'blessed', Swarz notes that one occurrence of it in N8128 reads כרוביי (KRWBYY) – i.e., 'cherub-of'. In this case the text depicts the 'Happy man' as presenting song before a cherub of God.[10] Which the correct reading is, we cannot tell from this, although it is worth noting that כרובי makes more grammatical sense than ברוכיי; and even if the latter is assumed to mean blessed, there is still an implied suggestion of a second figure who is the blessed one present in the text.

Given this implication of a second figure upon the Throne, who is God's 'companion in the name', we can offer a reinterpretation of the following section. In this light it appears there are two different '*Hes*' being discussed: God, and an angel. Read in this way, the passages become: '*his* name is like His might and His might is like *his* name. *He* is His power and His power is *him* and *his* name is like His Name' (§557); '*He* is His Name and His Name is *him*. He is in *him* and His Name is in *his* name' (§588). This reading is superior because it offers a clear sense to the otherwise useless phrases 'his name is like his name' and 'he is in him and his name is in his name', which are otherwise not even in the same spirit or formula as the preceding claims. We can see a similar method at work in the passages: 'He is one and His Name is one' (§550) and: 'You are one and Your Name is one' (§589). This is an obvious interpretation in terms of Metatron, the prince who shares God's Name and appears like Him, who has God's Name in him. Jared Calaway (2011) gives an important translation of HekhZ§420, where it says of MGYHShH: 'And he stands before the throne of glory, facing (or in the presence of) the speech of the seraphim, *for his name is as His name; it is the same name*'. I concur with Janowitz, Fossum and Calaway in their respective readings and believe we can extrapolate this out and explain most of the similar obscure passages as being discussions of the relationship between two different '*Hes*' – God and His angel.[11]

This reading is nothing that should not be obvious, given the repeated emphasis on this dual strata in heaven. In the next section I will look in more detail at the relationship between the strata and how this is articulated nominally.

The angel's names

The angels or servants of the second strata are often described as having a name similar to their master's. Metatron is the most well-known example of such an angel, this quality being ascribed to him in the Bavli,[12] and the condition is repeated throughout the Hekhalot literature, where he is often the angel 'whose name is like his master's'. Anafiel sometimes bears the Tetragrammaton after his name but even when without is described as 'the servant who is named after his master' (§244). Several times the formula is applied to the Youth, who may or may not be automatically subsumable within the figure of Metatron:[13] one Sar Torah passage applies Exodus 23:21 to the Youth before identifying him with Metatron (§396–7). At §400 he is the 'servant who is named after his master', and a Shi'ur Qomah passage also cites Exodus 23:21, claiming: 'The name of the Youth is like the name of his Master, as it is written: "for my Name is in him"'.[14] Dumiel may also follow this formula, some manuscripts having God instruct: 'Call him Dumiel after My name' (§230).[15]

In two separate texts we meet the angel MGYHShH,[16] who is labelled second in rank after God, their names being one.[17] It is difficult at first to fathom why this figure is claimed to share in the Name – the Tetragrammaton is not appended to him, and nor is any further etymological explanation given. The answer may be provided by a similar case in MMerk, where we find the character: 'ShQDH-WZYH Your servant.... Whose name is exalted because of [i.e. by bearing] the name of his creator'.[18] This angel is not appended with the Tetragrammaton, but has the letters of the Name integrated into its own. There is also the far more common ZHWBDYH, found in various forms in the Genizah fragments, the Shi'ur Qomah texts, HekhR and MerkR, which contains the letters YHWH. Although this name is not explicitly combined with a claim of divine name-sharing, it is often ascribed to the Youth or to Metatron,[19] who as we know are themselves frequently held to carry the Divine Name.[20] This presents the possibility that the former name MGYHShH also incorporated the letters YHWH, but has since become corrupted. One candidate would be MWYHShH, ‎ו and ‎ג not being extremely different, and with the remaining letters being, rather logically, ShM: name.

The question of what this name-sharing means has tested scholars for decades. Some assume it merely expresses devotion, while others have seen a much more powerful meaning. Odeberg writes that: 'The ascribing to Metatron of the Name YHWH ha-Qatan … denotes his Function of being God's representative. As this representative the Most High has conferred upon him part of His essence which is in His name' (1928, 188). Grözinger states that: 'the participation in God's Name is participation in God's power, and thus in the deity itself' (1987, 62), and Joseph Dan concludes that divine names 'cannot be interpreted as other than an appellation of divine power ... not just a technical appellation of a certain created functionary angel' (1998, 54). Likewise Schäfer writes it is 'plausible to regard the angelic-divine names with divine epithets as just one more indication that the boundaries between God and his angels in the Hekhalot literature ... become fluid' (2012, 137). Certainly the biblical tradition of the angel who bears God's Name indicates something more than a merely titular appellation: there, the angel is the representative of God and carries some of His authority, and so it seems likely that the use of the Name in these texts does imply some diffusion of divine power and identity into the angelic retinue.

This interpretation is supported by a further feature of the texts: the angelic princes are often described in the same terms as God, and sometimes are explicitly confused with him. In *3 Enoch*, Abuya mistakes Metatron for a second God because he sees Metatron 'seated upon a throne like a king, with ministering angels standing beside me as servants and all the princes of kingdoms crowned with crowns surrounding me' (16:2). The throne he sits on is like God's own (10:1), and even his wisdom is comparable to God's, the mysteries of the world as open to him 'as they stand revealed before the Creator' (11:1). As well as being directly comparable with God, Metatron is called: 'The lesser YHWH', (12:5)[21] with direct reference to Exodus 23's 'My Name is in him'.[22]

A Shi'ur Qomah passage repeated in *Siddur Rabbah*, *Sefer Raziel* and ShQ contains a section which describes the Youth in exactly the same terms that Metatron described God – including his crown bearing the name of Israel, his horns, and his fiery, rainbow-like appearance. Similarly, the Genizah fragment where an angel named Ozhayah warns of the Youth 'who comes from behind the throne' and whose crown, shoes, robe, splendour and glory are like his king's but who under no account should be worshipped, whose name is Zehubadiah.[23] In this case it is not explicitly mentioned but we know by now that his name also is 'like his king's'. Rowland and Morray-Jones have reconstructed the manuscript variations in another Shi'ur Qomah passage pertaining to the Youth, and reasons that the phrase ZHWBDYH should be read as זהו בד יה: 'This is the BD of God' (2009, 524). The word BD has a number of meanings including single/separate; stalk/shoot; and member/limb/part (Jastrow, 2005, 138), thus suggesting a kind of ontological continuity between the two. The phrasing is reminiscent of the talmudic version of Abuya's Metatron vision, where it is said that he 'cut the shoots', and it has been speculated that the shoots in this instance could refer to the severing of Metatron from God.[24] Although the term translated as 'shoots' in b.Hagiga 15a is *netiot*, the similarity, if a coincidence, is a very provocative one.

Anafiel is described as the Prince before whom 'all those on high kneel and fall down and prostrate themselves' (§242). The name Anafiel ('branch of God') is explained as referring to his crown 'which conceals and covers all the chambers of the palace of the firmament of *arevot;* [he is] like the maker of creation' (§244).[25] This however seems rather convoluted, more of an excuse than a satisfactory explanation. The literal meaning indicates some kind of attachment or emanatory relationship: a 'branching-off' of God.[26]

The subtext throughout is of a very close relationship, even a near-identity of the angel and God. In fact, after listing multiple meaningless strings of letters as names of God, HekhZ compiles a long list of names including his biblical appellations and ending with Michael, Gabriel, Raphael, Metatron and Shaddai (§357–367). The boundaries between the angel(s) and God are so blurred that it is impossible to be sure of the distinction, of which are the master and which the servant; which God and which angel. This is compounded by the dozens of different names each is given: God is TOTzSh YHWH God of Israel (§81, §92), Zoharriel YHWH God of Israel (§96, §99, etc.); Ozhayah YHWH God of Israel (§120); ShQRHWZYAY RHBYRWN[27] (§204), ADYRYRON YHWH God of Israel (§204, §553); Akatriel Yah YHWH God of Hosts[28] (§130, §501, §597 etc.), Yedidia, master of the World (§167[29]), Totrosiai NBWBMRṬShON NDYB MRṬTzAN YHWH God of Israel (§172), and sometimes simply YHWH/YWY God of Israel (§159); the prince or servant is named as Suryah (§108, §117–120, §152), Seganzegael (§122, §145), Metatron (§131, §140), Shamiel (§179), Anafiel, Yofiel, etc., or simply Prince of the Presence. However we soon find that the names cross over, that Ozhayah (§220[30]) and Totrosiai (§301) are also Princes or angels, and Metatron is 'Metatron YHWH God of Israel, God of the Heavens and God of the Earth, God of Gods, God of the sea and God of the land' (§279, §678[31]). Finally, in the Sar Torah passage appended to HekhR (§301) we read a list of princes to be called on which shatters any kind of system we may have built up, including the Prince Zehubadiah YHWH, the Prince Totrosiai YHWH and the Prince Adiriron YHWH, the mystic being instructed to conjure them by the name of Yofiel Splendour of Height,[32] and finally Ozhayah, Zebudiel YH, and Akatriel YWY God of Israel are all identified clearly as names of Metatron (§310).[33]

The seventy names of Metatron

Now, I'd like to suggest that there is a crucial point in the idea of Metatron's 'seventy names'. It is a persistent tradition that Metatron has many different names, sometimes seventy but (and this is probably the earlier tradition) occasionally eight.[34] At some point the idea that Metatron has multiple names has become fused with the long standing tradition of the seventy nations of the world, each with their own language,[35] and so in *3 Enoch* Metatron claims to have 'seventy names corresponding to the seventy nations of the world', all of which are 'based on the name of the King of kings of kings' (3:2).[36] In *3 Enoch* these names are engraved on God's crown and may (or may not) be the sacred names engraved on the throne.

It is not just Metatron who has seventy names, though. All the angelic Princes are claimed to have seventy such names, where one name is for each language of the world (3En.29:1) and the 'seventy-two princes of kingdoms in the height, correspond ... to the seventy-two[37] nations in the world' (17:8).[38] In a later addition to *3 Enoch*, God says: 'I took seventy of my names and called him [Metatron] by them, so as to increase his honor. I gave seventy princes into his hand, to issue them my commandments in every language' (48C:9). Likewise in HekhR§295, Metatron is 'given' the seventy angels by God. These passages suggest that there may be some equivalence between the seventy names and the seventy princes, while making the association with the languages of the world clear. The seventy angels themselves may be nothing but names for Metatron; names by which Metatron is known to the seventy nations of the world. In fact, one Genizah fragment it is a variant of ShQDHWZYH who is 'called by seventy names',[39] prompting the obvious suggestion that in fact all the angels are only different names for the single being.[40] More conclusively, we find in one Sar Torah passage a list of names including ShQDHWZYH, ZHWBDYH and a variant of Suryah (SWRYAYH), informing us that each 'is Metatron' (§682[41]).

Throughout this chapter so far I have been arguing that the Hekhalot literature presents a panorama of angelic beings, existing on an ontological rung below God, who are actually expressions of the same single 'being'. This hypothesis has, in a way, been discussed before. A few scholars have previously argued the inverse of my point, that Metatron is not a particular name, but only the title of an office, or a name describing a host of figures. Idel writes that: 'A chief stumbling block in understanding ... Metatron is the assumption that this is a personal name' (2009, 124); Segal claims that Metatron is 'the rabbinic name for many mediators in heretical thought' (1977, 72), a name 'first evidenced in Babylonia for a principal angel known by many names in Palestinian sects' (ibid., 1977, 63), and Scholem regards Metatron as 'not a proper name at all but a designation for the whole category of celestial powers performing a mission' (1987, 298–299).

I have previously suggested that the name Metatron may have been interpreted by some communities as Mi-TTR-on, or 'from the four-[letter name]', meaning that Metatron was read as being derived from or dependent on God (Miller, 2013). Now I would like to suggest an alternative interpretation, that the name Metatron may originally derive from a misreading (or miswriting) of the phrase 'his name is from the four-[letter name]', a phrase originally intended not as a name at all but as a description of one or more angelic beings who have the Tetragrammaton incorporated into their name. Metatron then came into being as a catch-all term that the rabbis used to discuss the various manifestations of the Name Angel which were in popular usage at that time.

Analysis

Saul Kripke's celebrated text *Naming and Necessity* (1980) presents a prolonged, analytic interpretation of the relationship between names and identity. In it he argues that names are not descriptions and so do not have sense, but only reference. The proper name is a 'rigid designator' in that it can only refer to one particular individual, whatever the contingent circumstances – a name refers to a non-ontological essence and not to a bundle of qualities which may or may not be attached to the individual object in question.[42] He argues that a name is not simply a linguistic entity, not merely a random collection of letters or phonemes which are attached arbitrarily to objects – rather, a name designates a reference and as such places the subject and object in relation to each other. A name therefore posits the subject as much as it does the object, for it must be located in terms of a specific referrer as well as a specific referent. For this reason, a name, even if historically false because the one we are using is not the one that person was known by, still cannot be incorrect because it succeeds in its function of locating the referent for *us*. Kripke gives the example of Socrates, of which either the written or pronounced form would be completely unfamiliar to the historical figure we use it for. Still the name Socrates, for us, points to that figure. So, a name is inherently localised in the context of its use and forms a point of contact between the speaker and the spoken-of.[43]

The name, then, in locating the object for the subject, is essentially a metaphor for the subjective phenomenon of presence – something which must always be particular. Presence must always be presence-to and cannot be removed from the subject. The name brings the object into the world of the subject and presents a particular face of that object.

We can conclude that while different names can be used of the same essence (thereby defining different relationships), one name cannot refer to more than one essence – although the same *sign* can mean different objects for different subjects, each proper *name* defines a single object for the subject. The Tetragrammaton as a name then cannot be a merely arbitrary signifier. Its use in the texts must always point to the same essence, and therefore any 'beings' of whom the Tetragrammaton is appellated are articulations of God, included in the divine essence. This suggests that we are incorrect in seeing the Tetragrammaton as a suffix; rather, the angelic names prior to it are prefixes. These prefixed names before the Tetragrammaton afford a kind of particularisation, a specific quality of God.[44] This is most obvious in Akatriel, whose name indicates crown. The name Akatriel YHWH would then mean, Crown of God. Likewise, Zoharriel YHWH would mean the Brightness of God – or God experienced as brightness. Thus, while many have seen the proliferation of angels during this period in Jewish history as a corollary of the increasingly transcendent God, in this reading the angelic strata is rather a positing of *linguistic* entities, names, as an epistemic level in between Divine essence and human other, such that each is protected while allowing the ability of the subject and object to meet epistemically. To use a particular name of God is to bring forth that aspect of God's nature, while the whole remains concealed.

According to this theory, then, all the angelic powers are merely names of God – nominal points of subjective contact with the Divine. We find an interesting piece of corroborative evidence in 3 Enoch where Metatron 'stands and carries out every word and every utterance that issues from the mouth of the Holy One' (48C:10), thus becoming the enactor of divine will. Here the master-servant roles are complete, because Metatron is a virtual extension of God. Likewise, Metatron is often presented as the mediator through whom all communication must pass (3En.10:4), and shares with Anafiel the role of protecting the other angels from the dangerously intense presence of the divine (e.g.

Sefer Haqqomah, line 160). Thus, Metatron and his cognates form a kind of buffer around the essence which can carry out its impulses at one remove. This reading helps to explain the strange similarity between God and angel: the angels appear similar to God because they are parts or aspects of God. They bear the Name of God because, quite simply, it is their name: in referring to the Godhead it also refers to them. We can see here the implication of the title *Sar haPannim*: Prince of the Presence, or Face. The angel(s) given this role are the powers which represent the divine presence or appearance.

In discussing Ishmael's vision of Akatriel in b.Berakhot 7a, Schäfer argues that 'there can be no doubt that for the Bavli editor Akatriel is identical with God' (2012, 180) – the prayer that Akatriel accepts from Ishmael is said immediately prior to be that which God himself prays and invokes the attributes of justice and mercy which are unique to God and nowhere ascribed to angels. Likewise in several Hekhalot passages where Akatriel is mentioned. However, where Akatriel takes the usual place of Metatron at the entrance to the *pardes*, surrounded by ministering angels (§597), we find a more confused picture: Abuyah charges past the enthroned Akatriel and demands an explanation of God, quoting scripture to establish that surely there must be only one God – whereupon God replies: 'Elisha, my son, have you come to reflect upon my *middot*?' Here, in contrast to *3 Enoch*'s recension, it seems that God speaks in defence of Akatriel, and apparently identifies Abuya's theological dilemma as being related to God's qualities or mysteries. While the story presents God and Akatriel as *apparently* separate entities, God Himself states that things are not as simple as that – effectively identifying Akatriel as one of His qualities.

In HekhZ, as R Akiva ascends and enters the presence of God, he hears a voice from beneath the throne. The voice asks, 'what mortal man is there who is able to ascend on high ... to behold His splendour ... who is able to explain, and who is able to see?' (§349–350). The text then juxtaposes three scriptural references to the experience of God: 'For man may not see me and live' (Exod.33:20); 'That man may live though God has spoken to him' (Deut.5:21–24); and 'I beheld my Lord seated upon a high and lofty throne' (Is.6:1), before asking: 'What is His Name?'. This passage suggests that although God cannot be directly perceived, the revelation of God's Name provides a route toward the divine and the possibility of a real relationship. In the context of the Hekhalot tradition which so emphasises the use of names and the adjuration of God with manifold names, it is obvious that it is the names themselves which are the desideratum, and the purpose of the human traveller.

However, this is not to equate the names with the essence of divinity. This passage also stresses that there is something not perceivable, something which is so beyond the finite human mind as to constitute an existential threat to it. The essence itself is not merely trans-linguistic – it is ineffable. God in Himself is never seen in the Hekhalot literature even if He is described. The Shi'ur Qomah material offers abundant descriptions of God without ever admitting the sense that he has been experienced. Not only are names not descriptions, but they must refer to something which is beyond the possibility of description: any nature which can be totalised is not an essence but a description, because it is solely technical and constituted. An essence must be singular, not complex, for it is what provides the unity to which qualities adhere. An essence therefore is always transcendent, which is to say that it is *hidden*. However, the essence which cannot be known can be known *of*, made known, through the name, which in positing an other necessarily posits such an essence to which it refers. The name is not merely a quality but goes to the heart of the object in its referential function because it is linked with the essence. The name therefore acts paradoxically as both condition and concealer: it is the action of naming which establishes an object as an other and therefore allows for knowledge of it, yet in so doing prevents the object from being known by providing its inviolable integrity. We can think of the name as a surface or a skin, which provides the possibility of contact at the same time as an opaque resistance. Interestingly, the lack of sense which for Kripke defines names is also derivative of language in its magical function: nonsense words are 'the symbol par excellence of magical language' (Janowitz, 1989, 90).[45] This being the case, naming is the essential magical action, for it literally creates identities: As soon as a name is used there is an ineffable something more than it, which it represents. Janowitz writes that, in HekhR, 'to know the names of angels is to know how to invoke them' (1989, 53). As we saw in Chapter 1, if the name creates identity, and this identity must be thought in terms of relationship – i.e., presence – then naming does in fact manifest the power of that angel, bringing it into the world of the subject.

According to Howard Jackson's analysis of the Shi'ur Qomah traditions: 'By their very nature numbers, even numbers reckoned in units of googols, function to delimit, and with that they confine what they measure' (2000, 380). The same is true of names, which function to relativise objects: they place them in relationship and articulate essence within the particulars of a situation and an individual or group who knows the name. The name becomes the shadow cast by an invisible object.

The function of a name then is to condense and reify. The name in representing an object necessarily draws on the essence, yet it does so within the field of subjectivity because a name can never be objective; to do so would be to become a (historical) quality, a mere sign. Thus a name forms a trajectory between the object and the subject, linking them in a single field of referential action. The name forms the manifestation of the object in relation to the particular subject, a trace which the object leaves, a scar on the surface of consciousness; an effect without compromising the externality of the essence.[46]

What this means is that the name is not the sign as such but the process of reference in which the material sign is utilised; and the process itself is the simple act of intending, i.e. it is the relationship between subject and object. This process-relation is non-complex; simple, because it is the one-dimensional point of contact between subject and object, the interface which links them. Naming is the meeting of object and subject: Just as without a subject a name is a mere empty, dead sign, so also without an object the sign is no longer a name, just a word.

When MerkR claims that 'no (mere) creature can comprehend him … we have no measure in our hand, only the names are revealed to us' (§699),[47] it states that the names are not the end-point of God, but that they are the end-point of human understanding. The names are not the identity of God, but are what is revealed to humans. This reflects the statement that: 'He is hidden from every eye and no man may see Him … His image is hidden from all' (HekhZ§356),[48] made while endlessly describing the pseudo-angelic beings who populate heaven. The strangely corporeal imagery of the Shi'ur Qomah then is in fact attempting to delineate not the essence of God, but the limitations which human understanding places on our perception. It relates that there is a very definite *sense* of perceiving the divine, one given in names – but this is not to be equated with the essence of God himself. Metatron articulates God into words (names) and numbers (descriptors) in order that God can be experienced, and so provides a kind of buffer around the divine essence.[49] We see here the same notion expressed by Adorno when he writes that the concept is always 'entwined with a nonconceptual whole. Its only insulation from that whole is its reification – that which establishes it as a concept' (1973, 12). In order to be made conceptual, that which transcends thought becomes reified into symbols (names), which by their nature exist as the point at which subject and object meet.

All these names, these points of reference or designators for God are not his essence; the dark ground of God transcends these, but the names form a surface, a shifting kaleidoscopic surface, a boundary which intimates a beyond. The essence, the dark ground or internality extends behind this surface of names, which in fact are particular points of view on God, each an individual relationship. Thus the pleroma some scholars have discussed is one not of beings but of names: God, like every non-totalisable object, is hermetically sealed within a polygon of names, and from every angle which we approach him we find a new name or variation, a new surface which refracts the essence in different hues. The 'seventy nations' of the world each receive a different name, a different relation with God.

Joseph Dan writes that: 'The mysticism of the names, numbers and letters is a mysticism of contact with the divine essence through its revelation in earthly symbols' (1998, 64). In this context, to say earthly is to say psychological – the plane of the human. The divine essence, which we know well cannot be conceived in itself (which is to say, cannot be within the world), must take some form when it enters consciousness. In order to be present in human life the unrepresentable and unseeable God must be compressed into some form which, while distinct from God, can still act as a vessel. Although Dan distinguishes this from the mysticism of the descent of the divine to the earthly mystic (and of the human's ascent), it does seem to be a metaphorical descent: the divine manifests into something conceivable by the finite minds of corporeal beings. It is thus a conceptual or ideological descent, of the formless into form. The tortured language we find in these texts represents how, in the process of emerging through the veil and into consciousness, the object (God) is twisted and broken into words – words that are themselves twisted and broken by the weight of what they are trying to express.

In the Hekhalot literature, God is both transcendent and present; but this dualism must be understood epistemologically. God is not so transcendent as to be unimaginable, unthinkable, unknowable, but what we can know of God must be tempered by a knowledge of our own minds' tendency to reduce and compress information into a subjective form. This is to say, all human knowledge of God takes the shape of human knowledge, which is linguistic: it is *language-shaped*. This does not invalidate it. This bringing into the subjective realm, or *making-knowable* of the divine is essential in any theology which claims revelation. However, the knowledge must not be mistaken for the thing-itself.

Shi'ur Qomah warns against the *qomatose* – a reductionist belief in only the immediately present, the body which is mechanical and divisible, without seeing the wholeness which constitutes and allows for identity. For an object to have integrity it cannot be constituted but must transcend. In doing this, we are given a subtle but devastating critique of idealism: if the name (that present in the mind) is the essence, God can be dissected and corporealised so that he is present but dead, inert before us; and so, not present; apparent but not present. The message is that a God constituted by names and numbers is not God. If we could gain God through this process, then what in fact would we have gained, and what more would we have lost? If truths were about names, if names were descriptions rather than pointing to something inexpressible beyond them, then we are left with a reductionist metaphysics, an atomism where everything is stateable in terms of the lowest common denominator. But objects, especially if that object is also a subject, must have an independence: they must transcend and at some level be concealed from view, withdrawing from the mind's eye which divides and compartmentalises them out of existence.

Thus we can understand the proliferation of meaningless and unpronounceable 'names' with which the Hekhalot literature provides us – even the apparently random collections of letters can be names, if they are used as such. But all the names used of God are names used relatively and are conditioned also by the finite human perspective. Even the Tetragrammaton is not God's internal nature but a name given to humans to use of him. In the Hekhalot literature we see evidenced a theory of naming where identity and name are interrelated, but beings are also divisible into an infinity of names. The unity is irreducible, and cannot be reduced to the names that it comprises, yet these names are the knowable manifestation of the ineffable unity which stands behind them.

Notes

1 Unless indicated, translations are my own. James R. Davila's comprehensive and definitive *The Hekhalot Literature in Translation* (2013) was consulted as the current best translation.

2 This chapter is a developed and rewritten version of an article originally published in *Bamidbar* (Miller, 2012).

3 Gershom Scholem's original dating (1965) placed the texts between the second and fourth centuries but has now been supplanted. Debate is still on-going about the precise nature of the relationship between the traditions found in the Hekhalot texts

and those similar passages in the Bavli (discussed in Chapter 3). For an overview of the opposing opinions, see Ra'anan Boustan (2011), especially 499n60.

4 The former elaborates Metatron's description of the body of God, in order that the mystic should know 'the measurement of our creator'. He is presented with both unpronounceably arcane names and impossibly huge measurements for each of the parts of God's anatomy, effectively translating God in words and numbers. The descriptions begin from the soles of the feet up to the features of the face and the crown on his head, often including the letters written on the crown and on his forehead. The latter describes the rituals to bring down the angel (again often Metatron) who will assist in the task of memorising Torah.

5 Also see Shem.Rab.29:2, on Ps.68:18: 'Another explanation of 'Adonai is among them'. The sages say: The name of God was joined with the name of each [angel], Michael and Gabriel [etc.].' Cf. Midr.Tanh. Mishpatim 18, that the angels all have the Name of God in common. These last passages however certainly relate to the common appending of the word 'el to the angelic names. As Idel (2009, 114) remarks, the Hekhalot literature differs from the normative rabbinic literature in using the Tetragrammaton rather than 'el theophorically. On inscription of the angels with the Name see Chapter 2, Note 13.

6 The gigantic fiery prince Keruvi'el wears a crown of holiness 'with the sacred name engraved upon it' (3En.22:5). Akatriel often has his name engraved on God's crown (somewhat oddly, as his name seems to mean 'Crown of God'. Is the crown then referring to the angel, or the angel to the crown?). At 3En.13 God writes on Metatron's crown the letters by which heaven and earth and their elements were created. Similarly, Metatron bears the letters 'with which were created heaven and earth and sealed with the [signet-] ring of Ehyeh Asher Ehyeh' (Sefer Raziel 261–2). In HekhR Anafiel holds the signet ring bearing the seal of heaven and earth (§242). These letters are likely those of God's Name (see Chapter 1), and the angels' crowns may well be related to Tg.s Neof. and Ps.-J. to Exod.32:25ff. which depict the Israelites wearing golden crowns bearing 'the great and glorious name'. It is also possible that the crown/robe bearing the Name is related to the garment of creation (on which see Fossum, 1985, 290; Gen.Rab.3:4; Pirq. R El. 3 and especially the Geonic *Sefer HaMalbush*, described in Scholem 1996, 136ff.). In Odes 4:8, angels are 'clothed' with the Name. On the imagery of the crown in Jewish mysticism, see Green (1997).

7 A full list of appearances is given in Miller (2013) but see especially §196: TWTRW-SIAI YHWH God of Israel, for He is called TWTRWSYAY, TWTRWSYH TWTRWSYA TWTRWSYCh TWTRWSYAL TWTRWSYG TWTRWSYKh TWTRWSYP TWTRWSYTz TWTRWSYSh TWTRWSYB TWTRWSYN TWTRWSYM TWTRWSYO TWTRWSYQ TWTRWSYṬ TzWRTQ ZYHRRYAL AShRWYLYAY.

8 The only scholar who has contested this is Dan, who argued, based on his interpretation of a single passage (§96), that Zoharriel, and by implication Totrosiai, must not be identified with the supreme God, although they clearly stand above all creation (1998, 102). His chain of reasoning is difficult to accept: the sole passage in which Dan finds a distinction between Zoharriel and God varies between manuscripts, and in every other occurrence the names are unequivocally used as titles or conditions of 'YHWH God of Israel'.

9 Davila's reading is very similar (2013, 266).

10 This is particularly notable because of the prominence of the Throne of Glory in this section, and puts this passage immediately in parallel with the Unique Cherub texts which describe a quadripartite heavenly emanation made up of God, the Glory, the Throne of Glory, and the Unique Cherub who is seated upon the Throne (Dan, 1999). Obviously one cannot base our reading of a text upon the beliefs of a school which came some half dozen centuries after, but the similarities are striking and in particular might suggest that this text was one of the major contributors to their theology.

11 It may be possible also to perceive a relationship between these passages and the Mekhilta de Rabbi Ishmael, which cites three Biblical texts as a refutation of the Two Powers heresy: 'As it is said: 'See now, that I, even I, am He' etc. [Deut.32:39]. And it says: 'Even unto old age I am the same' [Is.46:4]. And it says: 'Thus sayeth YHWH the King of Israel and his Redeemer the Lord of Hosts: I am the first and I am the last' [Is.44:16]…' (Bahodesh 5, line 4). The use of Deut.32:39 is particularly notable in its affirmation that 'I' and 'He' are the same, not two distinct entities, as some heretics had claimed. Similarly, the Bahir ascribes a fictitious quote to Habbakuk: 'Because Your name is in You and in You is Your name…' (71/48, Campanini, 2005). Last, the similarity should be noted between the interpretation I have offered and a saying of Jesus' in John 10:38, 'The Father is in me, and I am in the Father'.

12 b.Sanh.38b, analysed in Chapter 3.

13 נער is a title often applied directly to Metatron but also used without direct reference. The term is usually understood as 'youth' but can also mean 'servant'. At 3En.4:10, Metatron himself explains the title as referring to his short lifespan relative to the other angels, a consequence of his mortal origins. Of course, we would be unwise to not relate this in some way to the titles 'lesser (or little) YHWH', and 'Son of Man'. The paternal implications of all three are unavoidable, and at points God is said to have his right hand placed on the head of the Youth (e.g. *Sefer Raziel* 240 and parallels). Rowland and Morray-Jones (2009, 518–527) argue for the initial separation of the Youth and Metatron, although their argument is based on the absence of Metatron from a single text (*Siddur Rabbah*) which, on the basis of that absence, they assume to be prior to the identification and therefore to pre-date the other texts. The circularity of this argument works against it, and in the absence of any other evidence we are left unable to decide the point at all. In basic agreement though, see also Davila, who argues that 'there is a reasonable case to be made that the Youth is a distant but direct descendant of the angel Melchizedek' (2003, 262). In favour of their initial identification are Orlov (2004, 222–226), who sees Youth as a title which evolved from its use in *2 Enoch*, and Boyarin (2010) who sees Metatron as developing from the matrix of late Second Temple figures of which the Youth was a potent aspect. Idel (2009, 131) offers the only real argument for the Son of Man association, though even this is inconclusive.

14 From two manuscripts of *Sefer Raziel* and four of *Sefer Haqqomah*, as noted by Rowland and Morray-Jones (2009, 523). A similar implication is also made in *Siddur Rabbah* 14–33 (Cohen, 1985, 39–41).

15 Although the manuscripts are difficult to reconcile.

16 §420, where the manuscripts provide several variations (מניהשה [D436] or מניחשה [N8128]), but מגיהשה is the most common – and in the Ozhayah Genizah fragment which duplicates this section (8. T.-S. K 21.95.C 2b, Schäfer 1984, 105) it is given as מיהשגה (line 37), and מגהשה (line 38).

17 This part of the tradition extant only in the Genizah fragment (Schäfer 1984, 105).

18 §562; also given as שקדהוזאי (ShQDHWZAY); שקדאוזיה (ShQDAWZYH); שקראוזיה (ShQRAWZYH). The name is also found in several variants at §204, as mentioned below.

19 E.g. MerkR§682, and a Geniza fragment (Schäfer, 1984, 105, lines 15–16).

20 Idel (2009, 141–144) argues that this name is a theophorism based on YHWH and ZBD; however, Rowland and Morray-Jones (2009, 524–525) provide a different reconstruction, discussed below.

21 Cf. §295 in B238.

22 Interestingly, one recension of Abuya's vision (§597) puts Akatriel in Metatron's place. Nathaniel Deutsch (1999) concluded that this is the original version of the story.

23 8. T.-S. K 21.95.C (Schäfer 1984, 103–5). Ozhayah appears to be of the format mentioned earlier, being spelled אוזהיה throughout, although manuscripts of §220 give

variations as אוזהיא, (D436, B238, V228), אזהייא (O1531), אוזהריא (M40) and אוזהיה (N8128). M22 seems particularly corrupt, giving in its place אין היא. Towards the end, the Geniza Fragment even identifies Ozhayah with MYHShGH.

24 This was certainly the later kabbalistic interpretation, as will be discussed in Chapter 6.

25 Cf. 3En.18:18.

26 The branch motif here may be in reference to such passages as Jer.23:5–6, 33:15, Is.4:2, 11:1 and Zech.3:8, 6:12 where the term צמח (branch) is given a messianic implication. This was also known by R Yehoshua (Lam.Rab.1:51; p.Ber.5a) and Rav Huna (*Midrash Mishle*, Buber, 1883, 87). The interesting parallels between this biblical term, the term here ענף, and the Talmudic נטיעות, suggest some connection between the angelic servants and messianic conceptions, but have not to my knowledge been given the required investigation. This is particularly pertinent because of a tradition shared in the Talmud and New Testament that the Messiah has the Name of God (b.B.Bat.75b, Lam.Rab.1:16; Rev.3:12). See Chapter 2.

27 Obviously a variant of, previously the 'servant', ShQDHWZYH.

28 Cf. b.Ber.7a and HekhR§151, where R Ishmael reports seeing 'Akatriel Yah YHWH of Hosts, seated upon a high and exalted throne' within the Heavenly Temple.

29 In this Shi'ur Qomah passage, Metatron appears to call God 'Beloved of God'.

30 In the Geniza fragment 8. T.-S. K 21.95.C line 17 (Schäfer, 1984, 103).

31 Two identical Sar Torah insertions into HekhR (MS. M22 and B238) and MerkR (MS. N8128, O1531 and M40) respectively. Cf. §685 of the latter manuscripts, where 'Zevudiel YY, God of Israel king of kings … is Metatron'. On these texts, see Swarz (1996).

32 Similar passages at §414, §416 and §418 also contain Totrosiai YHWH the Prince. 3En.18–27 combines no less than 23 separate Princes with the divine name. However, it goes on to claim that while the Great Law Court is in session, 'only the great princes who are called YHWH by the name of the Holy One, blessed be He, are permitted to speak' (3En.30:1); there are apparently seventy-two such princes, 'not counting the Prince of the World' (3En.30:2).

33 This section only in V228. Cf. Geniza fragment G1 (T.-S. K 21.95.S), which in a parallel to the list of Metatron's names at HekhR§271, clearly states HZZHYYH, which is probably a variant of Ozhayah.

34 *Visions of Ezekiel* lists eight names, as do HekhR§277, §310 and MerkR§682.

35 Gen.10 relates that Noah produced seventy sons, each of whom formed a nation. The tradition that there are seventy nations, and therefore seventy languages, in the world persists throughout Jewish thought. We further find that the nations are each under the protection of a unique angelic power (e.g. Gen.Rab.37) – all except Israel, whose protector is God Himself. In later texts God is replaced in this role by either Michael or Metatron.

36 Cf. 4:1, where Ishmael asks: 'Why are you called by the name of your Creator with seventy names?'

37 The switch between seventy and seventy-two nations seems to have occurred with the LXX (Metzger, 1959).

38 Cf. 10:4, where we meet 'the eight great, honored and terrible princes who are called YHWH by the name of their king' (cf. 30:1); presumably the earlier version of this tradition, correlating with the eight names of Metatron. Also HekhR§240, where the nominal formula used by the guardians of the gates 'is derived from the name of the king of the universe'.

39 An eleventh century Sar Torah text from the Geniza contains the passage: 'I adjure you Metatron, *Sar haPannim*, I pronounce upon you Metatron, *Sar haPannim*, and I seal upon you, Metatron *Sar haPannim*, in the name of ShQHWZYY, who is called by seventy names' (Schäfer, 1984, 163).

40 In this I am roughly aligned with Idel (2009, 121–2), who suggests a similar conclusion but without investigation.

41 Present in M40, N8128 and O1531. §310, extant only as an insertion into V228, offers a similar list, this time including a variant of Ozhayah (HWZHYH).

42 Although Kripke is famous as the originator of this concept and the term 'rigid designator', Graham Harman (2014) pointed out that it can be found in Husserl, who wrote that:

> For a proper name also names an object 'directly'. It refers to it, not attributively, as the bearer of these or those properties, but without such 'conceptual' mediation, as what it itself is, just as perception might set it before our eyes. The meaning of a proper name lies accordingly in a direct reference-to-this-object...
>
> (1970, 198)

We may also find some suggestion in this direction in Rosenzweig's meditations on the desired substantial constancy which is to be found nowhere but in names (1999, 47–53).

43 It is worth noting that a given historical name would in fact be simply a quality of the object, and may indeed be an arbitrary sign if no one actually utilises that name in reference to them. Thus, $2+2=4$ is necessarily true, despite the fact that someone else may understand the sign 4 to mean the number 7, because it is not the signs themselves which are being discussed but the objects in relation to which those signs place us, the ones now using them. This, I would add for clarification, is the point at which signs become names: when they are used to form a link between a subject and an object. Without this employment in the action of naming, a mere sign is always arbitrary.

44 Grözinger has pointed out that Irenaeus of Lyons argued that heretics misunderstand the many names of God as being separate entities. Any 'angelic figure is nothing else than the function expressed in its name, a hypostasis of this function' (1987, 56). Interestingly, some statements of Eunomius also predict this: 'It is clear that the Divinity is given names with various connotations in accordance with the variety of his activities, named in such a way as we may understand' (Hall 2007, 127); 'Any name, whether discovered by human custom or transmitted by Scripture, is, we say, explicative of what we discover through thought concerning what is around the divine nature, but does not contain the significance of the nature itself' (Krivocheine 1977, 88). I am grateful to Ann Conway-Jones (2011) for highlighting these to me.

45 Hayman, similarly, writes that the 'greatest paradox' of both SY and the Hekhalot literature is that, 'the greatest power, magical power, lies not in the normal language with which we create our social reality and make sense of our chaotic universe, but in meaningless combinations of letters' (1989, 232–3). In this relation it is worth noting that the seventy-two letter name was likely reached due to the fact that all the three-letter sequences derived from Exod.14:19–21 have no meaning.

46 It would be wrong to call this a representation, as it does not share in the form of the object – the object itself is without form, this being a condition of manifestation. To have form is to be limited and therefore knowable.

47 Also repeated through most ShQ passages.

48 Cf. HekhR§159, 'no creature can recognize, neither the near nor the far can look at him'.

49 This function of articulation and categorisation is, I have previously argued, essential to the nature of Metatron throughout his history (Miller, 2009).

Bibliography

The Babylonian Talmud (32 vols). 1990. Edited by Rabbi Dr. I. Epstein. London: The Soncino Press.

Mekilta de-Rabbi Ishmael (3 vols). 1933. Translated by Jacob Z. Lauterbach. Philadelphia: The Jewish Publication Society of America.

Midrash Mishle. 1883. Edited by S. Buber. Vilna.

Midrash Rabbah (10 vols). 1939. Translated by R Dr. H. Freedman, and Maurice Simon. London: The Soncino Press.

Targum Neofiti 1 and Pseudo-Jonathan: Exodus. 1994. Translated by Martin McNamara and Michael Maher. Edinburgh: T&T Clark.

Adorno, Theodore. *Negative Dialectics*. 1973. Translated by E.B. Ashton. London: Routledge.

Boustan, Ra'anan. 2011. Rabbinization and the Making of Early Jewish Mysticism. *Jewish Quarterly Review* 101(4), 482–501.

Boyarin, Daniel. 2010. Beyond Judaisms: Metatron and the Divine Polymorphy of Ancient Judaism. *Journal for the Study of Judaism* 41, 323–365.

Calaway, Jared. 2011. Daily Hekhalot: §420 Synthesized and Revised. *Antiquitopia*. 28 June. Accessed 28 October 2013. http://antiquitopia.blogspot.com/2011/06/daily-hekhalot-420-synthesized-and.html.

Campanini, Saverio, ed. 2005. *The Book of Bahir: Flavius Mithridates' Latin Translation, The Hebrew Text, and an English Version*. Torino: Nino Aragno Editore.

Cohen, Martin Samuel. 1985. *The Shi'ur Qomah: Texts and Recensions*. Tübingen: Mohr Siebeck.

Conway-Jones, Ann. 2011. *Not Made With Hands: Gregory of Nyssa's Doctrine of the Celestial Tabernacle in its Jewish and Christian Contexts*. PhD diss., University of Manchester.

Dan, Joseph. 1998. *Jewish Mysticism Volume I: Late Antiquity*. Northvale: Jason Aronson Inc.

Dan, Joseph. 1999. *The 'Unique Cherub' Circle: A School of Mystics and Esoterics in Medieval Germany*. Tubingen: Mohr Siebeck.

Davila, James R. 2003. Melchizedek, the 'Youth', and Jesus. In: J.R. Davila. ed. *The Dead Sea Scrolls as Background to Postbiblical Judaism and Early Christianity: Papers from an International Conference at St. Andrews in 2001*. Leiden: Brill, 248–74.

Davila, James R. 2013. *The Hekhalot Literature in Translation*. Leiden: Brill.

Deutsch, Nathaniel. 1999. *Guardians of the Gate: Angelic Vice Regency in Late Antiquity*. Leiden: Brill.

Elior, Rachel. 1993. Mysticism, Magic, and Angelology: The Perception of Angels in Hekhalot Literature. *Jewish Studies Quarterly* 1, 3–53.

Fossum, Jarl E. 1985. *The Name of God and the Angel of the Lord: Samaritan and Jewish Concepts of Intermediation and the Origin of Gnosticism*. Tübingen: Mohr Siebeck.

Fossum, Jarl E. 1995. *The Image of the Invisible God: Essays on the Influence of Jewish Mysticism on Early Christology*. Göttingen: Universitatsverlag Freiburg Schweiz and Van-denhoeck & Ruprecht.

Green, Arthur. 1997. *Keter: The Crown of God in Early Jewish Mysticism*. Princeton: Princeton University Press.

Grözinger, Karl Erich. 1987. The Names of God and the Celestial Powers: Their Function and Meaning in the Hekhalot Literature. *Jerusalem Studies in Jewish Thought* 6, 53–69.

Hall, Stuart George. 2007. The Second Book Against Eunomius (Translation). In: Lenka Karfikova, Scot Douglass, and Johannes Zachhuber. eds. *Gregory of Nyssa: Contra Aunomium II*. Leiden: Brill, 59–201.

Harman, Graham. 2014. Husserl on 'Rigid Designators'. *Object-Oriented Philosophy*. 2 March. Accessed 2 April 2015. https://doctorzamalek2.wordpress.com/2014/03/21/husserl-on-rigid-designators/.

Hayman, Peter. 1989. Was God a Magician? Sefer Yesira and Jewish Magic. *Journal of Jewish Studies* 41(2), 225–237.

Husserl, Edmund. 1970. *Logical Investigations*, Vol. II. Translated by J.N. Findlay. London: Routledge.

Idel, Moshe. 2009. *Ben: Sonship and Jewish Mysticism*. London/New York: Continuum.

Jackson, Howard M. 2000. The Origins and Development of Shi'ur Qomah Revelation in Jewish Mysticism. *Journal for the Study of Judaism* 31(4), 373–415.

Janowitz, Naomi. 1989. *The Poetics of Ascent: Theories of Language in a Rabbinic Ascent Text*. Albany: State University of New York Press.

Jastrow, Marcus. 2005. *A Dictionary of the Targumim, the Talmud Babli and Yerushalmi, and the Midrashic Literature*. Peabody: Hendrickson.

Krivocheine, Basil. 1977. Simplicity of the Divine Nature and Distinctions in God, According to St. Gregory of Nyssa. *St. Vladimir's Theological Quarterly* 21, 76–104.

Kripke, Saul A. 1980. *Naming and Necessity*. Oxford: Blackwell.

Metzger, Bruce M. 1959. Seventy or Seventytwo Disciples? *New Testament Studies* 5, 299–306.

Miller, Michael T. 2009. *The Epistemological Role of the Archangel Metatron*. MA diss., Lancaster University.

Miller, Michael T. 2012. Chaos and Identity: Onomatology in the Hekhalot Literature. *Bamidbar – Journal for Jewish Thought and Philosophy* 3, 36–51.

Miller, Michael T. 2013. Folk Etymology and its Influence on Metatron Traditions. *Journal for the Study of Judaism* 44(3), 339–355.

Odeberg, Hugo. 1928. *3 Enoch or The Hebrew Book of Enoch*. Cambridge: Cambridge University Press.

Orlov, Andrei. 2004. *The Enoch-Metatron Tradition*. Tübingen: Mohr-Siebeck.

Rosenzweig, Franz. 1999. *Understanding the Sick and the Healthy*. Translated by Nahum Glatzer. Harvard: Harvard University Press.

Rowland, Christopher and Christopher R.A. Morray-Jones. 2009. *The Mystery of God: Early Jewish Mysticism and the New Testament*. Leiden: Brill.

Schäfer, Peter, ed. 1984. *Geniza-Fragmente zur Hekhalot-Literatur*. Tübingen: Mohr Siebeck.

Schäfer, Peter. 2012. *The Jewish Jesus: How Judaism and Christianity Shaped Each Other*. Oxford: Princeton University Press.

Schäfer, Peter, Margarete Schlüter and Hans Georg von Mutius, eds. 1981. *Synopse zur Hekhalot-Literatur*. Tübingen: Mohr Siebeck.

Scholem, Gershom. 1965. *Jewish Gnosticism, Merkabah Mysticism, and Talmudic Tradition*. Second edition. New York: Jewish Theological Seminary of America.

Scholem, Gershom. 1987. *Kabbalah*. New York: Dorset Press.

Scholem, Gershom. 1996 [1965]. *On the Kabbalah and its Symbolism*. New York: Schocken.

Segal, A.F. 1977. *Two Powers in Heaven: Early Rabbinic Reports About Christianity and Gnosticism*. Leiden: Brill.

Swarz, Michael D. 1992. *Mystical Prayer in Ancient Judaism*. Tübingen: Mohr Siebeck.

Swarz, Michael D. 1996. *Scholastic Magic: Ritual and Revelation in Early Jewish Mysticism*. Princeton: Princeton University Press.

5 The tree of names

The source of logic and emanation in Wittgenstein and Gikatilla

In Chapter 1 I argued that, although the doctrine of creation via the Name is not present in either Second Temple or early rabbinic literature, it remained a conclusion easy to reach from the sources available to speculative Jewish thinkers.[1] Indeed, by the tenth century it had become common currency and we find that in the writings of the Medieval Kabbalah a highly developed form of it is essential doctrine. Utilising the arboreal imagery which was common in these times,[2] Isaac the Blind interpreted Sefer Yetzirah's claim that 'all creation and all speech [dibbur] go out by one name' (§19) as signifying the unfolding from the letters of the Name YHWH, a tree-like structure representing the whole of manifest reality:

> In one name: their root is in one name, for the letters are the visible branches, like the flickering flames, which have motion, which are attached to the coal, and like the twigs of a tree and its branches and boughs, whose root is in the tree.... All the things [devarim] are made into form, and all forms issue from but one name, like a branch that issues from the root, so it turns out that everything is within the root, which is one name, therefore it says at the end one name.
>
> (Sendor, 1994, II, 107)

Likewise Moshe de Leon writes that 'all being is derived from the reality of the Tetragrammaton of the Creator' (Wijnhoven, 1964, 165) and Abulafia writes that:

> [T]he whole world is dependent on it [YHWH], it is the beginning of all beginnings and the purpose of all purposes, and it is the ineffable Name one in all manners of unity.... And it is YHWH ... and know that this blessed Name includes all the other divine names and all emerge from it.
>
> (2007, 30)

However, it is only with the thirteenth century writer Yosef Gikatilla that we find a fully developed theological system which deals with the emanation of reality in terms of the Name.[3] Taking Nachmanides' famous dictum that the

Torah consists entirely of names of God,[4] Gikatilla not only explains how this is possible, but also applies the same systematisation to all of reality, carefully explaining how the visible, differentiated world emanates from the single Name, YHWH.

Gikatilla describes a linguistic-nominal cosmos which begins with the primordial cosmic point of the Name YHWH. From this dimensionless beginning, the first stage of emanation is the ten *middot*, the unerasable names which are the potencies through which God expresses Himself in the world – these ten names are identical with the ten *devarim*, or sefirot. From these ten descriptive qualities of God, then emerge all the other words of the Torah, forming the blueprint of creation – and from which finally comes the whole of reality. Following the insight of Maimonides, the Name YHWH is understood as uniquely indicative of God in Himself, representing His unique nature and essence:

> This name bears witness to Him in the secret of His unity that indicates the truth beyond which there is no truth … this is the name that was singularly designated to indicate His truth, and it bears witness to His being separate from all, and that He bears all, and that He is in all and is outside of all.… All of His names, except for the unique name, were generated during the creation of the world, and the essence precedes them all, for it is what causes all existants to be.
>
> (GE19–20, Lachter, 2008, 20)

The Name is the secret of the essence of God, expressing 'the secret of His unity', and is the sole cause of creation to which everything is reducible and upon which everything is dependent: 'All reality … is reducible to that essence which is the secret of His Name' (ibid.). This fascination with the unity at the heart of reality, and the need to work out the relationship between the unity and the multiplicity that surrounds us suggests a deep knowledge of Neoplatonic thought.[5]

The intellectual gymnastics Gikatilla performs on the Tetragrammaton to express its generative relationship to the rest of reality are complex and multitudinous – their precise nature need not concern us here, and has already been discussed to some degree.[6] The Name is analysed, by turns, numerically via gematria, with and without the vowels, it is broken into constituent letters, which are then each spelled out and recombined; Gikatilla's sources for his methods of analysis are impressively diverse, stretching from Ancient Greek and Neoplatonic philosophy, to the previous centuries' Hebrew grammarians as well as rabbinic and kabbalistic writers.[7] Gikatilla never attempts an etymological explanation of the Name – its nature places it far beyond any kind of literal meaning or interpretation. The Name rather is explained as being a single cosmic point at the centre of the space of the Torah – Gikatilla here plays on the term *niqqud*, 'point' as both the vowel points which seem to spiritually and intellectually give life or form to the unpronounceable/dead/inert consonants, while being themselves incorporeal and barely included in the Hebrew language itself at all[8] and the smallest cosmic unit, from which any other would emerge, as the centre of reality. The Tetragrammaton itself is made up of consonants which are actually sounded as vowels, and so Gikatilla is able to argue for the primacy of the vowel over the consonant as that less dense, spiritual element which gives movement to the thick corporeal letters of the alphabet.

The most important method through which the Tetragrammaton emanates the rest of existence, however, is mathematical. Gikatilla writes that: 'He created [the universe] only through ... number relationships ... The Divine Name YHWH is the esoteric principle of number relationships' (GE46, Blickstein, 1983, 70). Beginning with the ten other divine titles found in the Bible, Gikatilla explains the mathematical/gematrial process of their emergence from the Name. So, YHW = 21 = AHYH; YH = YOD HA = 26; YHWH + 4 = 31 = AL; HShM = 345 = AL ShDY; 26 = KV = KP VV = 86 = ALHYM.[9] From these are emanated the other terms of the biblical text, so that the Torah itself precedes existence.

Here we are in a textual-linguistic landscape where normal semantic meaning, with its signifier-signified distinction, is no longer applicable.[10] Elke Morlok views Gikatilla's obsession with language as mediator between human and divine as 'a harsh critique of Rambam's description of language as idolatry' (2011, 99). For Gikatilla, negative theology would figure as a barbaric mistake: 'As language emanates from the divine it enables also the mystic to refer to the divine in a positive way and go back to its divine source' (Morlok, 2011, 99). Language itself shares in the divine essence. It is not that language is capable of accurately describing reality – rather, the root of language is formed deep within the ontological fabric, and so language is reality. Reality in its essence *is* linguistic.

Here, as was hinted at previously in Chapter 4, every word and indeed every *thing* in reality ultimately refers to God. The names and their cognomina are compared to both garments and wings, in that they conceal the form of the divine – 'His Names and his garments cover Him up and disguise Him' (SO, 1994, 177) – this is particularly so in the case of the gentile nations who cannot perceive God intimately as Israel do. Not knowing the Unique Name which was revealed to Moses, they can only relate to God through lower names which exist at two or three steps of removal; but these names still enable some kind of contact – although at greater remove, the gentiles are not totally disconnected from God – they are still ultimately as dependent as Israel on Him.[11]

While YHWH is the ultimate root of existence, being itself, the sefirot (which is to say, the names) are dependent on YHWH to be what they are, or to be at all. It is the nature of YHWH, existence, which allows them to exist and then produce from their differentiated kinds of being, all the other particular things that exist. The sefirot are finite in nature and thus are *belimah* – this term, made famous by Sefer Yetzirah, but whose intended meaning there remains contested, Gikatilla interprets as meaning 'without His essence', implying that the sefirot do not *contain* His essence (which would be for them to transcend it) but rather are contained *by it* (i.e. it transcends and unifies them – a point whose relevance will become apparent in Chapter 6).

Based on writings such as: 'The whole work of creation, which depends on My name...' (SN, Martini, 2010, 343); 'the whole world and its creatures are dependent on the Name *YHVH*, may He be Blessed, and nothing in the world can be sustained without His great Name, may It be Blessed' (SO, 1994, 172), some commentators have seen a hypostatic potency in Gikatilla's writings on the Name – Lachter comments that sometimes it appears as if 'the divine name is more the cause of all being than the Divine' (2008, 21). However, Gikatilla suggests a more complex relationship of God and His Name, claiming (on God's behalf) that:

> I am the being in the secret of the name YHWH, for My Name is the secret of My truth, and it alone indicates the secret of essence ... from my truth all beings came to be, and my Name and my truth are one, for my Name is the secret of my essence, and the secret of my truth. My Name and my true essence are one.... My Name is not outside of me, for it is the truth of my being.
>
> (GE24–5, Lachter, 2008 [amended], 21)

Likewise: 'He united Himself with the Name of the essence [the Tetragrammaton], since all beings other than Himself came to be from the truth of His essence.' (ibid.) This presents a challenge as to how we should understand the relationship between God and His Name. What is it that the Name indicates, considering that it refuses any semantic interpretation?

In order to answer this, we must ask, *what is the essential nature of God that His Name would share in?* The common answer among scholars has been to emphasise a grand theoretical statement relating the natures of language and God. For example, Martini comments that:

> [T]he four letters YHWH are not only a symbol of the godhead, but ... this name is fused completely with the idea of God, including all of His creative power and hidden strength. God is nothing but His name, which means that God is language; that is powerful word; and that comprehending YHWH means comprehending the structure of the cosmos and its origin.
>
> (2010, 121)

I would like to propose a different answer, based around the Maimonidean principle of God's radical unity and simplicity: God is fundamentally one, unique and simple; not one as we might think of a human as one through being a collection of multiples. This is supported by some statements of Gikatilla:

> Know, my brother, may God protect you, that none of the names by which He, may he be exalted, is called, bear explicit and absolute witness to the secret of His unity, except for the Name that bears witness to the essence (*havayah*).
>
> (GE19, Lachter, 2008, 19)

Know that there is among all higher and lower beings no simple thing without combination except the Name, blessed be He, which is the one pure simple thing, which has no multiplicity at all.

(ShN34b, Morlok, 2011, 47)[12]

The second of these quotes appears to be a restatement of a theme found in Eleazar of Worms' *Sefer haShem*, which claims that YHWH is the only word which, however you manipulate the letters, still can mean only being. The Name has a special kind of unity, because it is internally simple – unlike other objects which can be remoulded through the techniques of *tzeruf otiot* (letter combination), its elements effectively cannot be recombined in a new way, it is always what it is: the unity of being. Although the Name is articulated into all the other words of reality, the Name itself in its four letters can never be altered. This is particularly apparent in the second quote – Gikatilla's use of the term *havayah* draws on Eleazar's innovative use of it to mean the theological essence of being; the word itself is an anagram of YHWH.[13]

God's 'secret' – His radical unity – then is expressed perfectly in the Name which resists any kind of rearrangement or any kind of signification other than existence. But it is not merely expression of God's unity that the Name accomplishes: as Gikatilla claims, the Name is one with God, sharing in His unity which itself is the identity of His essence.

Thus, even the unity of God and His Name are testament to the unique simplicity of God. The Name here works as a kind of event horizon, the singularity beyond which knowledge is impossible, for there is in fact no-thing to be known. It is only after the single Name is broken into shards of multiple names in the primordial intellectual world, that these names then emerge into (as) the world of multiplicity which we inhabit. God and the Name are one only in the sense that the Name itself is unity, fully expressive of God's unity and nothing else. It is not the nature of language but the radical unity of the Name which makes it partake of God. So, the 'truth' from which 'all beings came to be' is the truth of God's unity – the only quality which may be ascribable to Him, that quality which itself makes impossible the ascription of any other quality. This demonstrates another level of Neoplatonic influence – the powerful notion that it is the singularity of the One which guarantees the integrity of every other substance in existence. Without sharing in the nature of primal oneness, nothing could itself be a unity, and therefore no independent things would exist. Likewise, Gikatilla seems to be arguing that not just is the Name the primal source of all reality, but it is also written into every existing thing simply because to exist as a thing is to stand in relation to it: 'this is the Name that was singularly designated to indicate His truth, and it bears witness to His being separate from all, and that He bears all, and that He is in all and is outside of all' (GE19–20, Lachter, 2008, 19).

The logic of emanation

There are some curious points of similarity between Gikatilla's nominal theology and the metaphysics of Wittgenstein's early system set out in *Tractatus
Logico-Philosophicus* (1974), the examination of which may help us see some of
the less obvious implications of the former.[14] In the *Tractatus*, Wittgenstein sets
out his picture of a world composed of facts, which themselves are composed of
objects conjoined into states of affairs. The structure of the world finds a perfect
mirror in the structure of language, which is composed of names conjoined into
meaningful sentences. Ergo, there is a fundamental isomorphism between language and the world. Both names and objects are simple, atomistic units – we
find this expressed in a number of passages: objects are simple (2.021), as are
names: 'A name cannot be dissected any further by means of definition: it is a
primitive sign' (3.26); names are not composite: 'So one could say that the real
name of an object was what all symbols that signified it had in common. Thus,
one by one, all kinds of composition would prove inessential to a name'[15]
(3.3411). There is no semantics in naming, only reference: 'A name means an
object. The object is its meaning', (3.203) and 'only in the nexus of a proposition does a name have meaning' (3.3). Thus, in a curious correlation with Gikatilla, 'Names are like points' (3.144). The simplicity of names in fact represents
perfectly the simplicity of objects: 'Objects can only be *named* ... I can only
speak *about* them, I cannot *put them into words*' (3.221). Because of their simplicity, objects cannot be described but only indicated, and the indication cannot
itself be further deconstructed.[16] This is like Maimonides' assertion that God in
essence can only be named, not described – and in Gikatilla's system God
unfolds, via His Name, into the states of affairs of the world, yet still is present,
and is not 'explained' or epistemically opened in these states; but rather is
present as the smallest, zero-dimensional point of indefinability at the core. This
infinitesimal characteristic, shared by both Gikatilla and Wittgenstein, is striking
– where for Gikatilla the Name is the primordial *point* from which all else emanates, via the descriptive names of scripture, for Wittgenstein names are the
irreducible points from which all semantic language flowers. In both writers
the irreducibility of the nominal forms the beginning point of meaning, either in
the world or in its isomorphic partner, language.

An initial striking difference between Gikatilla and Wittgenstein would
appear to be that while for Wittgenstein, names are totally simple and essentially
unrelated to objects, for Gikatilla names indicate the nature of their objects and
thus are effectively descriptions – *if one knows how to read them correctly*. The
essence of a thing is emptied into the letters of its name. So for Gikatilla, it
would seem that no objects are transcendent for all are fully present in their
names. However, this is only so if we fail to realise that normal words are neither
Tractarian nor Gikatillian names. If Tractarian Names *must* be semantically
simple, then any word which can be fully analysed into other words is not a
Name. Wittgenstein himself never goes in detail into the meaning of this, and it
is quite unclear how far we should take it – 'car' can be described in terms of its

mechanics and social role, but this perhaps lacks the singularity that 'car' conjures up for us. Certainly we can think of colour-words as Names – it is impossible to think of any other way of adequately describing them: referring solely to their frequency would seem unsatisfactorily shallow given the sensory and social aspect. This question anyway is identical to the question of what are the atomic objects of reality – one which Wittgenstein himself never addresses. On the other hand, for Gikatilla there are technically no names at all, except the Tetragrammaton: every other word is a concealed description, identical with the inner nature of its object. It is only the Name for God which is a Name, and which paradoxically denies access to God through its radical unity with His own nature, His nature itself being radical unity.

It may seem strange that the *Tractatus* never makes any suggestion as to an identity of Objects and their Names; rather, they take parallel roles in the world and the subject, respectively. Objects themselves do not exist in the world, any more than names exist in the subject. Rather they are the subsistent entities which underlie the world: 'Objects, the unalterable, and the subsistent are one and the same' (2.027) – thus names and objects are the substances of language and the world respectively (2.021). Objects are 'that for which there is neither existence nor non-existence' (Wittgenstein, 1975, 72).[17] For our purposes then, we can see that in the *Tractatus* most *things* that we perceive in the world are themselves *Sachverhalte*; they are complexes further analysable into constituent parts standing in relation to each other. Thus, just as words are not names, things are not objects: the words for everyday things deny the integrity of those things, making evident their complexity. Name-objects subsist as the base atomic unit of reality, into which all macroscopic things and circumstances are analysable. Because this replicates Gikatilla's claim that all things and circumstances are in direct relationship to the cognomina, we can understand the cognomina as taking the role of the 'subsistent objects' in Gikatilla's system.

So far we can see a striking similarity between Wittgenstein's and Gikatilla's cosmology of a world emanated from the primordial substance of titles for God. More interesting, though, is when we remember Wittgenstein's argument that logic is identical with the possible structure of the world. Logic is the condition of the world's existence, that which states the possible structures of the world yet without stating the particular contents of this structure. From this, Wittgenstein argued for the essential contentless-ness of logic: 'all the propositions of logic say the same thing, to wit nothing' (5.43). This means that every logical statement is identical, once fully analysed, to any other, and although in this passage he ridicules the idea that the infinity of possible logical propositions are derived from a finite set of fundamental axiomatic propositions, he later notes that 'the number of 'primitive propositions of logic' is arbitrary, since *one could derive logic from a single primitive proposition*' (6.1271, my emphasis). Because logic is only a structure, it has no meaning in itself – any correct logical statement is ultimately tautological, and can be reduced down to tautology, which is another word for identity; therefore, any logical statement states nothing more than $A = A$. In this quote it is the word 'could' which is pivotal: All statements of logic are equal, ultimately stating the same thing, the simple fact of logical truth – there are no surprises in logic, because everything is already present, and there are no prior or later statements in logic. Nothing 'follows from' another but all are equally derivable from each other.[18]

I have used Leibniz's formula $A = A$ here, partly because the Tractatus, according to this reading, is speaking almost as one with Leibniz, that the world is a completely determined logical emanation from the ultimate (divine) truth of identity.[19] For Leibniz the perfect self-identity of $A = A$ *is* God. Analysing Leibniz's logic, Heidegger seems to share in some Wittgensteinian insight: 'All other truths are reduced to first truths with the aid of definitions or by the analysis of notions; in this consists proof a priori, which is independent of experience' (1992, 38). First truths are truths of identity: 'For example, A is A, or A is not non-A'.[20] Of course, Wittgenstein does not claim that names or the objects they represent are included in the unfolding of logic – they are irreducible and subsistent. However, the structure that these substances conjoin into (the *Sachverhalte* which they form) are all ultimately reducible to logical identity, $A = A$. For Leibniz, what we consider contingent truths, truths which could apparently be otherwise, are reducible to identity only via an infinite series of operations – therefore their causal necessity is not obvious to us, but to God, who can manage these operations, the necessity is obvious.

We may understand this – and also smooth some of the difference between Wittgenstein and Leibniz here – by recognising that derivation is in fact a question of notation: if $A = B$ is a restatement of $A = A$, then $A = A$ is just as much a restatement of $A = B$. Just as $5 = 5$ is the same as $2 + 3 = 5$, neither is more originary or 'earlier' because both are merely different articulations of the same proposition. The use of signs is only a temporal (finite) problem: the fact that $2 + 3$ is a sign representing the same something as does the sign 5, would make the process of derivation no longer for a divinity that works not with the signs but with what they express. In fact the whole world then is the concealing of divinity in sign and symbol: the only truth is the divine truth of identity, which is all that any other truth expresses, behind the complexity of its notation. Truths of the world are just questions of notation, and they are ultimately dissolvable in such.[21]

Heidegger claims that: 'Original truths are those for which no reason can be given' (1992, 41) – i.e. where the identity is explicit and no reduction to simpler terms is required. But the explicit nature of the truth expressed in 'non-originary' truths is only not obvious for us – for the infinite intellect of God, truth is immediate. Fundamentally, if no reason is given for $A = A$, then neither is a reason given for $A = B$ when $A = B$ is reducible – that is to say, identical except for the notation used – to $A = A$. Thus there is no separation between the original and the derivative truths. All truths are equal, forming a web of simplicity. This is an important point which has implications for the Spinozistic philosophy: God's kenotic evacuation into materiality ('deus sive natura'), becomes then the same as Gikatilla's formulation, that the material is essentially nothing other than God in articulation. As modern String Theory proposes that all matter is in fact merely apparent forms generated by the vibration of one-dimensional loops of string, this mystical materialism presents all the bodies, particles, and events of the world as only apparent form which is ultimately reducible to the formlessness of divinity. The relationship between the macrocosmic material and the divine is opaque to us – God is concealed within the layers of matter – but with an infinite logic, the fact that all matter is nothing but God stated in complex form, is clear and immediate. The materialistic bent which we witness in Gikatilla is one that has been noted generally of the Kabbalah by Scholem (Biale, 1985, 77), and the relevance of which will become increasingly apparent through the next two chapters.

But the crucial point here is that God is conceivable as self-identity. In a turn of phrase of which Wittgenstein would approve, Heidegger writes that: 'What indicates their [primary truths'] truth is just this manifest identity itself (A is A). If we make this criterion for the truth of primary truths into a principle, the principle would itself be: A is A, *the principle of identity*' (1992, 51). Then, 'The criterion, identity, is itself the first truth and the source of truth' (ibid., 53).

Does this point have any parallel in the classical Kabbalah? It is immediately notable that the preceding discussion has focussed on the Name YHWH and has followed a path of *differentiation*, justified by the likely etymology which interprets YHWH in the third-person: He Is. When we begin to look for identity then, it is easy, especially given the foregoing chapters, to place A = A in line with God's self-revelation as *Ehyeh Asher Ehyeh*, I Am That I Am,[22] perhaps writeable as *Ehyeh = Ehyeh*, or א = א. The Kabbalists do not place this name on the tree, but do ascribe the contraction *Ehyeh*, I Am, to one sefirah.

The internal Name: AHYH

I have mentioned that there is an on-going tussle in the writings of the early Kabbalists between the divine names YHWH and AHYH. It is immediately clear from the Bible that, while YHWH is the personal name of God, the name which is revealed exclusively to Moses is different – AHYH Asher AHYH. Compacting this to AHYH, the kabbalists appear to have held that it is a more primal, incorporeal and interior name than the regal third-person YHWH. This is reflected in the association of the names with the sefirot, where AHYH is assigned to the first, unknowably inchoate sefirah of Keter and YHWH is given to the tree's central (sixth) sefirah, Tiferet.[23] Gikatilla discusses this in one passage in Sha'arei Orah:

> Know that all the Holy Names in the Torah are intrinsically tied to the Tetragrammaton, which is YHWH. If you would contend, however, that the Name AHYH is the ultimate source, realize that the Tetragrammaton is like the trunk of a tree [from which the branches grow] and the Name AHYH is like the root from which grow the other roots. It is the trunk of the tree that nurtures the branches which are the other Names of God, and each of these branches bears a different fruit. Know too that all the words in the Torah are

connected to one of the unerasable Divine Names just as the other cognomens are intrinsically tied to a specific Name ... until one finds that all the
words of the Torah are intrinsically woven into the tapestry of God's Cognomens which are tied to God's Names which, in turn, are tied to the ineffable Tetragrammaton, YHWH, to which all the Torah's words are
inextricably linked.

(SO, 1994, 6)

So for Gikatilla, AHYH is the essential nature which is embodied and given
form in YHWH. Gikatilla argues that for AHYH, representing the pure, simple
and transcendent existence of God: 'Its existence cannot be grasped by another
... for this reality is only perceived by Himself alone'. (SO, 1994, 160).[24] Furthermore, because YHWH is located in Tiferet, it is from here – rather than from
Keter – that all the other sefirot emerge. The other names are like garments
which enclothe YHWH.

As Gikatilla indicates, this is not an innovation on his part but an established
kabbalistic tradition.[25] From the earliest writings there is a clear ontological difference drawn between the two names AHYH and YHWH and, unlike Maimonides, the kabbalists believed God to be so transcendent that often even the
Name YHWH is too far into the human-world to designate God: In some kabbalistic texts the Tetragrammaton in fact appears as the principle of manifestation
or secret of emanation. YHWH, despite the powerful attestation of Maimonides
and the apparent agreement of the kabbalists, in fact represents a somewhat
lower, condensed, or more personified, aspect of the divine.

Sendor claims that we find an implicit ranking of AHYH above the Tetragrammaton as early as *Otiot de-R Akiva* (i.e. pre-tenth century), as well as explicitly in R Abraham ibn Ezra (Sendor, 1994, I, 184). In the former AHYH is used
to seal unalterable directions, whereas the Tetragrammaton seals the gate to the
lower world.[26] Ibn Ezra states:

Behold the two-letter Name [i.e. YH] is the Name received by the glorious
ones that are not bodies, so, too, the Name beginning with A, and because
of this, it can be pronounced by anyone in any place. It is compared to the
Glory of God exalted above all glory and all excess, like the divine Presence
that is among the angels, which are in the heights, moving the hosts of
heaven. While the Name which begins with Y and includes V is compared
to the divine Presence that is attached to Israel.

(Sendor, 1994, II, 152)

In this text, the Name YHWH represents the presence of God to Israel. Sendor
comments:

[T]he reason why the higher Name *ahyh* can be pronounced as written by
anyone in any place, without special precautions or sanctity, is because it is
so exalted, it cannot be tainted or mishandled. The Tetragrammaton,

however, is a lower Name, in touch with the lower world, and for that very reason greater care must be exercised in its pronunciation.

(1994, II, 185)[27]

It is the special quality of the Tetragrammaton revealed to Israel which prohibits its misuse. It has a special role and significance.

Isaac the Blind claims that 'by [the name beginning with] *aleph* the Name is elevated. It is the inner name by which the Name is elevated' (Sendor, 1994, II, [amended], 152). For Isaac, AHYH is complete in contrast to YHWH which is flawed.[28] For Isaac, the letter *aleph* has a 'higher ontological status' than the others (Sendor, 1994, II, 156).[29]

A lot of the earliest emphasis on AHYH focuses on the initial *aleph*,[30] a letter which combines a number of distinguishing characteristics, being the first letter of the alphabet, the number 1, the most simple vocal sound (in fact almost un- or pre-vocal, being basically the sound of breathing), and – the fact which must have sealed the deal for the kabbalists – being graphically conceivable as a *vav* between two *yods* and thus numerically equalling not just one but also twenty-six, the number of the Tetragrammaton.[31] Because of this last fact, the name AHYH then contains in concentrated form within its very beginning – which is the absolute beginning, the first letter – the whole manifest Name of God. We find this suggested in the Bahir, which claims:

[A]leph is the first of all letters. And not only that, but *aleph* causes the existence and the permanence of all letters. Furthermore, *aleph* is like the brain. When you say *aleph* you open your mouth; thinking [*machshavah*: the first sefirah] is similar: when you extend your thoughts to the infinite and the boundless,[32] you open your mouth. From *aleph* all letters are produced. You can see that it is their beginning. It is thus written 'And YHWH is at their head'. It is well known that whenever the name is written with the letters YOD HA VIV HA (=54), God, blessed be He, unites himself and is sanctified in holiness. What is the meaning of 'in holiness'? It is 'in the holy chamber.' And where is the holy chamber? You might say in thought [*machshavah*], which is the *aleph*.

(48/70, Campanini, 2005, 279–280)

This short passage is incredibly potent, as it identifies the letter *aleph* – the first letter of the name AHYH – with the primordial sefirah, while appearing to make *aleph* also one with the Name YHWH. The Name YHWH unites the sefirot into the highest sefirah of pure thought (*machshavah*).[33]

In another section we read:

What are the ten utterances? *Aleph* is *Keter Elyon*, blessed be it and blessed be its name and the name of its people. Who are its people? They are Israel, about which it is written: Know that the Lord is Elohim, He made us and not we (*lo anachnu*) [Ps.100:3]. In order to know and to recognize the unity of the unities united in all its names.

(94/141, Campanini, 2005 [amended], 326)

Here, after *aleph* is equated with the sefirah of Keter, the quote is read as 'He made us and we belong to *aleph*' (the word *'lo'* being spelled *lamed aleph*, readable as to-*aleph*).[34] Similarly, Jacob ben Sheshet analyses the word *echad*, claiming the *aleph* 'is an allusion to that which thought cannot fathom' (*Emunah u-Bittahon* Ch. 3; Dan, 1986, 119–120). Scholem explains that the *aleph* suggests an inchoate pregnancy of potential meaning: 'To hear the *aleph* is to hear next to nothing; it is the preparation for all audible language, but in itself conveys no determinate, specific meaning' (1996, 30).

Throughout, then, we find an association of AHYH with interiority; it is the name of God in His state prior to creation, prior to the emergence of reality.

It is important to note the relationship between the letter *aleph*, the first, and the letter *yod*, the tenth. *Yod* is thereby the completion of the series begun by *aleph*, and the beginning of another. The association with ten surely influenced the tradition that the Name YHWH represents the entirety of the sefirotic tree, constituted of ten potencies. Fishbane writes that: 'While the *alef* represents the elusive open-breath of cosmic generativity, the divine Name itself represents the inauguration of articulated speech—the transformation of Divinity from the complete concealment of interiority to the disclosure of exteriority' (2008, 469).[35]

R Asher ben David notes that:

> The four-letter Name is called *Shem ha-meforash* because it becomes revealed and spreads forth in its entirety from *seter* to *seter* [age to age] until the end of all *seter* that comes from the start of the vowel-movements of the *alef*.
>
> (1996, 104; Fishbane, 2008, 495)

So the Tetragrammaton is the Name which manifests – whereas AHYH is the root, symbolised by the *aleph* at its head. The Tetragrammaton rather emerges into fullness through a process that begins with the *aleph* of AHYH: 'This metaphysical alef channels the most subtle cosmic energy into the borders of the divine Name, stimulating the outward (or downward) flow of sefirotic life' (Fishbane, 2008, 496).

Asher explicitly claims that Tiferet (the middle pillar, also known as *rachamim*) 'is always called by the Unique Name [*Shem ha-meyuhad*] that is [also] called the Ineffable Name [*Shem ha-meforash*, I.e. YHWH], for [God's] actions are through [this pillar]' and yet, 'the inner force acts through it.... And [this pillar] is like a vessel [or instrument] for the inner breath [*ruah ha-penimi*] that is called One. (Asher, 1996, 109; Fishbane 2008 [amended], 510). So clearly here, the Tetragrammaton is not God but is a vessel for the actual essence of God. Fishbane reads the sefirotic tree in Asher as the emergence of speech from cosmic silence, speech which is contained potentially in the structure of the Divine Name which is the first word containing all else.

The kabbalistic theology of the Name admits of two fundamental aspects, then: YHWH and AHYH.[36] This separation of AHYH and YHWH into two distinct though inextricable meanings is one that reverberates through the Kabbalah right up until the near schism of Sabbateanism, and one whose full relevance will become clear in the next chapter.

For now, though, we must set aside the more detailed aspects of the manifest YHWH, in order to remain with the primordial aspect, AHYH. This name signifies that which is before any kind of reality, and completely beyond human thought – that in fact which cannot even be signified.

In closing this section, we can note that just as we found the root of all logic and all *Sachverhalte* in the tautological formula $A = A$, so we can admit a primitive identification in the early Kabbalah of AHYH with Ayin, a term not yet given to Keter. To say I Am, then, is to say nothing. To speak self-identity, to speak one's own existence is meaningless; as meaningless as to say, for Wittgenstein, 'there are objects' (4.1272) – because if there are words for things, if they can be spoken of, then necessarily they exist, and vice versa.

Tautology and reality

So, where for Gikatilla all objects and events in the world are reducible to their linguistic structure, which itself is reducible to the cognomina, then to the ten names, and finally to the single Name YHWH as the first manifestation from the essential root of nothingness, AHYH, for Wittgenstein all states of affairs in the world are reducible to the possibilities of logic, and this logical structure is reducible to the single truth of tautologous identity, $A = A$. In each system the world is composed of complexes which are articulations of simple essential (or, 'unerasable') objects. However, what has not been made clear in any study of the Tractatus' metaphysics[37] is that the logical structure, the contentless tautology of logic, is itself predicated from the subsistent objects themselves.

Wittgenstein writes: 'If I know an object I also know all its possible occurrences in states of affairs' (2.0123) – and he adds: 'Every one of these possibilities must be part of the nature of the object'. Because relations are not things but only the placement of objects relative to each other, the possibility of an object entering into any specific relation has to be written into the object itself – where else could it be? Furthermore: 'Objects contain the possibility of *all* situations' (2.014, my emphasis) and 'The possibility of its occurring in states of affairs *is* the form of an object' (2.0141, my emphasis): taken together these passages mean that objects in essence are nothing more than the possibility of their combinations. This seems counter-intuitive given Wittgenstein's insistence that objects are fundamentally simple, but the resolution of these facts will help us to solve a similar apparent flaw in Gikatilla's system. Because the logical structure of all possible states of affairs is the internal nature of objects, encoded as essence, the world itself is a condition of objects; the contingent world as it is in fact emanates from the conglomerate of subsistent objects which underlie it.[38] This powerful implication from within the text of the Tractatus clearly parallels Gikatilla's own claim that the world emerges from the cognomina which themselves are articulations of the Name of God. Given that Wittgenstein's logical structure is itself nothing but identity ($A = A$), it seems we can conclude that it is the very self-identity of objects which unfolds into the apparent world. This is to say, the actuality of the world generates from the inner nature of the atomic objects, an inner nature which is itself their own simple self-identity, and as such is indistinguishable from the single truth of logic, $A = A$; the separate instantiations of self-identity still state precisely the same thing: self-identity/ non-contradiction. They are also identical with each other in their radical simplicity. Thus, we find a possible solution to the dilemma which Gikatilla seemingly failed to address in his own system (Martini, 2010, 129), that God's Name was at once absolutely simple but also divisible and articulable into letter-elements:[39] The Wittgensteinian object faces the same problem in being entirely simple yet apparently containing the structure of its possible combinations, yet this is resolved by that structure being tautologous and thus entirely simple – the structure which identifies the very individuality of the object by determining its possible placements in the world, is its very own self-identity. Likewise, God's articulation into letters is nothing other than the apparent form which His own self-identity takes. This in fact is hinted at when Gikatilla writes that the Name YHWH is the secret of his essence: the multiplicity of the Name is only apparent, and actually reducible to the simplicity of God's essence because the complexity of the letters always expresses the same single nature of unity. Unity then leads inexorably toward multiplicity, just as one infers all other numbers.

Wittgenstein writes that a tautology is unrelated to contingent reality in that it is compatible with every state of affairs (in contrast to a contradiction which admits no possibilities and is compatible with nothing). The tautology, he writes, 'leaves open to reality the whole – the infinite whole – of logical space' (4.463). A tautology then can be thought of as the initial condition of possibility, the necessary initial axiom which generates the possibility-space within which a world, a world of contingent truths, can exist. $A = A$, then, is the 'completely general description of the world' (5.526), waiting to be filled in with the synthetic or empirical/accidental to give it meaning and truth value (Brockhaus, 1992, 168–169). Further refining this idea, he claims: 'Contradiction is the outer limit of propositions. Tautology is the unsubstantial point at their centre' (5.143). So just as Gikatilla makes the Tetragrammaton – which is the aleph of AHYH, symbolic of the internal selfhood of God – complicit in the smallest point at the centre of reality, prior to substantial existence, Wittgenstein makes the tautology the internal point which amounts to no quality or factual statement, but only the possibility of truth of a proposition.

Contingency is protected in the Tractatus by the fact that the possibility-space which is the objects' inner nature is not determined any further: the interior limit, so to say, is inscribed, but from or outside that limit the actualisation of the manifold possibilities are not determined but free; each *Sachverhalte* is independent from all others (2.061). However, if we accept that all objects' internal nature is self-identity, which is identical to all other objects',[40] we must realise that this self-identity cannot state only one specific object's possibilities but those of all objects. This means that every object contains all *possible* structures of the entire world (though without specifying any of them as actual). Because self-identity cannot have the complexity of specific uniqueness, it must be general. That this is so should anyway be evident from the nature of the structure as nothing but A = A; this is bound into its status as the 'completely general description of the world' (5.526).

However, while the tautological identity of A = A is a limit-point of logic, we also read that: 'The subject … is a limit of the world' (5.632). It is here that we discover that the transcendental subject *is* identity. It is not an external but an internal limit – it is the subjectivity of I Am which provides ground and possibility for the world to exist from; in parallel to the logical limit of tautology, it is subjectivity which opens the world as potential. It is the subject who generates the world and the world does not go beyond the bounds of the subject because outside the subject there is only subsistence, objects.[41] It is the subject who interprets/uses subsistent objects in forming a world, just like God uses His Name to seal the world, where the prima material are made into identities, i.e. present to subjectivity as things, from the possibility generated by God's own subjectivity – I Am. I Am is the beginning, the condition of possibility, YHWH is the limit, the It Is which presents to us the world as an Other; YHWH always stands at the boundary of selfhood, between self and other. At this point we can see exactly why God must use His own Name to seal creation: in forming otherness, the otherness which allows both individual objects to exist and the world as an other to God to exist, it must be stated by Him as an Other to Him, and so put into third-person existence terms: 'It Is'.

If Wittgenstein's object-names are all in fact only articulations of the primal identity, A = A, i.e. they are nothing but their own self-identity and are all of them reducible to the logical structure of A = A which conditions existence, then this is to say that all objects, as subjects, are ultimately reducible to AHYH or I Am – that statement of self-existence. And it is only when each can indeed make the statement, I Am That I Am – which is to understand oneself as existent, as a subject, that one can generate the possibility of names both for oneself and for the rest of the world. It is only here that internality becomes self-awareness; it is only once Moses has asked, for the first time of God, 'what is Your Name?' that He is able to make this statement.

It is here that we can gain some insight into the metaphysics of otherhood as expressed through the early kabbalistic tradition and inherited from Maimonides. We find in Gikatilla the fully articulated conclusion of the negative theology developed by Maimonides, where reality is describable in language – the finite world can in fact be exhausted by language, and God – the point where naming begins (or for us, ends) – is fundamentally indescribable, existing outside the realm of language which formally begins only with the manifestation of the Name YHWH. The Name then represents the limit of language and the limit of the thinkable world, where the linguistic-thinkable world is the articulable, the divisible. As the only true name, it is the seal of reality and the point beyond which we cannot know: the point at which description becomes impossible. In this we find an expression of Wittgenstein's stated intention in the completion of the Tractatus: 'Whereof we cannot speak, we must pass over in silence'.[42] the non-describable, that which can only be named, which is then God; and noting the distinction here from traditional Christian negative theology, which refuses the naming of God, but only because it understands naming as a kind of describing. Instead in the Jewish tradition we find that God can *and must* be named because only this states the very impossibility of description. Names are not within but outside of language, in fact forming a point of exit from language: For Wittgenstein, as Gikatilla, the substance from which language (and therefore the subject's world) is built, but which subsist beneath it, not within it.

Hilary Putnam writes that the fundamental claim of negative theology is not 'that there are *propositions* about God that are true, but that the believer cannot think or even understand' (1997, 411) – rather, negative theology refutes the applicability of propositional truth to the divine, and thus is not so much a statement about the limitations of human thought but about the ontological divide between God and human, and about the failure of thought more generally – the impossibility of some finite thing grasping the nature of being, as this would involve the paradox of an object enveloping the latter – a state which immediately negates the both the relationship and the very natures of the substances in question. After all, being is not a substance but that which allows and therefore conditions the possibility of substance.

Bertrand Russell (1917) claimed that because one is directly acquainted with oneself, it is possible to refer to oneself by a proper name whereas one can only refer to others by descriptions. So while Bismarck can understand a proposition which refers to him by name, we cannot. As Putnam correctly argues, the case with God is *not* analogous to this: it is not that there are propositions about God which are true to Him, but senseless to us because we have no access to God's nature.[43] Rather: 'To suppose that God literally thinks[44] in 'propositions' would be completely to reject the leading idea of negative theology.... *There are no 'propositions' about God that are adequate to God*' (Putnam, 1997, 412). This is to say, God does not have a private language; God enters language only in relation to humans. Propositional thought itself is irrevocably finite and not transcendental; it does not condition God, rather, God exists outside it.

And so Wittgenstein's insight – the distinction between, on the one hand, that which can be accurately described in linguistic terms, i.e. that which is isomorphic with language and can therefore be perfectly translated into linguistic structure and terms; and on the other hand, that which cannot be; that which, if approached via language, could only be misrepresented. Because that which is indescribable would only be mutilated by attempts to force it into the shapes conferred by language, we should therefore pass over it in silence; which is not to say we should ignore it entirely, for while it cannot be *said*, it can be *shown*. Thus the structural conditions of life which are not themselves things and are not composed of the relations between things (and therefore do not find any place in the onto-nominal structure of language) cannot be spoken, but can only be spoken *of;* that a world (or even a thing) exists, for example, stands outside the ontological framework provided by semantics. As that which is named cannot be described; it refuses the articulation into words. The nominal 'points' which are indivisible and unanalysable are not within but outside of both language and the world. While Wittgenstein identifies the linguistically describable as the world, and then identifies the world with the subject, this appears to make the internality of the subject complex; but it is only so for the subject. The subject can decompose itself, but it cannot be decomposed by another; for to describe something accurately is to have totalised and incorporated it into one's own analytical world.

Otherhood, then, is expressed in terms of sealing with the Name. In Gikatilla too we find the idea that all is contained – or sealed – within the Name, his interpretation of *belimah* as meaning the sefirot are contained by God's essence, indicating that the Name YHWH forms a seal around all His attributes. To say that God is 'contained' within his Name is the same as to say that everything else is contained within His Name, because reality is divisible into two basic elements: God and not-God, the film between them being His Name. This seal which seals otherhood allows for both the transcendence of God and also for the integrity of not-God. In this case we find an illicit prediction of Isaac Luria's most famous innovation, *tzimtzum*.[45] But here this is nothing other than the very creation of the Name in order to allow, or as the occurrence of, separate existence (these two things are identical). Whereas Luria perceived a flaw or corruption in God, this view now presents the process of creation as part of the completion of God, God shifting from the irresolute *one* of *echad* to the definite *unique* of *echad* only with the emergence of an otherhood which is posited in opposition. God speaks His Name – It Is! And the world is. And in this postulation of otherhood, the not-God, so then *God* is. Divine identity is predicated on the 'flaw' of requiring a finite opposite, a world which is independent from it. The empty space of *tzimtzum*, the void of primordial not-God is, in this reading, constituted by and as the Name, the point of not-God within God, just as names are points of not-language within language. God's withdrawal is confined, sealed, from the world through the establishment of the boundary of the Name.

Notes

1 Michael Fagenblat (2010, 128–129) has discussed the error present in Levinas' reading of Maimonides' statement: 'The foundation of the foundation and the pillar of wisdom consists in knowing that there is a being and that it is the first being,' where he misinterprets the Arabic loan-word *sham* as *shem*, thus forming the passage: 'The foundation of the foundation and the pillar of wisdom consists in knowing that the Name exists and that it is the first being' (Levinas, 1994, 119). In light of this chapter, it is possible to think that some kabbalists adopted the same misreading.

2 On medieval tree imagery, see Wolfson (1993).

3 For Gikatilla's theory of emanation and the linguistic background to the terms he uses, see Bo (2011).

4 His assertion that this is a long historical tradition likely means he took it from *Shimmush Tehillim*, a Geonic booklet of magic which opens with the words: 'The entire *Torah* is composed of the names of God, and in consequence it has the property of saving and protecting man' (Trachtenberg, 1939, 109).

5 As argued by Morlok (2011).

6 See for example Martini (2010, 118–130).

7 These sources are discussed in Morlok (2011).

8 This is a notion present in earlier Jewish philosophy such as in Ezra and Judah Halevi who states that the letters AHWY are spiritual letters as opposed to the other 'bodily' letters (Sendor 1994, II, 140n90, cf. Scholem 1973, 172). The spirituality of the vowels is a concept traceable back even to Philo (Barry 1999). The importance of these four letters for the kabbalists will be examined shortly (see esp. Chapter 5, Note 36).

9 '[T]he great, honourable Name *YHVH* is the Name which embodies all the Holy Names of the Torah. For there are no names that are not contained in the Name YHVH, may He be Blessed' (Gikatilla, 1994, 165).

10 This may partly be the influence of Barukh Togarmi. Morlok (2011, 38ff.), adduces that Gikatilla in fact comes from a circle of kabbalists distanced from the mainstream of Castilian Kabbalah and centring around the writings of Togarmi. Abulafia is also part of this circle, though Morlok claims that Gikatilla preserves more of Togarmi's linguistic techniques than does the latter.

11 Gikatilla emphasises that in the messianic age, even the gentile nations will become one with Israel, sharing their faith, and their intimacy with God (the 'seventy nations … in the future are going to eradicate their present beliefs and all will unite in the faith of Israel' [Gikatilla, 1994, 191]). This eschatological universalism, something he shares with Abulafia, will be further examined in Chapter 7.

12 Compare:

> It is … intelligible how in reference to God, those different actions can be caused by one simple substance, that does not include any plurality or any additional element. The attributes found in Holy Scripture are … qualifications of His actions, without any reference to His essence.
>
> (Maimonides 1956, 1.53, 73)

Divinity is simple yet its effects are multiple. R Asher ben David claims that the attribute-names can still be understood as articulations of the Tetragrammaton: 'even though we said that these attributes are named using other divine names [than the Tetragrammaton], I say that each and every one of them can also be called in the name of the Tetragrammaton' – with the sole difference of vocalisation, 'since the unique name is written with a different vocalisation that demonstrates His unity, while the other attributes called in His name each have their own vocalisation that demonstrates his action and his attribute' (1996, 72, Dauber 2004 [amended], 276); I agree with Dauber that 'his point is merely to employ, with some license, Maimonides' distinction between the Tetragrammaton and other divine names to the distinction between the standard vocalization of the Tetragrammaton and other vocalizations' (2004, 278). Eitan P. Fishbane claims that 'he structured the entire edifice of his sefirotic thought around the graphic form of the divine Name' (2008, 491) and:

> In R Asher's view, the letters of the Tetragrammaton (in addition to the *alef*) are also located within each phonetic articulation, as the energies of the first dimensions of emanation can always be found in the lower ones. Because, as the Neoplatonic grammarians noticed, these letters function in Hebrew as the consonantal signs for unwritten open-breath vowel sounds, the divine Name represents the primordial deep structure that animates the cosmos. The Tetragrammaton energizes Being as the vowel-breaths of language give birth to articulated sounds.
>
> (Fishbane 2008, 495)

13 Dan claims: 'The term *havayot* is one of the most important terminological innovations of Jewish esoteric and mystics in the early thirteenth century' (1998, 142). See
also Scholem (1987, 264–265). It is found first in this text and Isaac the Blind's
Perush Sefer Yetzirah, where 'the *havayot* are connected with the Tetragrammaton
and with the six permutations of YHV in *Sefer Yezira* 1:13, and that they are conceived as intrinsic to God, preceding the process of the emanation of the divine
powers, the *sefirot*' (Sendor, 2004, I, 143); on the term in Isaac see also Sendor (2004,
I, 313–315). In fact Gikatilla displays substantial dependence on *Sefer haShem*, but
Blickstein (1983, 93–96) has concluded that there was no other apparent influence
from the Ashkenazi Hasidim.

14 In this chapter, I will rely heavily on the brilliant – though sorely unrecognised – analysis of Richard R. Brockhaus' *Pulling Up the Ladder: The Metaphysical Roots of
Wittgenstein's* Tractatus Logico-Philosophicus (1991). I am tempted to comment that
it is this text's very metaphysical reading, grounding the *Tractatus* in the specific
historical and cultural moment from which it emerged, which has granted it little
interest in the realms of Wittgensteinian or analytic philosophy.

15 This is to say, they are not descriptions. Names are the fundamental irreducible
'objects' of propositions, and have no 'meaning' other than the object to which they
refer and for which they go proxy in a proposition. While propositions picture states
of affairs, states of affairs being composed of objects in relation to each other, so
propositions are composed of names which are simple signs. These signs do not
picture, but rather just represent. Because, objects are simple (2.021), are the subsistent entities which underlie the world (2.027), and the world is composed *as* the
subject ('I am my world', 5.63).

16 It is here that we can see how Wittgenstein's thought flowers into Kripke's – while
names are ultimately unrelated to objects in themselves, they can only be brought to
life, given signification by the process of naming which is nothing other than an act of
intending ('only in the nexus of a proposition does a name have meaning.' 3.3 – Cf.,
'Words have meaning only in the stream of life,' 1996, 913). Brockhaus comments
that if an object's 'real name' is 'what all symbols that signified it had in common'
(3.3411), naming is principally constituted of intention: 'What is common to every
symbol that can be used as a Name for a given Object is that the user of that Name
intends it to be the name of that Object' (1991, 171): ergo, it is the process of naming
and not the pseudo-object of the name, which is important. Names are mere hollow
tools of intention. This process requires both the use of a name by a subject, and a
specific object which is being referred-to, thus already in Wittgenstein naming states
both subject and object. This is also strongly inferred in other places: 'Naming is like
pointing' and 'the only function of signs is to induce such mental processes [as
meaning and understanding], and ... these are the things we ought really be interested
in' (Wittgenstein, 1969, 3).

17 *Philosophical Remarks*, post-*Tractatus* but pre-*Philosophical Investigations*, evidences the emerging transition in his thought, while still retaining much of the metaphysics of the former.

18 Scholem writes on Gikatilla's interpretation of the Torah, that its non-specificity
makes it a form without any necessary sense. I quote the passage in full:

> From this generally recognized thesis, however, he draws a far-reaching inference:
> In the world of the angels this meaning is read differently than it is in the world of
> the spheres, not to mention in the lower, earthly world, and the same goes for the
> millions of worlds which are contained in these three worlds. In each one of them
> the Torah is read and interpreted in different ways. The manner of reading and inter-
> pretation corresponds to the power of comprehension and nature of these worlds. In
> these millions of worlds, therefore, in which created beings hear the manifestation
> (revelation) and language of God, the Torah can be interpreted in an infinite fullness

of meaning. In other words the word of God, which extends into all worlds, is in fact infinitely pregnant with meaning, but has no fixed interpretation. As I have already remarked in this article, it is purely and simply that which is interpretable. In this respect Gikatilla even goes so far as to define the book of the Torah as 'the form of the mystical world.

but he hesitates when it comes to defining this proposal more closely' (1973, 180). In this interpretation, Gikatilla's view of the world's structure again comes strikingly close to Wittgenstein's description of a contingent world, whose accidents of being are drawn around the immutable-transcendental scaffold of logic as the open, non-specific structure manifest in every possible world, and present at the heart of everything.

19 A=A is of course also the 'nothing' which Rosenzweig held we know specifically of God (see Chapter 1).

20 Loemker (1969), translation amended by Michael Heim in Heidegger (1992, 38). Heidegger explains this as follows: 'All true statements are finally reducible to identities. Every true statement is ultimately an identity, only the identity is not necessarily explicit; but every truth is potentially an identity' and therefore, 'To be true means to be identical' (1992, 39).

21 The third side of the triangle connecting the Kabbalah, Wittgenstein and Leibniz is offered in the form of Coudert (1995) – who admittedly sees a direct influence only in the form of Lurianic Kabbalah via Francis Mercury van Helmont, but still holds this as a formative element in his work. The text *Thoughts on Genesis*, which she argues was ghost-authored by Leibniz, claims 'to call Things by their Names, is to give them their Nature' (1995, 147) and the last stage of a thing's creation is that 'it is call'd by name, that is, it receives an absolute and determinate nature.' She avers that 'Leibniz never relinquished the idea ... that names were "real"' and always rejected the nominalism of Hobbes and Locke (Coudert 1995, 150). Against Coudert's thesis on the authorship of this text, see Fox (2003).

22 On which Maimonides writes:

> The principal point in this phrase is that the same word which denotes 'existence', is repeated as an attribute ... as if to show that the object which is to be described and the attribute by which it is described are in this case necessarily identical.
>
> (1956, 1.63, 94–95)

23 In fact, YHWH is not solely localised in Tiferet – it is also spread across the whole tree, the *yod* found in Chokhmah (with the crown in Keter), the *heh* in Binah, *vav* in Tiferet (and thus symbolising the whole Name), and *heh* in Malkhut. Because of this the primordial AHYH is contained within the most primordial point of YHWH – or rather, it is 'alluded to ... but it does not exist as a letter in and of itself' (Gikatilla, 1994, 160). We will see more of the development and implications of this idea in Chapter 6.

24 Reminding us of Maimonides' claim that 'None but Himself comprehends what He is' (1956, 1.59, 85).

25 Notably, for the thirteenth century Hasidic writer Elhanan ben Yakar of London, the emanator was not Ehyeh but Elohim, who he describes as the 'soul' to the 'body' of YHWH. See Dan (1996, 244).

26 Cf. Sendor (1994, II, 159n48).

27 Sendor lists further precedents in Judah Halevi's *Kuzari* 4:3, in Abraham ibn Ezra's *Sefer haShem*, where 'the Tetragrammaton is the Name which expresses the divine Presence that adheres to Israel and the lower world', and in R Jacob haNazir, for whom Yah is Chokhmah and AH is Keter (1994, 152n34).

28 In contrast to R Azriel, for whom AHYH, although the highest name, is flawed only to be completed in the messianic era with another aleph – as AHYHA (Sendor, 1994, II,

156n41). The reasons for this are not clear, although gematrially AHYHA equals twenty-two, the same as the number of the alphabet and AHWY. Agata Bielik-Robson has suggested to me that this palindromic name could imply the shape of reality, book-marked by the two incursions of divinity or life force as creation and redemption.

29 Recalling the previous discussion of the Name YHWH as seal (Chapter 1), Sendor comments that 'in the writings of Asher b.David and Azriel of Gerona ... sealing with the letter alef of the divine Name imparts the immutability of divine unity to that which is sealed' (1994, II, 140n88). Isaac writes that 'the Name was not full until man was created in the image of God and the seal was complete' (Sendor 1994, II, 158n47) and 'the Name is sealed in all, and all is sealed in it' (ibid., II, 119–120); but, each sefirah is 'sealed with one letter' (ibid., II, 138).

30 Space does not permit us to fully examine the Zohar's own take on the Name YHWH which is so complex and kaleidoscopic as to require a separate study. However, it is notable that it mentions only in passing the derivation from *aleph*, pursuing a different notion of the relationship between Keter and YHWH based on a dual concealed/revealed YHWH, the upper (of the Ancient of Days, i.e. Keter, containing the Name of the whole tree in potential) and the lower (the Name as it is ascribed to Tiferet), respectively. The *Book of Concealment* suggests that 'the Ancient One' contains all in potentiality as signified by the spelling of the letter *yod* (YWD) as containing the union of male (W) and female (D) and thus, claims Rosenberg, 'The union of YOD ... presages the union of YHW' (1973, 37). The *Lesser Holy Assembly* (Zohar III: 289a), discussing the *Book of Concealment*, states that 'the only essences that are suspended so as to provide existence for the worlds' are the letters YHW:

> The name of the Ancient One is concealed from all, not to be discovered, but these letters are suspended in the Ancient One in order to provide existence for those below [i.e. for the YHW in the lower world of Tiferet]. Without them they could not exist.
>
> (Rosenberg 1973, 140)

However this appears to be contradicted by Zohar II: 146b, which claims that AHBH (i.e. love) are 'the letters upon which the Holy Name depends, and upon which the upper and lower realms depend, and upon which the praise in the Song of Songs depends'.

31 This was pointed out – although surely not for the first time – by Jacob ben Jacob ha-Kohen in his *Explanation of the Letters* (Dan, 1986, 155).

32 *Ein sof* – although at this point the phrase had not become a title for God.

33 Two other posited nominal references in the Bahir are questionable: Scholem (1987, 100–101) claims that the 36×2 powers or archons of the tree (section 79) connect with the seventy-two names of God, though this connection doesn't seem to be explicit in the text; Dauber (2004, 194–197), argues that Section 54's identification of the name with the body is a veiled reference to the non-separation of the lower seven sefirot from the divine Name, being the highest sefirah Machshavah – this is predicated ultimately on the reading of *'sam shemo me'inyano'* as referring to God's placing His own Name in each created thing, rather than His placing the particular thing's name into it. Dauber's claim stretches the evidence beyond what I can grant credibility because the passage immediately quotes Gen.2:19 and Adam's ascription of particular names to the animals. If, despite this, Dauber's interpretation is correct then it is a message very well-concealed. Kaplan (2001, 145) shares my reading of the passage.

34 Fishbane (2008) posits that R Asher ben David may have been responsible for the redaction of some Bahir traditions and thereby have placed this passage which is so strikingly similar to some of his own – most notably, 'The *alef* is the first *sefirah*' (Asher ben David 1996, 105).

35 Interestingly, R Asher ben David (1996, 105–106) related the *yod* of Tetragrammaton

as the beginning of manifestation, to the Talmudic claim that *yod* generates the *olam ha-ba* (discussed in Chapter 1).

36 There is an interesting sub-tradition which seeks to efface and combine the two names in the one name of AHWY. This appears to have roots in the Hebrew grammarians who valued these four vowel-letters above the other, harder, sounds (see Chapter 5, Note 8). It is likely that the gematria value of 22, the number of Hebrew letters, helped seal the importance of this 'name'. Certainly this is the case for Abulafia who appears to have played with AHWY as gematrially signifying the Hebrew alphabet, and thereby the roots of language generally. Idel writes that, 'according to Abulafia, the letters aHWY constitute the hidden divine name, which will be revealed to the messiah' (2011, 81). The *Fountain of Wisdom*, a central text of the early kabbalistic group known as the Iyyun Circle, describes a complex creational mechanics involving four holy names (Ehyeh, Adonai, YHWH and YeYa'eY), but: 'The root principle of all of them is YHWH' (Verman, 1992, 61). However, this sign (YHWH) itself is created via a complex process of articulation and division (though still not at the initial point of creation) from the 'sources' AHWY and HWY. For Gikatilla (GE343) AHWY, as that which contains the Torah, appears to be *more* external than YHWH. Finally the tradition is also found in the Unique Cherub Circle, in R Buchanan's *Sod ha-Sodot* we read:

> And with the Aleph, which corresponds to the Sabbath, AHVY was completed, the full complement of the letters AHYH. YHVH is signed in the work of Creation in two names YHVH which are four AHVY, the number of the twenty-two letters.
>
> (Dan, 1999, 63)

Other than this the Iyyun Circle appear to have little in the way of name theology, although there is mention made of the letters of the Tetragrammaton (*Contemplation-Short*, Verman, 1992, 44–47) and a short passage which mentions the name-ring, Ehyeh Asher Ehyeh, and the first instance of the acrostic ARARITA (*Contemplation-Standard*, ibid., 101–102) as well as a passage reminiscent of RaBaD's conviction that various vocalisations of the Tetragrammaton refer to separate divine attributes (*Contemplation-Standard*, ibid., 111).

37 It will be no surprise to learn that we are, here, on highly speculative ground which would be uncomfortable for the most seasoned of Wittgenstein scholars.

38 This view is confirmed at 2.022 and 2.023, where the unalterable form of any imaginable world is identified as the subsistent objects. This fact, further, implies that we are correct in viewing the Tractarian Names and Objects as identical; because Objects are identical with the logical form of the world, and the form is 'What a picture must have in common with reality, in order to be able to depict it' (2.17). Therefore, names and objects share their form.

39 Although all *Sachverhalte* are independent (2.061), they are stateable by the aggregate of objects, as each *Sachverhalte* is nothing more than the aggregate of its objects. This is the same as to say that logical operators are not themselves objects: a state of affairs is simply the objects themselves in relation to each other. Since the relations are not *things* which unite the elements but merely the fact of their existing in those conjunctions, the possibility of any particular relation must be written into the object itself and is therefore internal to it, part of its own nature. Likewise for Gikatilla, there is no space in which the names of God exist or which determines their relationships – their numerology (*cheshbon*) is internal to them.

40 We see here another similarity to the thought of Leibniz in the deep analysis of the *Tractatus*: it is a Leibnizian principle that all monads not only are identical to one another, but that they each contain an image of the entire world. On this in Leibniz, see especially Ishiguro (1990, 130–132). I have found nothing about this in the secondary literature on Wittgenstein, though I believe it fair to conclude he deliberately incorporated this notion. As we will see in Chapter 7, the idea was also picked up by Walter Benjamin.

41 It is worth here briefly mentioning Fichte, who made $A = A$, or $I = I$, the initial axiom of all philosophical investigation – the assertion of self-existence and self-identity which all subjects must reach in order to progress further.

42 The structure of the *Tractatus* is largely understood and agreed upon by commentators now – this being the distinction between two realms, one which is entirely describable in words and one which is entirely indescribable in literal terms. This distinction is between those aspects of life which are literal, manifest to analytic description and stateable in clear and distinct language which is either true or false; and on the other hand those aspects which are not stateable, which are not confineable in human language, not susceptible to literalism but only to suggestion. The famous aphorism in full, reads 'what can be said at all can be said clearly, and what we cannot talk about we must pass over in silence' (3); his attempt is 'to draw a limit to ... the expression of thoughts', where that limit is drawable by means of language, and what lies on the other side of the limit is inexpressible; 'nonsense' in linguistic terms. This division into the expressible and the inexpressible is in no small way reminiscent of our division between the descriptive and the nominal. Where the former can be entirely put into words, can be adequated with a linguistic description, or 'semantified', the latter is so precisely because it is not equatable into words; it can only be referred-to, and even this is fraught with the difficulty of establishing valid reference.

43 Because the use of rational language divides the world into objects; in the case of something which admits no such demarcatory lines, language cannot hope to gain a foothold and is left slithering along an undented surface. Putnam, guided by this insight, claims that '"proposition" (in the sense of meaningful assertion) is a term that refers to human thought and speech' (1997, 412). Of course for many logicians this would not be the case. For Wittgenstein propositions, being written into the nature of objects, exist *outside* the human mind and are fundamental, primary, constituents of reality – the possibilities which the human mind accesses and must match up against the empirical world in order to ascertain their 'truth' via their similarity to that world (Brockhaus, 1991, 162). For Wittgenstein then, like Frege, it is not propositions that express thoughts, but thoughts that express propositions. That this is the case is a large part of why the empirical world is so perfectly describable in linguistic terms, because *propositions are formally identical with the facts they represent in the world.* This means that language is not just isomorphic with the world, but springs from the same root; language, in its propositional nature, is identical with the relationships between objects in the world.

44 Or, more importantly, *exists.*

45 Wald locates this doctrine first in the Zohar, writing that:

> The term *Tsimtsum* in the Zohar designates God's initial creative act, an act which of necessity occurs within God Himself. It is this first act of creation which allows the Name, and with it the finite world, to emerge from out of the infinity of the Transcendent Creator.
>
> (1989, 54–55)

The priority of the Zohar or Gikatilla is a matter unresolved, and although some passages from the Zohar certainly predate its redaction in the thirteenth century we are as yet unable to make a definitive decision on passages such as those used by Wald. Either way, the doctrine is certainly nascent within the thirteenth century circle of Gikatilla, Abulafia and de Leon.

Bibliography

The Zohar (12 vols). 2003–2014. Translated by Daniel C. Matt. Stanford: Stanford University Press.

Abulafia, Abraham. 2007. *Get Ha-Shemot*. Translated by Fabrizio Lanza. Monfalcone: Providence University.

Asher ben David, R. 1996. *Complete Works and Studies in his Kabbalistic Thought*. (Hebrew). Edited by Daniel Abrams. Los Angeles: Cherub Press.

Barry, Kieran. 1999. *The Greek Qabalah: Alphabetical Mysticism and Numerology in the Ancient World*. York Beach: Weiser.

Biale, David. 1985. Gershom Scholem's Ten Unhistorical Aphorisms on Kabbalah: Text and Commentary. *Modern Judaism* 5, 67–93.

Blickstein, Shlomo. 1983. *Between Philosophy and Mysticism: A Study of the Philosophical-Qabbalistic Writings of Joseph Giqatila (1248-c.1322)*. PhD diss., Jewish Theological Seminary of America.

Bo, Frederick Dal. 2011. The Theory of 'Emanation' in Gikatilla's *Gates of Justice*. *Journal of Jewish Studies* 62(1), 79–104.

Brockhaus, Richard R. 1991. *Pulling Up the Ladder: The Metaphysical Roots of Wittgenstein's* Tractatus Logico-Philosophicus. La Salle: Open Court.

Campanini, Saverio, ed. 2005. *The Book of Bahir: Flavius Mithridates' Latin Translation, The Hebrew Text, and an English Version*. Torino: Nino Aragno Editore.

Coudert, Allison P. 1995. *Leibniz and the Kabbalah*. London: Kluwer Academic Press.

Dan, Joseph. 1986. *The Early Kabbalah*. Mahwah: Paulist Press.

Dan, Joseph. 1996. The Name of God, the Name of the Rose, and the Concept of Language in Jewish Mysticism. *Medieval Encounters* 2(3), 228–248.

Dan, Joseph. 1998. *Jewish Mysticism Volume II: The Middle Ages*. New Jersey: Jason Aronson Inc.

Dan, Joseph. 1999. *The 'Unique Cherub' Circle: A School of Mystics and Esoterics in Medieval Germany*. Tübingen: Mohr Siebeck.

Dauber, Jonathan Victor. 2004. *Standing on the Heads of Philosophers: Myth and Philosophy in Early Kabbalah*. PhD diss., New York University.

Fagenblat, Michael. 2010. *A Covenant of Creatures: Levinas' Philosophy of Judaism*. Stanford: Stanford University Press.

Fishbane, Eitan P. 2008. The Speech of Being, the Voice of God: Phonetic Mysticism in the Kabbalah of Asher ben David and His Contemporaries. *Jewish Quarterly Review* 98(4), 485–521.

Fox, Nicholas James. 2003. *Leibniz's Cosmology: Transcendental Rationalism and Kabbalistic Symbolism*. PhD diss., Open University.

Gikatilla, Rabbi Joseph. 1994. *Sha'are Orah: Gates of Light*. Translated by Avi Weinstein. London: Harper Collins.

Heidegger, Martin. 1992. *The Metaphysical Foundations of Logic*. Translated by Michael Heim. Bloomington: Indiana University Press.

Idel, Moshe. 2011. *Kabbalah in Italy 1280–1510: A Survey*. New Haven: Yale University Press.

Ishiguro, Hidé. 1990. *Leibniz's Philosophy of Logic and Language*. Second edition. Cambridge: Cambridge University Press.

Kaplan, Aryeh. 2001. *The Bahir: Illumination*. York Beach: Weiser Books.

Lachter, Hartley. 2008. Kabbalah, Philosophy, and the Jewish-Christian Debate: Reconsidering the Early Works of Joseph Gikatilla. *Journal of Jewish Thought and Philosophy* 16(1), 1–58.

Levinas, Emmanuel. 1994. *Beyond the Verse: Talmudic Readings and Lectures*. Translated by Gary D. Mole. Bloomington: Indiana University Press.

Loemker, Leroy. 1969. *Gottfried Wilhelm Leibniz: Philosophical Papers and Letters.* Second edition. Boston: D. Reidel.

Maimonides, Moses. 1956. *The Guide for the Perplexed.* Translated by M. Friedlander. New York: Dover.

Martini, Annett, ed. 2010. *Yosef Giqatilla The Book of Punctuation: Flavius Mithridates' Latin Translation, The Hebrew Text, and an English Version.* Torino: Nino Aragno Editore.

Morlok, Elke. 2011. *Rabbi Joseph Gikatilla's Hermeneutics.* Tübingen: Mohr Siebeck.

Putnam, Hilary. 1997. On Negative Theology. *Faith and Philosophy* 14(4), 407–422.

Rosenberg, Roy A. 1973. *The Anatomy of God: The Book of Concealment, The Greater Holy Assembly and The Lesser Holy Assembly of the Zohar with The Assembly of the Tabernacle.* New York: Ktav.

Russell, Bertrand. 1917. *Knowledge by acquaintance and knowledge by description. Proceedings of the Aristotelian Society, 1910–1911.* In: *Mysticism and Logic.* London: George Allen & Unwin Ltd.

Scholem, Gershom. 1996 [1965]. *On the Kabbalah and its Symbolism.* New York: Schocken.

Scholem, Gershom. 1973. The Name of God and the Linguistic Theory of the Kabbalah. *Diogenes* 80, 164–194.

Scholem, Gershom. 1987. *The Origins of the Kaballah.* Edited by R.J. Werblowsky, translated by Allan Arkush. Princeton: Princeton University Press.

Sendor, Mark Brian. 1994. *The Emergence of Provencal Kabbalah: Rabbi Isaac the Blind's Commentary on Sefer Yezirah.* PhD diss., Harvard University.

Trachtenberg, Joshua. 1939. *Jewish Magic and Superstition: A Study in Folk Religion.* New York: Behrman's Jewish Book House.

Verman, Mark. 1992. *The Books of Contemplation: Medieval Jewish Mystical Sources.* Albany: State University of New York Press.

Wald, Stephen G. 1989. *The Doctrine of the Divine Name: An Introduction to Classical Kabbalistic Theology.* Atlanta: Scholars Press.

Wijnhoven, Jochanan H.A. 1964. *Sefer ha-Mishkal: Text and Study.* PhD diss., Brandeis University.

Wittgenstein, Ludwig. 1969. *The Blue and Brown Books: Preliminary Studies for the 'Philosophical Investigations'.* Second edition. Oxford: Blackwell,.

Wittgenstein, Ludwig. 1974. *Tractatus Logico-Philosophicus.* Translated by D.F. Pears and B.F. McGuinness. London: Routledge.

Wittgenstein, Ludwig. 1975. *Philosophical Remarks.* Edited by R. Rhees, translated by R. Hargreaves and Roger White. Oxford: Blackwell.

Wittgenstein, Ludwig. 1996. *Last Writings on the Philosophy of Psychology,* Vol. I. Chicago: University of Chicago Press.

Wolfson, Elliot R. 1993. The Tree that is All: Jewish Christian Roots of a Kabbalistic Symbol in Sefer ha-Bahir. *Journal of Jewish Thought and Philosophy* 3, 31–76.

6 Name and letter

Deconstructing language with Abulafian prophecy and Levinasian othering

> What is to be known? 'That YHVH is Elohim' [Deut.4:35]. This is the totality of the whole mystery of faith, totality of above and below, totality of the whole Torah […] for it is the complete Name; this is the mystery of faith. And who is it? 'YHVH is one and His Name one' [Zech.14:9].
>
> (Zohar II, 161b)

We found in Chapter 5 a pull towards the differentiation of Keter from the rest of the sefirot. This was articulated most commonly in the doctrine of the primacy of the name AHYH over YHWH. This chapter will examine the development of this idea through a careful analysis of the nominal theology of Abraham Abulafia (1240–c.1291), which emphasises the deconstruction of names into their constituent parts.

The literal construction of names (and Name) has already been briefly touched on in Chapter 4. There, I argued that the construction of names was unimportant because names always transcend their materialisation, being a process and not an object. In this chapter I will analyse this distinction in greater depth, specifically in relation to the kabbalistic tradition that describes the relationship between the letters of the Name, as embodied in the sefirotic tree, and the Name itself. Abulafia's work demonstrates in powerful effect the distance, not only between name and object, but also between word and the letters which constitute it. One of the striking facts immediately obvious in any analysis of language is that the linguistic is ultimately reducible: it is constructed of discrete elements which themselves are *not* further reducible. Spoken language reduces to phonemes; written language to letters. Language is thus atomistic. This argument will be counterbalanced by a reading of Lacan which sees the letter as the material root of language, and thus as the 'real' which perpetually threatens to disrupt the process of signification, destroying meaning by refocussing on the elements in their separateness instead of the signification which together they create and in which they too disappear. I will then introduce Levinas in order to develop this theory, as the holism of the name indicates an essential quality about the subjective construction of identity – a concept which also is at the heart of Abulafia's mystical reconstruction of the Divine Name.

This chapter will therefore propose an investigation of what stands outside the semantically totalised cosmos: that indefinable which is conditioned by the Name. This will necessitate, first, the analysis of two kabbalistic motifs: Cutting the shoots, and unifying the Name.

Cutting the shoots

In the early kabbalistic literature we find repeated use of the motif of 'cutting the shoots' (*qatzatz ba-netiot*). Originating in the Talmud as a generic term for heresy, by the time of the first kabbalists the phrase had come to signify one specific theological crime: the separation of the sefirot either from each other, or from the source, Ein Sof.[1] This clearly has its roots in the usage of Hagiga 15a, where Aher 'cut the shoots' by making Metatron a second divine power. In what is possibly the first kabbalistic usage of the motif, R Isaac the Blind's famous upbraiding of heresy, addressed to Nachmanides and R Jacob Gerondi, we read:

> It is evident that their hearts have moved from the supernal one, and they 'cut the shoots.' But the things [*devarim*][2] are united 'like a flame bound to a coal, since the master is one and has no second, and what may you count before one.' [SY§6] The explanation: before one is the Great Name who is united in all ten.
>
> (Scholem, 1934, 143)

In this passage, Isaac is at pains to emphasise the unity of God and the sefirot: the sefirot are not a separate being, but are contiguous with the essence of God. While distinguishing between the 'master' and the Great Name, Isaac emphasises their unity. God is a singular, without multiplicity – the Name, the sefirotic potencies which emanate from Him, are united with His essence, admitting of no independent existence. This 'Great Name' is immanent throughout all ten sefirot, pervading and uniting them; the essence and the sefirotic manifestation then are like a coal and the flame which springs from it, the latter dependent on, and constituted from, the former.

Developing this theme, the thirteenth century Geronese kabbalist, Jacob ben Sheshet, writes: 'They [Aher *et al.*] also cut the shoots in order to make one of the branches a tree unto itself and the root a tree unto itself' (*Emunah u-Bittahon* Ch. 3, Dan, 1986, 120). He then explains that this cutting can be the isolation of (any) one of the ten sefirot from the others:

> I am of the opinion that this cutting is of ten *devarim*: each one of the ten, either between the tenth and the ninth or the ninth and the eighth and so on until between the first and Ein Sof itself.
>
> (Ibid.)

We find the phrase increasingly as the Kabbalah develops; specifically referring to Hagiga 15a, Todros b.Yosef Abulafia writes that Aher 'cut [*qatzatz*] the two distinct beings and separated them from each other' (*Sefer Orar ha-Kavod ha-Shalem* 24a; Abrams, 1994, 306). Gikatilla criticises Elisha (that is, Elisha ben Abuya – i.e. Aher), for his errors in not only failing to grasp the intelligible world (by 'draw[ing] the intelligibles to perceptibles'[3]) but also cutting the shoots (ShN, Martini, 2010, 396).

Abulafia uses the phrase repeatedly, but the most interesting passage is from *Gan Na'ul*, where he advises:

> The one who receives should try to receive the sefirot first in order to receive the divine overflow from them and in themselves according to His attributes he will cleave to each and every sefirah separately and he will cleave to all the sefirot together as one so that he will not cut the shoots.
>
> (Wolfson, 1995, 350)

This passage articulates an important point for Abulafia: the sefirot must be united as one, separating them and uniting to them both individually and together. This is because of the kabbalistic practice known as the Unification of the Name. Before moving on to look at this practise, it is worth noting that the interpretation of *qatzatz ba-netiot* seems to be confined to the kabbalists. There is no use of the phrase in the literature of the Ashkenazi Hasidim, or any surrounding groups, suggesting that we can trace the use, along with its specific interpretation, back to R Isaac the Blind's letter cited above.[4]

The unification of the Name

Completing the triangular relationship of the Name, Metatron, and the sefirot, there is a kabbalistic tradition that the sefirot *in toto* constitute the Name YHWH,[5] indicated in Isaac the Blind's statement that the Name is 'united in all ten' of the sefirot. Here, the Name is not assigned to Tiferet, as we saw in Chapter 5, but rather spread across the entire sefirotic tree – with individual letters representing particular sefirot. The first letter *yod* is Chokhmah, *heh* is Binah, *vav* is Tiferet and also the five sefirot surrounding it, and the final *heh* is Malkhut. The primordial sefirah Keter both is and is not part of the Name, being represented by the crown of the *yod*: it is indicated, but transcends the corporeality of the Name. The primal root or *Ein Sof* is nothing other than God in His unity, prior to the emergence of His Name; the point wherein 'God and His Name were One', to quote the famous passage in *Pirqe de-Rabbi Eliezer* Ch. 3, because the Name had not yet become separated out into an external presence. Ein Sof here means the same as AHYH in the last chapter, being assigned to Keter which both is one of the sefirot yet stands above all the rest of them.

The kabbalistic practice of Unifying the Name indicates the metaphysical sealing of the ten sefirot together with Ein Sof, thereby refuting any distinction between the sefirotic potencies and God's essence: as such it is the inverse of Cutting the Shoots. R Ezra of Gerona writes that 'an individual must know how to unify the Name, that He is One and not two, as it says: 'There is none besides

Him' [Deut.4:35] and to unify the ten *Sefirot* within the Ein Sof' (*Commentary to Canticles*, Brody, 1991, 239). Ezra claims that 'the knowledge of YHWH is the basis and root of everything', and that this knowledge consists of knowing 'how to unify the Unique Name' (*On the Kabbalistic Meaning of the Mitzvot*, Travis, 2002, 176). He explains that: 'This imperative *mizvah*' is 'To unify Him by way of the ten *Sefirot* within *Ein Sof*' (Travis, 2002, 178). The means of doing this, is:

> to cause thought [*machshavah*, i.e. Keter] to conform to faith [*emunah*] as if it were cleaving to what is above, to conjoin the Name in its letters and to include the ten *Sefirot* within it, like a flame connected to a coal.
>
> (*Commentary to Canticles*, Brody, 1991, 239)

Although *emunah* is a term most usually used for the sefirah Binah, Scholem remarks that Isaac the Blind used *emunah* 'to represent the second *and tenth sefirot*', (my emphasis) and so: 'Perhaps this 'cardinal principle' signifies therefore that in the meditation on the name of God the mystic brings the ten sefiroth – from the first to the last – into harmony' (1987a, 302).

This emphasis on uniting the sefirot with their root indicates the danger which these Kabbalists perceive in separating the more tangible manifestation of divine potency from the unknowable essence. In uniting the sefirot, the Name pervades and transcends them by being a singularity composed from their multiplicity. Thus the essence, the irreducible unity, is embodied by and contains the attributes, even while it transcends them; the finite (perceivable) qualities, discrete 'things' or describable 'words,' which themselves can have no reality apart from the essence, are attached to it 'like a flame to a coal' but do not exhaust it. It is the essence which holds together the attributes and makes them bind into a single perceivable thing, yet that which is perceived is still not the essence. The Name, then, although being composed of letters, when understood as a single word – or as an act of reference which indicates an object – becomes more than the sum of its parts: it becomes the nominal aspect of its object.

We find this tradition, of the ten sefirot as a somewhat lower, *manifest* aspect of the deity, identified with the Name YHWH, throughout the early kabbalists: In Nachmanides' Torah commentary the God of revelation 'is the unity of the ten sefirot' which arises from the dark ground of Ein Sof.[6] In an oft-quoted passage, Azriel utilises ontic terminology to discuss the distinct levels of divinity which we can conceive and which we cannot:

> He made his Nothing [*eino*] into his Being [*yesho*].... This teaches us that the Nothing is the Being and the Being is the Nothing.... But the place at which the Being is linked to the point where, from the Nothing, it begins to have existence is called 'faith' ('*emunah).* For faith is not related to a visible and apprehensible Being, nor to the invisible and unknowable Nothing, but precisely where the Nothing is connected to the Being.
>
> (*Derekh ha-Emunah va-Derekh ha-Kefirah*, Scholem 1987a [amended],
> 423–424, cf. Pachter, 2004, 21–27)

'Nothing' here indicates the first sefirah or Ein Sof,[7] and Being would seem to be that which proceeds from the Nothing, i.e. the first stirrings of concrete existence which we can think of as the Name. *Emunah*, as mentioned, is a common name for the third sefirah Binah, known as the highest point that consciousness can access. Azriel in this passage is claiming that humans should not worship the Name, and cannot worship the Nothing, but should attempt to find the very point at which Being emerges from Nothing; i.e., where YHWH emerges from Ein Sof. Scholem interprets: 'Being and Nought therefore are only different aspects of the *superesse* of the divine reality. There is a Nought of God that gives birth to being, and there is a being of God that represents the Nought' (1987a, 424). This use of strictly ontic phraseology to describe the nature and relationship of the manifest and concealed aspects of divinity is important to note, and is one which we find again echoed in Rosenzweig's work on the dark ground of the elements, prior to their emergence into subjective knowledge; reminding us that epistemological absence is conceptually associated with non-existence; being that is not-known appears to be known as *not-being*. However, though a name presents existence, that which does not exist in this nominal (or what we may call *phe-nominal*) way is not necessarily non-existent *in-itself*.

Gikatilla explicitly associates *yesh* with Chokhmah, using the text: 'But wisdom [*chokhmah*], where [*me-ayin*] can it be found?' (Job 28:12) to explicate that God:

> [B]rought forth being [*yesh*] from nothing [*ayin*], that is to say, [He] emanated the Chokhmah, which is being, from Keter which is called nothing … without boundary [*ein sof*] and without measure … there is never any division, for the *yod* cleaves to the crown…
>
> (*Sefer Sha'are Tzedek* 368–369, Lachter, 2008, 35)

The Zohar goes so far as to suggest that the primordial *yod* of the Name is the letter left over when the אויר (atmosphere) of Keter becomes the אור (light) of Chokhmah, thus placing YHWH firmly within the created realm (I:16b). One early kabbalistic manuscript, relying on *Pirqe de-Rabbi Eleazar*, identifies God's Name with Chokhmah and asserts that all things existed eternally there, in potential:

> Before God created His world He was alone with His name, and His name is equivalent to His Chokhmah. And in His Chokhmah all things were mixed together and all the essences were hidden, for He had not yet brought them forth from potentiality to reality, like a tree in whose potency the fruit is already present, but which it has not yet brought forth.
>
> (Scholem, 1987a, 451)

In this text Chokhmah, the point at which the Name begins, is pre-existently present within Ein Sof as that which will become, once it is emanated.

For the early kabbalists, then, the Name YHWH is identified as God's emergence into reality – the condensation of the formless into form. The sefirot, as the manifest potency of God, are themselves the body of the Name: the manifestation of God into being. This association of the Name YHWH with Being is a crucial development, though one not unprecedented in the pre-kabbalistic material; while several tenth century writers saw the Name as the gateway to creation (as described in Chapter 1), we have found already in the Talmud the phenomenal aspect of God – i.e., God's emergence into the created world of subjective consciousness – associated with the Name as it is embodied in Metatron (Chapter 3). However, the nature of this tradition within the Kabbalah requires further analysis.

While the Name manifests the presence of the 'Nothing' Ein Sof, Ein Sof itself is formally nameless, meaning that the Name must be in some way distinct from the unmanifest essence.[8] Azriel of Gerona writes that 'Ein Sof cannot be conceived, certainly not expressed, though it is intimated in every thing, for there is nothing outside of it. No letter, no name, no writing, no thing can confine it' (*Commentary on the Ten Sefirot*, Matt, 1995, 29–30). Likewise, Jacob ben Sheshet writes:

> And because it [this Supreme] is removed from all thought, no limited name whatsoever can be attributed to it, and all things and allusions found in relation to it in the words of the Bible refer to the realities [sefiroth] which come from its cause.
>
> (*Sha'ar ha-Shamayim*, Scholem, 1987a, 437)

The process of unifying the Name of God then consists in uniting the ten sefirot into one, i.e. the rejection of differentiation or multiplicity in the singular presence of God; this is the error which the kabbalists knew as Cutting the Shoots. Unifying the Name is not just an intellectual affirmation, but achieves the ontological uniting of the sefirot into a single being. God becomes in the Name; enters reality only in the guise or via the mechanism of the Name. The Tetragrammaton seals the unity of the sefirot, making them one as an identity. The Name is then like a sphere, surrounding our reality – humans direct our thought or prayer towards it but are aiming to go beyond, to the outer Ein Sof, that which is un-limited by name; beyond it, and because of this, within it; in sealing God from World, the Name appears to contain both, separately. It is from the positing of the Name that limitation into identity becomes possible, and this is replicated in the giving of names. Thus the idea that 'all being is derived from the reality of the Tetragrammaton of the Creator' (Moshe de-Leon, *Sefer ha-Mishkal*, Wijnhoven, 1964, 165).

This presents an unresolved picture of the Godhead, in which human agency is the final stage, either corrupting it (when the shoots are cut), or correcting it (when the Name is unified). It is then the responsibility of humans to complete – or to *seal* – the Godhead, uniting it and forming a singular divinity through which divine energy can travel from Ein Sof into the world. As Hartley Lachter writes: 'It is a theurgic act in which the flawed and divided Godhead is repaired through human agency' (2004, 156). Because the ontological emerges in and as the phenomenal, altering the experiential by meditative processes such as Unifying the Name effects a change which transmits back to the ontological itself.[9]

Furthermore, the making of God a unity, via the unification of the Name, brings God into the presence of the mystic; through the mystery of consciously unifying the Name, God's unity is presented to the consciousness. As Wolfson puts it: 'divine unity is intrinsically related to the active unification of the ten sefirot, i.e., the ten intellects, on the part of the individual' (2000, 58).

This doctrine, unlike Cutting the Shoots, is found throughout Jewish mysticism of the time, and far beyond the Kabbalah. It is found in Eleazar of Worms' *Sefer haShem*,[10] and the writings of the Unique Cherub Circle.[11]

The motifs of Cutting the Shoots and Unification of the Name both express the continuity of the *middot*, the sefirotic potencies which manifest in the world, and which constitute the Name YHWH, with the unnameable essence of God, Ein Sof, that which is unlimited and not present in the finite world or present to finite human consciousness. The transcendental essence is *not* something different from the finite qualities we perceive in the world and through which God acts. Yet the Name should not be confused with the thing itself, neither should it replace it nor be seen as separate from it; rather it is how the thing manifests in subjectivity, in the world of the subject. The debate carried out by R Azriel of Gerona in *Sha'ar Ha-Sho'el* articulates the importance of this well: Azriel at once rejects the philosophical position that an infinite and impersonal deity (i.e. Ein Sof) completely transcends the world without the qualities of rulership, and the simple theistic faith in a personal ruler without an infinitely larger, transcendent aspect which is invisible to us (Pachter, 2004). His proof reads: 'Know that everything visible and perceivable to human contemplation is limited (and anything limited has an end and everything that has an end is differentiated). Thus that which is not limited is called *Ein Sof*' (*Sa'ar ha-Sho'el* 2b, Pachter, 2004, 16).

Language and the world

The Unification of the Name takes on some unique characteristics in the thought of Abraham Abulafia, another deeply systematic thinker, who will occupy us for the remainder of this chapter.

Abulafia, like Gikatilla, saw Hebrew as divine,[12] the language being a fundamental part of reality and having a direct relationship to its objects. However, this is not a semantic literalism, with words having identifiable meanings in regard to their objects; rather names are to be understood 'not according to their literal sense in any manner', because:

> [T]hey are mentioned to inform us about the truth of the mysteries of language and its secrets, and this is that the Lord, blessed be He, did not call these entities by the aforementioned names according to the convention but according to the nature.
>
> (*Sefer ha-Melammed* 296a, Wolfson, 2000, 63)

Abulafia's philosophy of language then is not based on semantics but something altogether more material. Drawing on traditions such as the Sefer Yetzirah, Abulafia perceived words not as the primal unit of language, but rather as materially constituted of letters: 'letters are the reality of the world entirely, and by means of them the Lord governs the world' (*Sefer ha-Hesheq* 19b, Wolfson 2000, 60n171). Abulafia's unique emphasis on letter rather than word leads to the sublimation of word beneath the letters which construct it – and even to the destruction of normal semantic language. It is not in the surface meaning that we must seek truth, but in the elemental constitution which undergirds meaning: 'For just as natural reality instructs the philosopher in an easy way as to the truth of things, so too the [Hebrew] letters instruct us of the truth of things, with greater ease' (*Sitrei Torah* 163a). In order to get to the root, the source of our finite reality, Abulafia pursues a path of deconstruction – deconstruction of object-words into the letters that constitute them.

This approach to language is unique even in Judaism, for its disregard for surface forms and persistent contortion of word into a more basic ontology. Abulafia sees the mystic's role as deconstructing the communicative function of language – and in doing this, they will transcend the world of mere things to achieve – a kind of – divine union.[13] For Abulafia, the manipulation of letters – or *tzeruf otiot* – is a real metaphysical process, one of going beyond the concrete forms which surround us, dissolving actual objects into their primal constituents – the letters which make them up. These are the fundamental atomic constituents of reality, but it is only via the deconstruction and reconstruction of names that humans can access them. He writes,

> My son, it is not the intention that you come to a stop with some finite or given form, even though it be of the highest order: Much rather is this the 'Path of Names': The less understandable they are, the higher their order, until you arrive at the activity of a force which is no longer in your control, but rather your reason and your thought is in its control.
>
> (*Sefer Shaare Tzedek*, Scholem, 1995, 149)

Names then offer the key to the inner nature of things, and the means by which we can perceive their relations to each other and to their source is through the dismantling and analysis of their components. In performing this process, the dissolution of normal semantic meaning activates the dissolution of individuated consciousness, and in going beyond the forms of reality one is going beyond the stratifications of everyday perception, into a more primal realm. We might suggest that, beginning with the descriptive words of the Torah, by deconstructing the words away from meaning, they then become names, by virtue of having lost their descriptive aspect. They can no longer describe, and so can only refer.[14]

Because of the linguistic-ontological dependency of all things on the Name, by deconstructing words we can actually progress backwards towards the primal unity of the Name which predates and transcends the world. The means of finding this relationship is only possible through *tzeruf otiot*, the manipulation of the letters which make up the inner identity of things. For Abulafia, by manipulating names into letters, one can begin a mystical reversion of the process of emanation, and in doing so the true function of language is unveiled: 'the intent behind language is the discovery of the function of the Active Intellect, that makes human speech conform to the Divinity' (*Mafteach ha-Chokhmot*, Idel, 1989, 22).

The Active Intellect is a concept taken directly from Neoplatonic thought, as the rational source of reality – the *logos*, effectively, that intellect which creates and orders reality in its multiplicity.[15] The Jewish thinkers placed it within a matrix of identities most of which are familiar to us – the Name of God, the Torah, etc.[16]

For Abulafia this accessing of the Active Intellect is the method of prophecy, i.e. the attaining of true knowledge about the structure of reality from God. He writes:

> [P]rophecy does not come to anyone who prophecies in truth except by way of letter-combination in conjunction with knowledge of His ways, the paths of His configurations, the arrangements of His plans, and the pathways of the secret of the sefirot together with comprehension of the mysteries of the matters of the names.
>
> (*Mafteach ha-Shemot*, Wolfson, 1996, 58)

Further, 'it is impossible for any person in the world to reach the level of prophecy except if he has received the tradition concerning the knowledge of the Name' (*Imrei Shefer* 226b, Wolfson, 2000, 69). This method of prophecy then allows us to follow the path which Leibniz claimed was impossible for finite beings: to trace the means of causality back from the visible world to its logical cause, the structural predecessor which is the divine realm, the Divine Name:

> [N]ature is the activity-function of the Blessed Name and is the corporeal existence, whereas the Torah is the activity-function of the Blessed Divine Name and is the spiritual existence. Physical and spiritual existence are nothing more than systems and orders, ordered and systematised in accordance with all that is ordered and systematised by the One who orders and systematises. For the systematiser is the Name, and all is ordered in accordance with the Name of God.
>
> (*Otzar Eden Ganuz*, Idel, 1989, 35)

By investigating the intellectual nature of the natural world, then, the structure which generates it can be found.[17]

Further, prophecy is accessed through this method because this practice creates a union with God – by massaging the letters of the Torah, which are the letters of the world, the mystic is effectively meditating on the Name of God. By dissolving the entities of the visible world back into their constituents, one can perceive the radical unity – the Name – which lies within and above them. This is what Idel calls the murder of language,[18] because one must: 'Read the entire Torah, both forwards and backwards, and spill the blood of the languages. Thus, the knowledge of the Name is above all wisdoms in quality and worth' (*Perush Sefer Ish Adam*, Idel, 1989, 27). Abulafia wants to take hold of language and cut it into its smallest parts in order to see past the apparent existences of this world and to their primordial root. This untying of worldly identities frees the atomic letters to reunite as the Name, which is their natural originary form – the twenty-two letters of the Hebrew alphabet are released and reform into their root in the Tetragrammaton.[19]

In de-descriptifying language by breaking words into letters we commit its murder but also its apotheosis into Name. Literal meaning is destroyed, the blood is spilled but only to be reformed – into a non-descriptive form, that of the Name. The Unification of the Name then, for Abulafia, is a process related not just to abstract meditation on the sefirot, but is tied to our very experience and thinking about the world around us. In order to Unify the Name we must intellectually perceive everything that exists in its relation to the Divine, the linguistic nature of manifest reality being nothing but a complex articulation of the Name of God. The world, being dependent upon the ten sefirot, is itself the emergence of the Name.

However, it is not just knowledge that the mystic is seeking, but something altogether more potent. Abulafia has absorbed the Aristotelian notion of the identification of the knower, the known and the knowledge:[20]

> [J]ust as his master who is detached from all matter is called the Knowledge, the Knower and the Known, all at the same time, so shall the exalted man, the master of the exalted Name, be called intellect, while he is actually knowing; then he is also 'the known' like his master, and then there is no difference between them...
>
> (*Hayyei Olam ha-Ba* 32a, Idel, 1989, 295)

Thus in contemplating the Name, massaging the letters that make up the world to reveal their ontological relation to the Name, the mystic is actually becoming one with it. Abulafia envisions a dissolution of selfhood into the mental-mathematical truth of creation. As he famously wrote, the seeker, in the process of combining letters, 'will be messiah to God, his very messenger, and will be called the Angel of God. And his name shall be like the name of his master, Shaddai, who shall name him Metatron, Prince of the Presence' (*Hayyei Olam ha-Ba* 32a, Idel, 1989 [amended], 295). The mystic here achieves a virtual union with God – or rather, a union with the Name. The preceding lines of those just quoted make clear the influence of the Hekhalot literature on Abulafia: 'now he is no longer separated from his Master, and behold he is his Master, and his Master is he; for he is so intimately adhering to Him that he cannot, by any means, be separated from Him, for he is He' (ibid.).

The contemplation and unification of the Name into one creates Metatron, the Prince of the Presence – the presence of God or the point at which God and human meet – and thus the unknowable unity of God is made available to the human; only when the Name is unified can human find God, because within that process the human becomes unified, as one with the Name.[21] I have previously argued (Miller, 2009) that the Enoch literature and the progressive dehumanisation of Enoch into Metatron that we see in the 1,000 year progression from 1 Enoch through to 3 Enoch is related to Enoch's initial indoctrination into the 'heavenly secrets' – in fact a celestial mechanical order which generates the phenomena of the world. This is likely based on the trend in Greek philosophical thought (and even Philo) which suggests that, because the truth of the world is rational, by immersing oneself in rationality a human can transcend the mere finite limits of human consciousness and existence and, to the extent that one's consciousness becomes identical with the rational superstructure which generates the world of appearances, become immortal.[22] Abulafia appears to draw on the undercurrent of this tradition within Jewish mysticism when he believes that, through immersion in the Name which generates all else, the mystic can become identified with the Name and the superhuman archangel of rationality, Metatron.[23] Idel confirms this reading, stating that: 'This technique [of letter-combination] is conceived to induce a transformation that changes the human into an angelic being, namely into an intellectual entity' (2008, 12). Wolfson comments that:

> In this moment [of prophecy] the epistemological dichotomy of outside-inside is overcome for the angelic presence is an external projection of the inner self of the mystic, a projection that is made possible by the fact that in the conjunctive experience the intellect that is actualized is identical with the intellect that actualizes.

> (2000, 208)

Lachter writes that 'the assimilation of the self in the highest levels of the divine economy [i.e. Keter/Ein Sof] is the culmination of the task of "unifying God's name"' (2004, 156). The Unification of the Name is not merely the projection of God as a unified entity; at its peak it is the unification of the whole of creation, including the mystic, into the primordial unity which preceded being: the nothingness of Ein Sof. Thus, 'to unify God's name is to unify God, and this is accomplished by uniting *with* God' (ibid.).

In the process of Unifying the Name, then, the mystic becomes it – and yet this is not to become God, but only Metatron, who remains on and *as* the boundary.[24] The mystic then can access divine truth and act as a conduit to pass this on to the world (as Enoch-Metatron did). Currently 'the world of Names is suspended and obscured and its letters and combinations and virtues are not understood' but: 'When the one whom God desires arrives ... God will reveal His secrets to him ... And the wisdom of the letters and Names which now are not understood will be revealed' (*Sefer Sha'are Tzedek*, Idel 1989, 18).

The Messianic aspect of this theory is hinted at in another passage, where Abulafia says of the mystic:

And he [God] says: 'Anoint him as a king' – rejoice him like a king with the power of all the names.... And his saying 'and his name I have called Shadday, like My Name' – whose secret is Shadday like My Name, and understand all the intention. Likewise his saying 'He is I and I am He,' and it cannot be revealed more explicitly than this. But the secret of the 'corporeal name' is the 'Messiah of God'.

(*Perush Sefer ha-Edut*, Idel, 2011, 82)

This identification of the mystic with the archangel Metatron, who is the Name of God, can perhaps be best understood through the work of Jacques Lacan, who at several points emphasised the theological, and specifically Jewish, influence on his work. The Abulafian conception of a world reduced to language recalls Lacan's Symbolic Order, the semantic mirror which perfectly reflects the world, though replacing things with words, and in so doing, provides a structural method for representation and meaning. For Lacan the central signifier is the Name of the Father (*nom du pere*): it is this which guarantees meaning for everything else, and which mediates the possibility of all communication.

The Name of the Father is representative of the Symbolic Order, the signifier which precedes the signified, representing the essential priority of the Symbolic Order and the symbols it contains over the real, where the real is subsumed, forced to fit into, the order and system of the symbols by those beings (humans) who utilise it ... or even, are utilised by it. In Abulafia too, there is a symbolic order which transcends the real: the Active Intellect, which is the structure of language, conveys the true form of reality, above and beyond appearance.

While the early kabbalists maintained a dual tradition of, on the one hand, the Name's constitution from the sefirot-letters, and on the other, the association of the Name with the single sixth sefirah, Tiferet, (as opposed to the primal sefirah of Keter), Lacan, on the one hand, argued that letters are the material substrate of any signification or dialogue, and on the other, imposed a radical separation of the signifier from the signified – something represented most potently in his placing of the Name of the Father ontologically prior to the symbolised Father himself. In Lacan we see that the 'bar' which fundamentally separates the name from the object, the bar which is the act of signification itself, is an intraversable abyss, but also one which inverts the presumed direction of influence by making the Name that which establishes the identity of the Father. Further, it is only via the Name – i.e. via the intervention of the symbolic order – that the individual can achieve any kind of closeness or communion with the Father. It is the nature of signification to provide access, while yet denying it – by making identity a *metaphysical* question, something which transcends the material. God, in manifesting *into* the Name, takes an identity which we can conceive, and one which we can even become ourselves. Thus by the alteration of the self which follows from the integration of the symbolic order, that achieved by the mystic in his translation into Metatron which itself is the culmination of his knowledge of the celestial order, is also the achievement of contiguity with God, symbolised by the mystic taking the name Metatron himself in his identification with the Active

Intellect. As the subject attempts to join society and communicate with other members, the Symbolic Order is integrated and written into him; and so he takes on the qualities of the order.

Tzahi Weiss (2009) has placed the work of Lacan in line with the linguistic theory of Sefer Yetzirah. For Lacan, the letter is equivalent to the Real, that which is never present to consciousness, never given in meaning, for it is constantly subsumed under the larger totality which it is to form: the letter disappears in the comprehension of the word or sentence, and it becomes apparent only in the disruption of signification, when meaning disappears. The letter itself then threatens the chain of signification, as the material strata could break through the symbolic with its raw, meaningless physicality. Like broken paving stones that erupt the smoothness of pavement and make walking an assault course.

> The signifier's priority over the signified, as well as the understanding that at the foundations of the signifier an absolute component exists, which does not take part in the chain of signifiers and therefore cannot be interpreted, leads to the Real, and to the letter, which is part of the Real. Thus, reading individual letters, or combinations of letters that do not form words, causes a cognitive break stemming from the amputation of the normative process of interpretation. The reader who faces a letter or a successions of letters does not focus on the signifier; instead, he looks for the signified—the meanings of those letters or successions of letters.
>
> (Weiss, 2009, 113)

Weiss explains that this 'evokes traumatic qualities caused by the reader's intersection with the Real level of the language, which is prior even to the signifier: successions of letters that cannot be related to the Imaginary or Symbolic levels' (2009, 112). In contrast to the breaking of descriptive words into letters, allowing the letters to maintain their independence breaks the Name of God – destroying the unity.[25] While SY argued that letters are the first ontological level of reality, for Abulafia and Gikatilla it is the Name which exists first, and is then broken *into* letters in order to generate the multiplicity of the world. In order to undo this multiplicity we must first take the step of freeing letters from their constitution in mere words. So in breaking words into letters, their material essence is laid bare; yet in unifying the Name of God one is moving from the division of the material world into something wholly other – that which transcends the world and cannot be captured within it.

Just like primordial matter disappears into the metaphysical – and invisible – identity which it, itself, helped to construct; an identity manifest via the combination of letters or matter, but still transcendent of it.

This violence of the letter aptly reflects the violence inherent in the motif of Cutting the Shoots; the unity is broken, pulled apart. In spilling the blood of language we untie worldly identities in an entropic process of deformation whereby elements take their natural 'shape' (which is no shape), in the Name of God.

There is, then, a kind of cosmic flattening in Abulafia – the Torah is flattened from its discrete words so that the single Name which it is becomes apparent; the world is flattened from its discrete objects and what is individual is lost, so uniting with the universal Intellect which is the Name. This entropic vision of a complete lack of structure thereby constitutes *perfect* order; everything becoming one in the reduction to the smallest elements, and the denial of metaphysics in the removal of contingent relations between parts. As letters must be effaced in order to generate the meaning of discrete words, so objects must be effaced to construct over and above them the grand order, that which *in toto* they constitute and which constitutes them. By breaking words into their components, we are going into the deep structure of reality, and the human gets closer to a God who is both eternally transcendent yet unfathomably immanent – masked only by the appearance of individual identities which make up our world. Once we see the structure of the Name present behind everything, and understand that the Name is unity itself, a pure simplicity beyond which nothing can be, we are in the presence of God; to be so is to be the *Sar haPannim*, Metatron, it is to have become so rational as to be completely identified with the truth of the cosmos, the Active Intellect, and to have the power to pass this knowledge prophetically on to others.

Thus we see that Abulafia pursues almost the inverse path to Gikatilla – whereas the latter conceived a cosmology beginning from the Name and ending in visible reality, Abulafia desires to transcend the immediate visible world, and actively reconstruct the divine unity from the elements, from the letters which, when united as Name, it will transcend. As I have argued previously that naming creates identities within the field of immanence, Abulafia's ecstatic method of mysticism aims to bring the divine into direct contact with the mystic's consciousness: the building of the Name from the letters which inhabit the subterranean level of the world around us forms a unified entity which is itself transcendent of those very letters. But what does this formation of divine identity, *as the Name*, mean, theologically?

Levinas writes that although theology 'does not reach the level of philosophical thought', this is only because the act of thinking God 'brings God into the course of being' (1996, 130) – necessarily then, theology (which is to say, the attempt to talk about God) fails, and fails because it attempts to talk *about* God. Theology appears here as the attempt to describe God, rather than to name Him. Enwording God is enworlding Him.

> The idea of God is God in me, but God already breaking up the consciousness which aims at ideas.... This difference is certainly not an emergence, which would be to imply that an inclusion of God in consciousness had been possible, nor some sort of escaping the realm of consciousness, which is to imply that there could have been *comprehension.*
>
> (Levinas, 1996, 136)

This correlation of making-meaningful and making-finite is clearly related to the Wittgensteinian attempt to make language coextensive with the world. If what is in the world can be expressed in perfect language, and what is not cannot, then the attempt to express God can only fail – ... if by *express* we mean *describe*. But what of the alternative attempt, to name?

In his later work, from *Otherwise Than Being* onwards, Levinas replaces the 'face' of the other as the site of the ethical encounter with the 'name'. This change in terminology indicates a more important shift in his thinking, as Michael Fagenblat (2010, 130) indicates: the name is not as simple a bearer as the face, and its significance lies in the fact that it displays a 'trace,' which suggests the presence while actually inscribing the absence of the other. Drawing on Maimonides' depiction of the Name YHWH as qualityless, signifying pure existence and nothing else, Levinas interprets the name of the other as the pure ethical presentation:

> [O]nly by negating the positive ideas one has of the other can one accede to the uniqueness signified by the proper name. Such a uniqueness can be signified only by the proper name, since phenomenological descriptions always refer to general predicates that never correlate with the uniqueness of the other.
>
> (Fagenblat, 2010, 129–130)

For Levinas, the name 'points to a sense in which human beings are not substances with fixed identities that can be described like common nouns but are individuated singularly like proper names – without essential attributes and unconvertible into a set of descriptions' (Fagenblat, 2010, 130). This 'realism without positivism' (ibid., 2010, 131) admits a oneness by means of its refusal to constrict to a given essence or predicate. I have argued that in naming we do not describe, and so cannot fail; but the name points outside of the world and to that which can only be shown. The name as a *point*, that smallest and indivisible aspect, then leads towards the infinite blackness which cannot be worded; the name, which is not in language, *shows* the essence which is not in the world although ironically it shows it only by concealing it, by showing that there *is* something concealed. What cannot be said is internality – the I Am of another.

This is the curious bipolarity of language – that while it opens, giving meaning and articulating for the understanding what otherwise could not be comprehended, at once it conceals, distancing the user from the inarticulate core of being which exists under, behind, language. Language then mediates but to that extent only provides a mediated access. What *is*, is in language and the world language describes, but *what* is, is in neither. The object itself *as object* is concealed by that which represents it, this being the name. But all this is platitudes; it is nothing more than to say that the manifest, the phenomenal, is not identical with the noumenal, the in-itself. What is more important is to see how this dialectic is enacted *within* the phenomenological immanence of selfhood. The attempt to name God, then, does not fail so long as we understand that name is not description: it forms a portal from the world, pointing outside of it and creates the possibility of referring to that which is indescribable. The Name is still not identical with that to which it points, but it does create the presence of otherhood in the world, tearing the literality of the world with a semantic black hole; rupturing the immanence of 'my world' with the transcendence of the Other. There is thus the presence of an other who is not present, who is not immanent within the world. The world of the self is then disunited, torn by transcendence; a united world, as Abulafia claims, is itself a unity – when the world is torn by objects it ceases to be a singularity and becomes a multiplicity. Naming thus destabilises what would otherwise be a pernicious locked-in-ness of being; by providing pinpoints of transcendence which break out of the literality of the world. Levinas calls it:

> The breakup of the actuality of thought in the 'idea of God', an 'unincludable idea' which 'overturns that presence to self which consciousness is, forcing its way through the barrier and checkpoint, eluding the obligation to accept or adopt all that enters from the outside'.
>
> (1996, 137)

At another point he writes that: 'To hear divine speech, does not revert to knowing an object, but to being in relation with a substance that exceeds its idea in me' (Levinas, 1969, 77) – the divine speech is a language consisting purely of names, as Gikatilla and Wittgenstein demonstrated. Language then is predicated on transcendental substance, substances which are conditioned by being named.

For Fagenblat:

> Levinas reduces discourse from nouns (or essences) to verbs (or actions) and finally to an approach to the proper name.... Ethical negative theology is the avowed response to proper names that designate the 'realism' of the Other in a nonessentialist, nondescriptivist, non-metaphysical sense.
>
> (2010, 131)

Because the Biblical God YHWH is thinkable, is personal, has a personality and a presence in the world, this manifest deity cannot be the undepictable Ein Sof. YHWH then, in this radicalisation of Maimonides' work, is entirely an effect of Ein Sof; the flame that dances on a coal in a black room as to illumine us, and indicate the coal without exhausting it.

It is perhaps strange to place Levinas in this chapter; while Abulafia argues explicitly for the deconstruction of worldly forms as the messianic goal, Fagenblat argues that Levinas saw this as the gateway to unfathomable evil – releasing the *tohu vavohu* which the names sealed safely away:

> To hold that evil is uncreated and present in the chaos of the unformed, indeterminate existence is to affirm that the goodness of the created world consists of its particularities and inherent distinctions and that all value resides in the singularity of phenomena. It is precisely this singularity that is jettisoned by reverting from creation to the indeterminate *tohu wa'bohu* or *il*

y a existence. Both the Priestly author and Levinas regard evil not as a lack but as the neutralization of the goodness of creation that takes place when the singularity of things and, above all, of persons is revoked.

(2010, 37)

This 'existence without a world' which Levinas trembled before seems to be exactly what Abulafia is aiming for by way of disintegrating identities. Now, I would like to suggest a method of resolving these claims, one which is challenging, but which will open the way for a new understanding of the kabbalistic theology and the development of some later aspects.

Levinas, in line with the argument I have been pursuing, claims that pure being, the existence of the world in itself, is evil – but this is only when it is stripped of the existant perspective, when one tries to view it without the ethical; the ethical is the framework that personhood places onto the world, by making it a creation, composed not of dead matter but of beings, singularities. This strongly implies that to get to the true essential being of the things we see we should not try to transcend personal viewpoints, but to go through individuality – the essences disappear when we remove ourselves from the role of subject, because a name cannot exist one-sided; it needs both object and subject. This 'suggests that a world without values "is" a world without facts, or is not a world at all but a sheer chaos of indeterminate existing' (Fagenblat, 2010, 49). All this suggests that the primal evil is in fact Ein Sof itself; Ein Sof creates from itself, which is also *tohu vavohu*, by generating a name which differentiates it from itself; it is then only names which constrain the evil, and only names which isolate Ein Sof from itself. This creates a tension with Abulafia's project of return to the source, because by doing this the mystic is in fact destroying all that exists and returning the world to evil, a world without identities; but these identities are dissolved into *the* Name, so that the Name YHWH is all that is left of reality. This primal evil, the *tohu vavohu* which constitutes Ein Sof, must demand an expression – the salvation of Ein Sof from itself comes in the generation of names, a process begun by the generation of *the* Name, YHWH, and which process is only reducible to the Name YHWH. YHWH, the third person articulation, delineates otherhood and by so doing, grounds selfhood – as the Name seals both God and the World, providing integrity and independence for each, the two now exist in distinction from each other; safe from the chaotic nihil of multiplicity which exists within each.[26]

The unification, then, is the denial of difference, the unification of the sefirot and world into a single body – the body of the Name. The letters, formerly spread across the sefirotic potencies and combined into the names of objects, are reunited to form the Name YHWH; the Name which is itself emanated from Ein Sof as a perceptible, external manifestation of the divine, and yet not separate but united fully as one with the essence by being the full expression of the being of God. The kabbalistic Unification of the Name is then the generation – or the invocation – of God into the presence of the mystic.

This process of naming, of unifying into a name, creates identities by tearing the fabric of subjective reality; but it does not create substance. The raw material is literal, in the world already; it is the base level of absolutely describable matter, represented by the atomic letters. But naming draws these letters together into objects, and these objects then admit something more than the material which constitutes them – there is an internality, a metaphysical unity which cannot be described because it doesn't conform to aggregates of letters. For Abulafia, in the dissolving of these identities, the letters reform in the process of Unifying the Name – so that all reality becomes unified as the single Name, the flat entropic state from which reality first emerged. This sealing of reality lifts all up into direct contiguity with God – we become the Name, indifferent from the symbolic structure of the Active Intellect.

Thus we see that the signifier, the Name of God, transcends and divides all reality; giving separation to the objects of existence. The Name, the Symbolic Order, allows for identity in principally separating God and world, giving internality as the principle for existence, it creates the paradigm of individuality and thus the interdependence of naming-selfhood-otherhood, which exist in a triangular (or perhaps rather, linear) relationship.

Abulafia's is the method of the reconstruction of signification from all else (from the mundane world). Objects are realised as identical with their signifiers, and those signifiers are broken into non-signifying elements which themselves reform into the primal root of signification, the Name of God the Father; that which signifies (and is) the symbolic order, which allows for meaning, allows for identity, and also generates or pre-exists the otherness of God Himself.

Notes

1 Scholem wrote that: 'This is the expression used by all kabbalists since Isaac for errors concerning the relationship between the sefiroth and God; it is not simply a general metaphor for heresy' (1987a, 394). For a bibliography of research on the original meaning of the phrase, see Abrams (1994, 295–6, esp. n14).

2 Many of the early Kabbalists (including Abulafia) denote the sefirot by the terms *devarim* (words) or *dibburim* (sayings) which, as we have seen previously with the root *davar*, can also mean simply 'things'. This usage surely descends from the ten creative *ma'amarot* (sayings) of the Talmud (e.g., m.Avot5.1, cf. b.Rosh Hash.32a, 'With ten *ma'amarot* the world was created' – which later became, in b.Hag.12a, 'the world was created with ten *devarim*'); an origin which may be reflected in the Bahir's unique usage of the term *ma'amarot* for the sefirot. The term *devarim* also indicates the conception of the sefirot as the primordial realities; they are *things*, objects, as opposed to that no-thing (*ayin*) which generates them. Sendor has noted that even the earliest Kabbalists associated the sefirot and *ma'amarot* – R Asher ben David writes that:

> [T]he philosophers called these ten *sefirot* spheres, saying they are ten, and they called them collectively the sphere of the intellect.... The author of *Sefer Yezirah*, the Rabbis and the philosophers, all equally agree that these things are ten ... but their [individual] names differ according to the language of the discipline.
> (*Perush Shem haMephorash*, Sendor, 1994, I, 94)

Isaac the Blind expresses the lower sefirot as *dibburim*, and states 'Chokhmah is the beginning of the thought of the word', and Keter 'is the thought of the beginning of the word' (Sendor, 1994, II, 274). On the development of the sefirotic schema from the philosophical commentaries to SY see Sendor (1994, I, 286–308), and for the Islamic influence Verman (1992, 129). Finally, it is worth highlighting the following passage from SY: 'His word [דבר] is in them [the sefirot] as though running and returning' (§8).

3 Because this is during a passage about the motions of the planets, I presume it to be condemnation of astronomy – suggesting that he failed to respect the difference between the intellectual world above and the phenomenal world below, thereby eliding the former into the latter.

4 The first use of it in reference to Hasidic tradition comes in the thirteenth century, with Eleazar of Worms' disciple R Shem Tov ben Simchah. His *The Intention of Prayers, from the Tradition of Rabbi Judah the Pious*, attempts a synthesis of Hasidic and kabbalistic ideas, identifying the Unique Cherub as Metatron. The earlier identification of the Cherub and Metatron in the German Pietists is uncertain – for and against, see Abrams (1994, 311) and Dan (1999, 228) – and explains the phrase 'My name is in him' as 'for His Name is the great Metatron who is called the little YHWH' (Dan, 1999, 227). For Simchah the sefirot:

> [A]re all degrees of the Creator. And the tenth degree is the sanctified cherub, to which the angels above direct their praise [so that their praise] will go before the Cause of Causes without separation and without cutting.... And so they should not err with their prayers and 'cut' and separate [a potency] by saying – God forbid – that there are two ruling powers.
>
> (Simchah, *Intention of Prayers*, Abrams 1994, 307–308)

Perhaps drawing from Shem Tov, the sixteenth century Hasid R Moshe haDarshan's *Sefer haQomah* uses the phrase more than once, and explicitly in reference to Metatron.

5 Sendor notes what may be the earliest example of this theme, in a liturgical poem of Solomon ibn Gabirol bearing the lines: 'This is Your name forever/to hide, for it is not expounded/In which are the ten *sefirot*/and the secret of the whole world is expressed' (1994, I, 292).

6 Ein Sof of course is understood as being not present in the Bible; in the words of an anonymous kabbalist quoted by Scholem: '*En-sof* is not even alluded to in the Torah or in the prophets, in the hagiographers or in the words of the sages; only the mystics received a small indication of it' (1987a, 443).

7 As Nachmanides also used the term – his claim of a created, primordial hylic element, a 'very subtle and immaterial point' emerging from the first sefirah and differentiated into the two distinct matters of the higher and the lower world (on this see Scholem, 1987a, 426) surely indicates the *yod*, the first letter which emerges from Ein Sof and then forms the Name.

8 This formal namelessness of Ein Sof should not be understood as a literal distinction between the Name and Ein Sof; rather, Ein Sof *happens* as the Name YHWH; in its presence to humans, Ein Sof appears as and through the Name YHWH, so the two are never distinct. The Name has no being other than in its connection with Ein Sof, and this fact shows the very reason for the importance of Unifying the Name: without this confirmation, the kabbalist may appear to divide between the Name and the essence, postulating an ontological divide between them similar to that discussed and rejected in Chapter 2.

9 This intrinsic relation of the subjective to the objective or ontological has been discussed by Goldberg (2001), who argues that the distinction between them is constantly blurred in the kabbalistic writings.

10 Eleazar connects the Name with the sefirot by use of the kabbalistic neologism HWYH, or 'essence'. Implicit in this text is the reading of YHWH as ten HWYH, ten beings. In this there is a suggestion that YHWH is the essence of everything – is essence itself; so, the ten *havayot* of direction are all comprised of him, and 'there is

none besides Him, and He is in everything and rules everything.' (*Sefer haShem*, Dan, 1998, 150). However, according to Joseph Dan:

> Rabbi Eleazar regarded the tetragrammaton as the ultimate linguistic expression of God: This whole treatise is dedicated to proving it. Yet in the beginning of the book he repeats twice the demonstration how inadequate even this sacred name is in expressing the essence of God.
>
> (1998, 170)

Contemporaneously, a pseudo-Hai responsum (*c.*1230) writes that 'the four-letter name and, still more, all of the other epithets [of God] are related specifically to the created Glory' (Scholem, 1987a, 351).

11 One passage explains that: 'The essence of His names express the wonder of His enterprise, hidden from everybody. He alone will announce His name and his power and the essence of His names'. He comments:

> [H]is true essences and powers are completely hidden, and God Himself will choose what and how to reveal. The revealed name is therefore such a choice: God chose to reveal an aspect of his name and essence by the structure of the Tetragrammaton.
>
> (Dan, 1999, 88)

Dan's investigation of this group demonstrates a similar understanding to these kabbalists, wherein 'The Tetragrammaton is used in these texts to indicate the Divine Glory' (1999, 75n83). However I cannot agree with the statement of Dan, that UCC present an idea:

> [R]ather radical in the context of Jewish understandings of the name YHVH. Here it is described unambiguously as a 'given name', one bestowed by Elohim on the Glory after its emanation, which is a part of the process of Creation. YHVH, therefore, is not an eternal being, nor is it the Creator. The sanctity usually attached to this name in Hebrew religious texts is hereby diminished, despite an emphasis on the identical nature of the emanated power and its source.
>
> (Dan, 1999, 147)

My investigation has so far established quite the opposite, that while the Name YHWH is an aspect of God, and therefore shares His Divinity, it is repeatedly envisioned as something of a lower entity to God Himself. The real innovation of the UCC is the utilisation of Elohim as the Name of the essence, rather than the kabbalists' (more logical) AHYH or Ein Sof. The only parallel I have found to this tradition is in the Samaritan writings analysed in Chapter 1.

12 On this see Idel (1989, 12–27), as well as the list of references collected by Wolfson (1999, 58n166).

13 Scholem famously rejected divine union in the Kabbalah, claiming that *devequt* 'is not union, because union with God is denied man even in that mystical upsurge of the soul, according to kabbalistic theology. But it comes as near to union as a mystical interpretation of Judaism would allow' (1987b, 203–204). Idel claimed that Abulafia was the proof against this (1998, 35–73). Lachter (2004) has, to my mind, conclusively shown that *devequt* in the Zohar is unification – in the most total sense – of the self with God. A detailed analysis of earlier traditions of divine union has been provided in Goldberg (2001).

14 Abulafia instructs us to:

> Separate [the elements of] the words, for at times a name may consist of even only one letter, which is regarded as if it were one whole word. This tells us that each letter is a world unto itself, according to the Kabbalah.
>
> (*Peras haSefer*, Idel, 2008, 23)

15 Wolfson (1990) has demonstrated that in the twelfth century ibn Ezra used the Neoplatonic term 'all' (*kol*) as the Active Intellect = Metatron = Name, being both Malkhut and
the whole of the tree. Thus in the sense that the word *kol* signifies 'the All that is a
whole before its parts', it 'serves for ibn Ezra as a name not for God in His essence ...
but rather for the demiurge which is also identified by ibn Ezra as the angelic Metatron'
(ibid., 1990, 80–81). In fact it seems as if Ezra already identified Metatron with the
'God of Israel,' thereby pre-empting Abulafia's identification of Metatron as the primal
manifestation or demiurge who contains, in nascent form, all things. Wolfson writes:

> The notion that the Universal Intellect is the cause or agent of all things in virtue
> of containing them all within itself is repeated ... in the Arabic paraphrases of
> Plotinus that were widely circulated and read in both Islamic and Jewish circles.
>
> (1990, 90)

The *kol* = Name identity is also heavily implied by ibn Ezra (1990, 01–2); and he
explicitly states *hitbodedut* (self-seclusion or concentration; i.e., meditation) as cleav-
ing to the Name (1990, 106). In another text Wolfson also notes the following passage
in the anonymous *Sefer haNavon*, a non-Pietistic text which draws on their ideas:

> The name [YHWH] appears in its letters to the angels and prophets in several forms
> and radiance and it appears in the image of the appearance of an anthropos ... this
> refers to the *Shekhina* and the angel of the glory, which is the Tetragrammaton.
>
> (Wolfson, 1995, 74)

Abulafia does mention that Metatron = 314 = I am created (*ani nivra*) (Wolfson 1995,
77n87). For precursors to the identification of Metatron with the Active Intellect see
Idel (1998, 349n27).

16 On this see Idel (1989, 111). Abulafia also writes that the Torah:

> [I]s a name referring to the Active Intellect, which is called the Word of God, or
> the Spirit of God, or His Speech or His Name or His Glory, for it instructs the
> sages of the Name, in the knowledge and comprehension of Him.
>
> (Idel, 1989, 36)

17 As he puts it in another text:

> You should bind together all of the letters with the letters themselves, for they are
> the roots of all their existence according to what they indicate, *for all of the bodies
> are signs by which to discern through them the Name as well.*
>
> (*Perush haSefer Yetzirah*, Wolfson, 1996, 58, my emphasis)

18

> Abulafia clearly expresses the idea that only by breaking apart the conventional
> form of words can one attain a higher level of knowledge, i.e., knowledge of the
> Name of God.... Only by means of the murder of the languages, the spilling of
> blood, can one attain to the knowledge of the Name.
>
> (Idel, 1989, 27)

19 'Know in truth that the comprehension of the Agent Intellect is found within the
twenty-two holy letters', Cited in Idel (2008, 11). He argues that Abulafia may have
understood the term Jew (יהודי) 'as an allegory for the perfect knowledge of the divine
name' (ibid., 2008, 22). It seems that Abulafia also interpreted the 'name' AHWY as
related to this process, due to its gematria value of twenty-two.

20 See especially:

> [T]he essence of the Blessed Creator is the conception of all existence, which is
> why He is called intellect ... the conceiver and conceived are never different as
> long as the intellect is actualized, though if it is only potential, they are different.
>
> (*Get Ha-Shemot*, Abulafia, 2007, 4)

21 This emphasis on becoming the Name may play on a Maimonidean motif that the attributes of action (i.e. the sefirot; the Name) are at once all that we can know of God, the trace of Him that is present in our world, and that behaviour to which we should try to attain – the ethical paradigm for humanity: 'For the utmost in virtue is to become like unto Him, may He be exalted, as far as he is able; which means that we should make our actions like unto His' (Maimonides, 1956, I.54, 128).
22 On this in Philo, see Burnett (1984).
23 I am minded to relate to this Gikatilla's claim that 'those who cleave to the letters of the Tetragrammaton exist and live forever' (ShN 38a, Martini, 2010, 46).
24 This same point is expressed by Gikatilla, who claims that knowledge of God can be attained only via the Torah, which is the outermost manifestation of His attributes:

> Those who know the Torah attain the Name (*hashem*) may It be blessed, face to face, since they are in the center of the point that is the sacred inner courtyard, while the rest of the nations circle the perimeter that surrounds the point, and they remain outside.
>
> (GE343)

Morlok comments:

> [T]hey will see the divine face to face, as they stand at the middle point (a clear reference to creation, the secret of the inner palace). To stand at this point is to be incorporated in the textual embodiment of the name, the Torah, i.e. the imagined body constituted by the letters of the divine name, which contains all the letters of the Hebrew alphabet.
>
> (2011, 185)

25 In fact Lacan describes the role of the letter as 'materialis[ing] the agency of death' (2002, 52). In this the Real of the letter, threatening yet buried beneath the symbolic strata of the word, reflects the Real of the Father who threatens castration yet is hidden behind the symbolic Name of the Father.
26 Levinas writes of the Hasidic thinker Hayim Volozhiner, that humanity's internal nature is not defined independently but rather always in relation to God, and by relationship with that Big Other: 'It is not through substantiality – through an in-itself and a for-itself – that man and his interiority are defined, but through the "for the other": for that which is above self' (1994, 161).

Bibliography

The Babylonian Talmud (32 vols). 1990. Edited by Rabbi Dr. I. Epstein. London: The Soncino Press.

Pirkê de Rabbi Eliezer: (The Chapters of Rabbi Eliezer the Great) According to the Text of the Manuscript Belonging to Abraham Epstein of Vienna. 1916. Translated by Gerald Friedlander. London: Kegan Paul.

The Zohar (12 vols). 2003–2014. Translated by Daniel C. Matt. Stanford: Stanford University Press.

Abrams, Daniel. 1994. The Boundaries of Divine Ontology: The Inclusion and Exclusion of Metatron in the Godhead. *Harvard Theological Review* 87(3), 291–321.

Abulafia, Abraham. 2007. *Get Ha-Shemot*. Translated by Fabrizio Lanza. Monfalcone: Providence University.

Burnett, F.W. 1984. Philo on Immortality: A Thematic Study of Philo's Concept of *palingenesia*. *Catholic Bible Quarterly* 46(3), 447–470.

Brody, Seth Lance. 1991. *Human Hands Dwell in Heavenly Heights: Worship and Mystical Experience in Thirteenth Century Kabbalah*. PhD diss., University of Pennsylvania.

Dan, Joseph. 1986. *The Early Kabbalah.* Mahwah: Paulist Press,.

Dan, Joseph. 1998. *Jewish Mysticism Volume II: The Middle Ages.* New Jersey: Jason Aronson Inc.

Dan, Joseph. 1999. *The 'Unique Cherub' Circle: A School of Mystics and Esoterics in Medieval Germany.* Tübingen: Mohr Siebeck.

Fagenblat, Michael. 2010. *A Covenant of Creatures: Levinas' Philosophy of Judaism.* Stanford: Stanford University Press.

Goldberg, Joel R. 2001. *Mystical Union, Individuality and Individuation in Provencal and Catalonian Kabbalah.* PhD diss., New York University.

Hayman, A. Peter. 2004. *Sefer Yesira: Edition, Translation and Text-Critical Commentary.* Tübingen: Mohr Siebeck.

Idel, Moshe. 1988. *Kabbalah: New Perspectives.* London: Yale University Press.

Idel, Moshe. 1989. *Language, Torah, and Hermeneutics in Abraham Abulafia.* Albany: State University of New York Press.

Idel, Moshe. 1998a. Abulafia's Secrets of the Guide: A Linguistic Turn. *Revue de Métaphysique et de Morale* 4, 495–528.

Idel, Moshe. 1998b. *Messianic Mystics.* London: Yale University Press.

Idel, Moshe. 2008. A Unique Manuscript of an Untitled Treatise of Abraham Abulafia in Biblioteca Laurentiana Medicea. *Kabbalah: Journal for the Study of Jewish Mystical Texts* 17, 7–28.

Idel, Moshe. 2011. *Kabbalah in Italy 1280–1510: A Survey.* New Haven: Yale University Press.

Lacan, Jacques. 2002. *Ecrits: A Selection.* Translated by Bruce Fink. London: W.W. Norton & Company.

Lachter, Hartley. 2004. *Paradox and Mystical Union in the Zohar.* PhD diss., New York University.

Lachter, Hartley. 2008. Kabbalah, Philosophy, and the Jewish–Christian Debate: Reconsidering the Early Works of Joseph Gikatilla. *Journal of Jewish Thought and Philosophy* 16(1), 1–58.

Levinas, Emmanuel. 1969. *Totality and Infinity.* Translated by Alphonso Lingis. Pittsburgh: Duqense University Press.

Levinas, Emmanuel. 1994. *Beyond the Verse: Talmudic Readings and Lectures.* Translated by Gary D. Mole. Bloomington: Indiana University Press.

Levinas, Emmanuel. 1996. *Basic Philosophical Writings.* Edited by Adriaan T. Peperzak, Simon Critchley and Robert Bernasconi. Bloomington: Indiana University Press.

Maimonides, Moses. 1956. *The Guide for the Perplexed.* Translated by M. Friedlander. New York: Dover.

Martini, Annett, ed. 2010. *Yosef Giqatilla The Book of Punctuation: Flavius Mithridates' Latin Translation, The Hebrew Text, and an English Version.* Torino: Nino Aragno Editore.

Matt, Daniel. 1995. *The Essential Kabbalah: The Heart of Jewish Mysticism.* Edison: Castle Books.

Miller, Michael T. 2009. *The Epistemological Role of the Archangel Metatron.* MA diss., Lancaster University.

Morlok, Elke. 2011. *Rabbi Joseph Gikatilla's Hermeneutics.* Tübingen: Mohr Siebeck.

Pachter, Mordechai. 2004. *Roots of Faith and Devekut.* Los Angeles: Cherub Press.

Scholem, Gershom. 1934. Te'udah Hadashah le-Toldot Reshit ha-Kabbalah. In: Jacob Fichman. ed. *Sefer Bialik.* Tel Aviv: Hotsa'at Va'ad ha-Yovel uve-Hishtatfut Hotsa'at Omanut, 7–34.

Scholem, Gershom. 1987a. *The Origins of the Kaballah.* Edited by R.J. Werblowsky, translated by Allan Arkush. Princeton: Princeton University Press.

Scholem, Gershom. 1987b. *Kabbalah.* New York: Dorset Press.

Scholem, Gershom. 1995. *Major Trends in Jewish Mysticism.* Third edition. New York: Schocken.

Sendor, Mark Brian. 1994. *The Emergence of Provencal Kabbalah: Rabbi Isaac the Blind's Commentary on Sefer Yezirah.* PhD diss., Harvard University.

Travis, Yakov M. 2002. *Kabbalistic Foundations of Jewish Practice: Rabbi Ezra of Gerona On the Kabbalistic Meaning of the Mitzvot.* PhD diss., Brandeis University.

Verman, Mark. 1992. *The Books of Contemplation: Medieval Jewish Mystical Sources.* Albany: State University of New York Press.

Weiss, Tzahi. 2009. On the Matter of Language: The Creation of the World from Letters and Jacques Lacan's Perception of Letters as Real. *Journal of Jewish Thought and Philosophy* 17(1), 101–115.

Wijnhoven, Jochanan H.A. 1964. *Sefer ha-Mishkal: Text and Study.* PhD diss., Brandeis University.

Wolfson, Elliot R. 1990. God, the Demiurge and the Intellect: On the Usage of the Word *Kol* in Abraham ibn Ezra. *Revue des Etudes Juives* 149, 77–111.

Wolfson, Elliot R. 1995. Metatron and Shi'ur Qomah in the Writings of the Haside Ashkenaz. In: Karl Erich Grözinger and Joseph Dan. eds. *Mysticism, Magic and Kabbalah in Ashkenazi Judaism: International Symposium Held in Frankfurt a.M. 1991.* Berlin: Walter de Gruyter, 60–92.

Wolfson, Elliot R. 1996. The Doctrine of Sefirot in the Prophetic Kabbalah of Abraham Abulafia. *Jewish Quarterly Review* 3(1), 47–84.

Wolfson, Elliot R. 1999. The Glorious Name and the Incarnate Torah. In: Ade Berlin and Marc Zvi Brettler. eds. *The Jewish Study Bible 1979–1990.* Oxford: Oxford University Press.

Wolfson, Elliot R. 2000. *Abraham Abulafia – Kabbalist and Prophet: Hermeneutics, Theosophy, and Theurgy.* Los Angeles: Cherub Press.

7   Redemption in the Name

Walter Benjamin's kabbalistic Messianism

> But the meaning of 'This is its name' [Genesis 2:19], is that it is its true name, in accordance with Divine wisdom, based on the Supernal Book. For Adam received it all by way of Kabbalah, and the Holy One Blessed be He informed him of the secret orders of the universe, the secrets of His Chariots, the ways of causality and the hidden potencies behind all orders; and after He had informed him of these he was properly able to call each thing by its true name, in accordance with the Divine intent.
>
> (Gikatilla, *Be'ure ha-Moreh*, Idel, 1998, 299)[1]

The influence on Walter Benjamin of the Kabbalah has been noted, on occasion, but only a small amount of time has been spent in investigating the nature of this influence which Benjamin himself seems to have understood as crucial. Richard Wolin relates Benjamin's assertions that 'only someone familiar with Kabbalah ... would be able to understand the notoriously difficult prologue to the *Trauerspiel* study' (1994, 37), and Idel (2010, 168–175) has argued for the influence, via Scholem, of Abulafia's theory of language on Benjamin's own.[2] Having investigated at length the linguistic theory of the early Kabbalah, I would now like to move the investigation forward some 700 years in order to argue that Benjamin presents the logical conclusion of those doctrines developed in the thirteenth century.

Naming in Eden

> God did not create man from the word, and he did not name him. He did wish to subject him to language, but in man God set language, which had served *him* as a medium of creation, free. God rested when he had left his creative power to itself in man. This creativity, relieved of its divine activity, became knowledge. Man is the knower in the same language in which God is creator. God created him in his image, he created the knower in the image of the creator.
>
> (Benjamin, 1996, 68)

While the kabbalists saw Hebrew as the original, natural, language, one given by God and into which is encoded the exact nature of all things, Benjamin rather talks of the 'pure language' of nature, the silent tongue in which objects communicate themselves phenomenally. For Benjamin the role of the human in interpreting this self-expression can be found in Genesis 2:19–20, where God brings the animals and birds He had formed before Adam, in order for Adam to name them. In this passage, unlike the initial narrative of creation, it is not God but the human who names. Adam here takes the role of overseer, providing titles to the animals. That these names are not arbitrary is implied by the Biblical text: the verb קרא, 'to call/name', means also to *read out*. Therefore when Adam names, he is not merely applying a sign to the object, but is interpreting its being into words: he 'reads' it.[3]

But language for Benjamin is not simply a human system of signs, and the reading of nature is not a passive reception and description. Rather, language is an essential component of phenomenal reality; it is the coming together of nature and human, object and subject, in communication – in order for nature to be read it must speak itself, and speak itself *to* human beings. Recalling the linguistic interface between elements described by Rosenzweig, Benjamin claims that all knowledge occurs *as* language, and the extent to which something is knowable is *its* language; its capacity to speak is its capacity to be known: 'Language is thus the mental being of things' (Benjamin, 1996, 66).

Objects, then, interact through a self-expression of their intellectual nature, and this self-expression is structured as language. Therefore, language is coextensive 'with absolutely everything'. Because all objects that are apprehended by the mind give of themselves to some degree, and this action of giving is a communicative one: 'There is no event or thing in either animate or inanimate nature that does not in some way partake of language, for it is in the nature of each one to communicate its mental contents' (ibid., 1996, 62). It is the 'speakable' being of an object which it itself communicates – language being the faculty in which things express themselves to each other and thus is not merely a human capacity, but is the prerequisite of relation between any two or more objects. We 'cannot imagine a total absence of language in anything. An existence entirely without relationship to language is an idea; but this idea can bear no fruit even within that realm of ideas whose circumference defines the idea of God' (ibid.).

Unlike Hebrew, Benjamin's natural language is one which contains no words and is not in itself complete. Rather it depends on the interpretative action of humans to complete it. The human, in giving names to things, is effecting this completion. Like Adorno, Benjamin always rejects the unity of appearance and being, of a reality with its idea: 'The view that the mental essence of a thing consists precisely in its language ... is the great abyss' which we must avoid, for: 'Mental being communicates itself in, not through, language, which means: it is not outwardly identical with linguistic being' (1996, 63). Benjamin draws a clear distinction between the language of a thing (that which is communicated), the mental being (that which is capable of being communicated in language) and the thing itself. Because the mental being of objects is not their name, language must always be something of a misreading; or a translation. There is always some subtle play of difference between an object and its name. While Adam reads the animals and then produces the correct names for them, these names are not what those beings communicate to him: humankind must transform this base phenomenal expression into final, verbal language. Names, therefore, are not provided by the world but depend on being processed by humanity.

In translating the being of objects into their names, humans evince a transformation – a name is not the essence, nor is it merely description, it is a step away from the simple being of things into a new realm. The misreading which is a name can take us further, away from the merely real, and into the *true*. This process of translation from the factual into the nominal should not be confused with the untranslatability of names into factual descriptions, for the creation of name is the refusal of a being's reduction to facts, and instead the admission of a being which transcends facts. It takes us away from the insignificant natural world and begins the generation of a metaphysics – that practice by which alone redemption is possible. This is 'the task of the coming philosophy', which is:

> [T]he discovery or creation of the concept of knowledge which, insofar as it relates the concept of experience *exclusively* to the transcendental consciousness, renders possible not only mechanical but also religious experience. Which is not to say that knowledge renders God possible, but rather that it first makes the experience and doctrine of God possible.
>
> (*Gesammelte Schriften* 2, 164, Wolin, 1994, 35)

This process of translating, of naming, provides both the meaning of the linguistic being of the world, and the meaning of human consciousness. The fact that 'Adam' is used as a proper name for the first time only at Genesis 2:20, the point when he is naming other things, suggests to Benjamin that Adam's full individuality is corollary to (and dependent upon) the fulfilling of his role as namer, as the one who completes creation by providing the names for its elements. So: 'Man ... communicates his own mental being ... by *naming* all other things' (1996, 64). In fact, language is the totality of humanity's mental being where this mental being is then uniquely 'communicable without residue' (1996, 65), and it is the being of humans to name things; which is to say, to translate *their* mental being into names.

This naming is not humanity merely *knowing* the correct names of things; it is not a passive understanding of the nature of things; it is rather the *giving* of correct names. Benjamin writes that the mystical (kabbalistic) theory that 'the word is simply the essence of the thing ... is incorrect, because the thing in itself has no word' (1996, 69). Nature itself speaks in 'a nameless, unspoken language,' so in itself, the thing is nothing – it is simply an aggregate, a chaos which requires articulation into identity by an other. To be a thing, it must speak *and be heard;* and it is the peculiar role of humanity to translate the silent speech of a thing's being into its name. Humanity then acts as the finaliser of the linguistic process of being, by stating – which is not a repeating – the names of the world. Unlike Abulafia, who sees the name as the nature which humanity is able to read, indeed must read in order to go behind the phenomenal and progress back towards God's unity, for Benjamin the name is the final stage in the world's emergence into being; a stage which is realised in human perception and which is articulated in the process of naming. In this sense, naming takes humans not back and down into the roots of reality, but up and forward into the divine realm which the human activity projects.

Thus: 'God's creation is completed when things receive their names from man' (Benjamin, 1996, 65). But humanity is also completed in our giving of names to things; we express our own nature through the activity of naming. This aspect of the completion of creation is part and parcel of divinely prescribed human nature.

This process of naming as a redemptive translation into the spiritual realm is founded on a transformation of Abulafia's atomistic cosmology. In *The Origin of German Tragic Drama* (1977) Benjamin argues that in the interpretative action of consciousness, the phenomenal must be broken into its constituents in order to be reformed not as what it *is* but as what it *should be*:

> Phenomena ... do not enter the realm of ideas whole, in their crude empiri-cal state, adulterated by appearance, but rather [are] redeemed only in their elements. Broken up into parts they are deprived of their false unity in order to take part in the genuine reality of truth. In this their disintegration, phe-nomena are subordinated to their concepts; the latter are what bring about the dissolution of things into their elements.
>
> (1977, 33)

It is via forming concepts that we deconstruct the phenomenal into its constitu-ents and it is via the subsequent forming of an *idea* that we reconstruct them into a new form: creating an idea from those elements then reforms them into some-thing new, and something which is both eternal and transcendent. Benjamin argues that an idea has the same relationship to the phenomenon that it repres-ents, as a constellation does to the stars it contains: 'Ideas are timeless constella-tions and by virtue of the elements' being seen as points in such constellations, phenomena are subdivided and at the same time redeemed' (Benjamin, 1977, 34). As Wolin explains:

> It is only upon being dissolved into their constituent elements that phe-nomena are first rendered fit for the ultimate philosophical reordering in the redemptive embrace of the constellation, for the latter consists of nothing more than the simple rearrangement of these elements themselves.
>
> (1994, 94–95)

This is the retranslation of the base material of the phenomenal into the intelli-gible. The intelligible representation, though, does not incorporate the object itself: rather, it signifies it. Clearly then this is something different from idealism, which would specify the object as identical to the intellectually graspable. This redemptive translation into the intelligible realm is a process of *naming*: 'The

translation of the language of things into the language of man is not only a translation of the mute into the sonic; it is also the translation of the nameless into
name' (Benjamin, 1996, 70).

The name, as I have argued previously, does not comprehend or give access
to the inner nature of its referent, but rather provides the simple unity behind
which its complexity is concealed. This then constitutes not access to the objects
but their liberation, and even their liberation from subjectivity (for ideas are the
'objective interpretation' of phenomena).[4] It is only in the translation into idea
that an object 'becomes something different: a totality' (Benjamin, 1977, 46).
And exactly as we saw in Wittgenstein's Tractarian nominal theory, every totality contains 'an indistinct abbreviation of the rest of the world of ideas' (1977,
48) and 'every idea contains the image of the world' (ibid.). The name is a 'state
of being beyond all phenomenality' which 'determines the manner in which
ideas are given. But they are not given so much in a primordial language as in a
primordial form of perception, in which words possess their own nobility as
names, unimpaired by cognitive meaning' (1977, 36). Wolin comments that
here, 'the name, by virtue of its sheer lack of intention, thereby prefigures a condition of universal being-for-self' (1994, 103). This intentionless quality of
naming is something Benjamin also refers to as 'the primordial form of perception' (ibid.).

The suggestion here is that there is a semantic, though prelinguistic, nature to
reality, one to which the human mind is attuned – or even, isomorphic – in order
to express this nature linguistically. Named language is the final manifestation of
reality. And to say this is perhaps not to admit that there must be a distinction
between such a semantic substructure in nature, or in the mind; it is merely to
assert that the deep structure of *the reality which is perceived* is essentially
semantic, is patterned according to the logic which facilitates language; and this
too is not to say that *a* language is more or less correct than another, as languages act as a mere expression of the underlying semantic logic which is the
logic of language singular. The seventy languages of Jewish tradition, then, are
diffracted aspects of the single language, which itself is not *a* language but only
the possibility of language, encoded into the interpretation of reality. And thereby
it is the divine nature of human beings to give names, to divinise reality; in
naming we lift the world into a messianic state. The world as named by human
beings effects and finalises God's creation, which may also be the creation of
God, God's Name as the final state of reality – the seal which can only be
applied once the world is complete in its creation, and the seal which also finally
differentiates God and world once each is named. The names we give all speak
of, participate in, and actualise, the Name of God. It is because: 'Only the
Messiah himself consummates all history, in the sense that he alone redeems,
completes, creates its relation to the Messianic' (Benjamin, 1978, 312), that we
may conclude the Messiah must bear the Name of God, and even *be* the Name of
God. The Name takes its role as that which posits correct relationship between
creation and divinity. The Name is the final thing, almost no-thing, that one
dimensional brane or point of contact between two which defines each in accord

with the other. When Benjamin claims that 'the language of things can pass into the language of knowledge and name only through translation – as many translations, so many languages – once man has fallen from the paradisiac state that knew only one language' where that language was 'perfect knowledge' (1996, 70–71) – a direct pre-nominal language, one that we must transcend by translating knowledge into name, the correct name – which is knowledge not of things as they are, but the forming of things as they should be. 'The paradisiac language of man must have been one of perfect knowledge; whereas later all knowledge is again infinitely differentiated in the multiplicity of language, was indeed forced to differentiate itself on a lower level as creation in name' (Benjamin, 1996, 71). The original language has no separation between subject and object, it lacks the play of difference – it in fact is no mediation at all.

Benjamin argues that Knowing is a constructive activity – not merely a passive reflection on the world, but the epistemic completion of it. I have talked previously about the role of the Name of God in sealing creation – but for Benjamin it is the human, as the namer, who epistemically seals reality into being, and who therefore elicits a *material* redemption by transforming the raw chaos of the material sphere into the ordered types, forms, identities and *natural kinds*. This process of naming, of enwording and sealing is a partaking of divine reparation or prelation – by translating the linguistic being of things into names, humanity elevates these things into the divine sphere; we make them metaphysical. The essence of metaphysics is identity, and in prescribing individual identity to objects, they participate in the transcendental, which is to say they are incorporated into the identity of identities: God. In becoming named, objects participate in the Name of God, that which confers the possibility of identity on all and which acts as the gravitational pull towards the manifold singularity of identities which ultimately – Messianically – speak of the unity of all in the identity of God.

The change of name

> For Benjamin, language, once released from the correspondence model of truth, might provide the path to another realm of possibilities, to the recognition of altogether different 'correspondences'. Set free from the nefarious effects of instrumental reason, language was to regain some of its lost aura. Once humans recognized language's unfathomed revolutionary potential, perhaps it might field a blow, issue a redemptive shock, undoing the numbing anaesthetic and aestheticized shock effects of modernity's culture of dispersal.
>
> (Hanssen, 2004, 55–56)

Benjamin records that he was given two 'very unusual' names in addition to his known ones, in order apparently to facilitate his postulated writing career. Benjamin hid them 'as the Jews used to watch over the secret name that they gave to each of their children', which was kept concealed until Bar Mitzvah.

This name is that 'which contains in itself all the life forces, and by which the latter can be summoned forth and guarded against the unauthorized'. He relates his own transformation, as he 'stepped out of the old name' whereby the transfiguration of the secret name 'reveal[s] itself on the occasion of a new maturity' (Benjamin, 1999, 712).

According to the philosophy outlined above, language – and especially names – are not merely descriptive, not here merely to correspond with the world. Instead, language offers the potential to change realities and to ameliorate the world. Benjamin's change of his name, wherein he claims his true or secret name, correlates to, or perhaps even causes, a change in nature – a shedding of the skin. This motif, this notion of the name as something which can be changed, hidden and revealed, signifying a shift in fate or even ontology is common in Jewish thought: in the Bible God changes human names, Avram and Sarai having their names changed with the addition of a *heh* (Gen.17:5–15), and Jacob becoming Israel once he has wrestled God's angel (Gen.32:28, 35:10). These nominal shifts represent not just a change in moniker, but assert the character's renewed and transformed destiny; their future role has taken on a new significance, one which was not inevitable but must be conferred by God on His chosen.[5]

Robert Hall (2011) has offered an unusual reading of *Similitudes* which highlights the role of the name in a similar aspect. In Chapter 43 Enoch witnesses the stars of heaven, which heed God and whom he calls by name; these stars, Enoch is informed, 'are the names of the holy ones who dwell on the earth and believe in the name of the Lord of spirits forever and ever' (43:4). The stars' obedience to God is a direct corollary of their being named by him; their natures are defined and prescribed. Hall argues that Enoch's inheritance of the name 'Son of Man' is similar to God's naming of the stars. So: 'When Enoch inherits his heavenly name, he becomes Son of Man. When his followers inherit their heavenly names, they will each become the star God names each to be' (Hall, 2011, 324). This nominal inheritance is bound up with conforming to God's knowledge, such that a being only inherits their name when they become identical with what God commands of them. This conforming to God's knowledge or wisdom is, Hall argues, the Similitudes' model of salvation:

> [H]aving ascended to see God, conforming to his knowledge, they shall find out who they really are as they inherit their real names. By seeking God's knowledge and conforming themselves to it, Enoch and all the righteous take their proper stations in God's presence. Conforming to God's mind is salvation: as they conform to God's knowing they become what he knows them to be.
>
> (2011, 325)

Salvation, then, is the assuming of a role or office which has been predetermined; in becoming one with a heavenly archetypal form, Enoch and his followers actually take on names which are new yet old; names reserved for them as they stepped into a new skin (bringing to mind Is.49:1: 'From my mother's womb he has called my name'). As the righteous inherited their names once they altered themselves to align with God's plan and precognitive knowledge, so Benjamin assumes his new name, his secret, *hidden* name, only 'on the occasion of a new maturity' (1999, 712). If, as I have argued previously, the name represents the relationship in which subject and object stand to each other, the *correct* name then indicates the just relationship. To change one's *own* name is to change one's relationship with oneself; and to allow new qualities to emerge in one's relationship with the world. Thus, taking a new name is not as simple as a mere internal ontological shift, but is principally an external event: one which redefines ones' place in the world, altering the relations into which identity is bound and from which it is constructed.

Wolin writes that in Benjamin's earliest work, 'the utter sinfulness of the creaturely world described in the allegories of the baroque epitomizes a confused, godless condition in which name and thing have become separated' (Wolin, 1994, 68).[6] This separation of name and object is familiar to us – it is a form of Cutting the Shoots, of desecrating the relationship between the *phe-nominal* and the essential. The kabbalist Jacob ben Jacob Kohen writes similarly:

> But if one wants to make some precise relation with the proper names of men, one will find that they and the being (or essences) (which they denote) are one, with the result that the name cannot be separated and differentiated from the being (or essence), nor, similarly, the being (nor essence) from the name. Because the name is directly linked with the being (or essence)...
>
> (Scholem, 1973, 177)

Abulafia wrote often about the change of his own name, and famously claimed that at the heights of mystical union, the seer (who is likely meant to be Abulafia himself, at the point of his own messianic identification[7]), 'will be messiah to God, his very messenger, *and will be called the Angel of God. And his name shall be like the name of his master, Shaddai, who shall name him Metatron, Prince of the Presence*' (*Hayyei Olam ha-Ba* 32a, Idel, 1989 [amended], 295).[8] This passage suggests likewise the importance of naming in the change of nature; nothing is exacted upon the seer except his being (re-)named by God. The shift in nature and God's act of naming are identical.

This notion that everything has a secret or hidden name, we may call Messianic Naming – the implied notion is that these names are realised only at the advent of the messianic age, the Messiah then being the one who knows how to correctly name every thing and person – including God. In revealing the correct names, the true identity of every thing becomes apparent, and correct relations between all can be resumed. This is the form of redemption as it appears in Benjamin's philosophy.

When everything takes its correct name, all is in its right place – and reality equates to the *Book of Life*, the list of the righteous who are to be preserved from the world, a motif repeatedly referenced in the apocalyptic literature of Late Antiquity.[9] That point is when this world becomes united with the world-to-come, with the supernal (archetypal) structure – and in becoming textual, reality itself ascends to a prior, more abstract, form. We *become* our names, there is no distinction (as Enoch did: He became like the angels whose names defined their nature, who were without will, and therefore purely textual). The world dissolves into Torah, which itself dissolves back into the names of God that comprise it – so eventually the big crunch resolves (*tikkun*) the face of God – no longer differentiated, no longer diffused, simply God and Name will again be one.

Here, name *is* description. When there is no distinction and name is essence, otherhood is vitiated. All is flattened and reabsorbed, as the Torah becomes reabsorbed into God by becoming His Name. His name will be one (Zech.14:9), one with Him as everything will be one with their names, once they will be known solely by their true (messianic) name.[10]

The single name and the single language

> And they [the languages] will continue to be so confused until the coming of the redeemer, when the entire land will return to the only clear language, as it is written: 'For then I will turn to all nations a pure language, that they may all call upon the Name of God and serve Him with one consent, with One Name.' [Zeph.3:9]
>
> (Abulafia, *Sefer Shomer Mitzvah*, Idel, 1989, 26)

Abulafia and Gikatilla both claim that in the Messianic Age the seventy languages of the world generated at the collapse of Babel will be reaccommodated into Hebrew so that only the Divine language remains. However, as this passage explains, the crucial aspect of this is that at this messianic point, all nations will then name God with the same Name.[11] Having discussed the multiple names of God in the Hekhalot literature, manifest as angelic princes, I will now begin to tie this theme into more recent developments in nominal theology.

We find this association of names with angels in many kabbalistic writings. Jacob ben Jacob Kohen, in a passage which identifies the seventy-two letter name formed from Exodus 14:19–21 with the seventy-two princes of the Hekhalot literature, depicts the names themselves as angelic entities:

> Note that the seventy-two holy names (that is in the sovereign world of the Merkaba) serve and are united with the essence of the Merkaba itself. And they are like gleaming pillars of light and are called (in the Bible) *bnei Elohim*, and the whole host of heaven regards them with reverence, like retainers paying homage to the king's sons...
>
> (Scholem, 1973, 176)

In the *Alphabet of Rabbi Akiva*, the names are represented somewhat similarly, in fiery depiction; fiery like the bodies of the angels: 'God sits upon a throne of fire and around him stand the ineffable names, *Shemoth meforashim*, like pillars of fire.' (Jellinek 1855, III, 25).

In a text dedicated to the Throne of God, Jacob ben Sheshet writes:

> This is the rule – the attached entity is called by the name of the thing to
> which it is attached; and the thing by the name of that which is attached to
> it. So too the guard [is called by the name] of that which is guarded, as when
> the verb is called by the name of the act, and the guarded by the name of the
> guard. Since the Holy One, blessed be He, guards all creation, the text says,
> 'Everyone that is called by My name, for I have created him for My Glory.'
> [Is.43:7].
>
> *(Response of Correct Answers: The Holy Throne and the Commandments*
> Ch.2, Dan, 1986, 134)

This passage seems to refer to the relationship between Metatron and God, the
former being the attachment which is called by the name of that to which it is
attached. Sheshet goes on to assert that the 'Name [which] is great among the
nations' (Mal.1:11) actually represents the angelic guardian (the seventy
'thrones' being the seventy angels united with God and therefore called by his
Name) placed over them, to which they have offered worship in the place
of God:

> His *Name* is great among the nations, and they offer incense to His
> *Name.* But it does not say *I* am great or that they offer to *Me;* rather
> everything is linked to His Name, may He be blessed. Therefore I say
> that their intention was to the Name of God, but they followed in error
> after the messengers appointed over them. These messengers were their
> celestial leaders...
>
> *(Response of Correct Answers: The Holy Throne and the Commandments*
> Ch.3, Dan, 1986, 134)

Sheshet then links this to the admonition given in b.Sanhedrin 38b: 'do not
exchange Me [God] for him [the angel]'. But, 'the sum of all these thrones is the
Torah, which is the belief of the truth and the unity [of God]' (ibid.). Here we
find that the Torah is composed of names or thrones which are the princes over
the seventy nations, and which are bound in unity to God Himself – and thus the
Torah itself is composed of names or angels which mediate between God and
human communities. As mentioned previously, kabbalists such as Abulafia identified the Torah as the Active Intellect, Metatron. As he puts it:

> [God] is like one who combines [letters] through the Torah, for the truth of
> its being is the combination of letters, whose secret numerologically equals
> the [seventy] languages through the combination of letters, which are called
> by the seventy names and written by seventy scripts. Each script is seventy,
> and the seventy languages are written in the *hashmal* [Metatron], and they
> are sealed in his name and in his name is his seal.
>
> *(Hayyei ha-Nefesh* 69a, Wolfson, 2000, 198)[12]

Likewise, R Asher ben David writes that:

> [T]hose who are called by His name and by the name of His messengers and His chariot, [are so-called] according to the attachment with which they are attached to Him and according to the mission upon which they are sent before him.
>
> (1996, 77)

Goldberg comments that here, those righteous prophets or servants who attach themselves to God:

> [A]cquire a new identity as a human person, but they also acquire what seems to be a semi-divine identity as indicated by the fact that they are now not only called by their own name or function in this world, but they are now 'called by His name'.
>
> (2001, 52)

This suggests that 'one result of the unitive process is a transformation of the personal identity of the person who enters into the union' (ibid., 2001, 51).

Throughout this study I have argued that Metatron, as the meta-angelic potency who contains the multiplicity of angelic potencies, embodies the Name of God – where the Name is the phenomenal presentation of God. Because, according to the Jewish myth, every nation has its own angelic ruler, its own phenomenal access to the divine, but only Israel has the correct Name by which to know God, in the end times the nations must come to know God through the one single Name. The seventy (or seventy two) nations, each with their own corrupt translation of the one, natural (Hebrew for Abulafia; prelinguistic for Benjamin) language and of the one correct Name of God, will in the end times be reabsorbed into Israel – their languages becoming reunified and their address of God becoming reunited with the correct Name YHWH. At this point, in the oft-quoted terminology of Zechariah, God's 'Name will be One'.

The manuscripts of 3 Enoch 48D:2 vary, but in one of the two versions we find that the seventy names given to Metatron are all engraved on the throne of glory.[13] As discussed in Chapter 1,[14] the names on the throne are those same letters by which the world was created (or sealed), and therefore this passage suggests that it is via the extrusion of Metatron into the seventy names that creation occurs. This theory offers a reprisal of Gikatilla's cosmology: the articulated titles of God, His modes of appearance in the world, are descended from and comprised in the Tetragrammaton – the name which Metatron has been specifically given. If Metatron, as I argued in Chapter 4, in fact *is* the Name YHWH, the manifestation of the final nominal potency of God which comes to be only at the conclusion of reality – the Messianic Age – then our Prince of the Presence functions as the Messiah whose Name existed before creation, and yet whose Name seals creation, reforming history into a single entity, and thereby proffering a kind of salvation by making the created realm no longer a disordered chaos of raw matter, disjointed souls, distant lost stars, but a new constellation of right-eous souls, an idea (not a concept) transcendent in its unity and all-encompassing in its scope – as Metatron is said to cover heaven and earth (3En.9:2–3) and know all of history (3En.11:1–2).

This powerful cosmo-soteriological myth would seem difficult to read philo-sophically; yet, Benjamin does absorb aspects of it into his philosophical cos-mology. In one brief fragment on the logic of language, he writes that:

> [E]very essence contains from the outset a limited – and moreover determinate – multiplicity of essences, which do not derive from the unity in a deductive sense but are empirically assigned to it as the condition of its representation and articulation. The essential unity reigns over a multiplicity of essences in which it manifests itself, but from which it always remains distinct.
>
> (Benjamin, 1996, 273)

Here the apparent unity of an essence contains, latent, all the possibilities of its own representation. Just like Metatron who reigns over the seventy princes of the nations, the 'essential unity' still stands in pre-eminence over its appear-ances. Moreover:

> The multiplicity of languages is such a plurality of essences … [it] is not the product of decadence any more than is the multiplicity of peoples.... If we interpret this doctrine in the spirit of the mystics as pointing to a revealed unity of a linguistic kind, it will mean not just that this primordial language is the one originally spoken, but that the harmony originally created by those spoken languages was of incomparably greater power than any of the individual languages could possibly possess.
>
> (Benjamin, 1996, 273)

The primordial language which unfolded into the tongues of the world held a power unlike any of those descended from it; this single language of pure per-ception could not help but disperse into the different aspects of interpretation which lay dormant within it, but at one time in the process of redemption we might hope to reclaim this unity and see the world again through the eyes of Adam. In fact we can reinterpret the tradition of Metatron and the Princes: it appears to be the articulation of Metatron, God's Name, into seventy fragments which marks the emergence of perspective; the ability to differentiate and to interpret subjectively. Without this diffraction into multiple perspectives, the single Name would be reabsorbed into the unity of God; objects would remain internal only, never with a particularised or subjectified face, which is to say forever without presence to an other.

In one passage Gikatilla expresses his nominal cosmology with a visual meta-phor, writing that the Name YHWH is surrounded by the numerous cognomina, which He wears as a king wears garments. These cognomina are related to the seraphim of Ezekiel 1:23 and Isaiah 6:2, but also the *kenafim* ('wings'), covering here the form of the manifest God: 'His Names and His garments cover Him up and disguise Him' (1994, 177); 'the *kenafim* hide and cover [His Name]' (1994, 179); 'the Cognomens are the essence of the *kenafim* and they are the essence of the 'cloak' which YHVH wears' (ibid.). In this reading there is some kind of equivalence between the wings, the cognomina, and the seventy princes/angels, who cleave to the unerasable holy names (1994, 184). This image of linguistic entities surrounding a core of divinity finds a typological reflection in Benjamin's musing on the nature of translation:

> For if words meaning the same thing in different languages are arranged about that signified as their centre, we have to inquire how they all – while often possessing not the slightest similarity to one another – are similar to the signified at their centre.
>
> (Benjamin, 1999, 721)[15]

The myth of the single language is a powerful and persistent one.[16] The single language represents the reversion of all languages to the sacred tongue, which is the identity of the world's names for God. The single language, as Benjamin has argued, knows only identity, without the differentiation of translation, and without the distance of otherhood. Without the epistemic gap created by names, objects as discrete entities do not exist. The single language cannot communicate, it cannot state anything. It says nothing but identity because it is the play of indetermination which makes communication possible; it is the gaps between words and things which make it possible to use them to refer, to go proxy for objects. The single language can say nothing more than the perfect logical language that Rosenzweig describes in his appropriation of Cohen's infinitesimal calculus: it can state only specific nothings, $A = A$, $A = B$ or $B = B$. As the radical transcendence of Rosenzweig's noumenal elements became unthinkably dark, so the radical *transparency* of the perfectly described renders it non-existent for us. It is tempting to think this is not what Benjamin envisaged – that the perfect language which makes reality diaphanous, as a function of that purpose also destroys all reality; consuming and breaking down the things of the world into nothings, an inexistent chaos of which only nothing can be said – but it is the logical conclusion we reach here. Would Benjamin have preferred a constructive vision, where through naming the world, humanity would finally construct the Name of God, that Name which transcends and unites all? He writes that:

> [I]n this pure language – which no longer means or expresses anything but is, as expressionless and creative Word, that which is meant in all languages – all information, all sense, and all intention finally encounter a stratum in which they are destined to be extinguished.
>
> (Benjamin, 1969, 80)

That the 'creative Word' is to be identified as the Name is suggested by Benjamin's citation of John 1:1, in the same text two pages earlier (ibid., 1969, 78).

As we already found in Abulafia's philosophy, the unification is also destructive process when it is predicated on the singularity of language.

Given also Kripke's (1980) thought as explored in Chapter 4, it is logical that the single Name for God would posit not only a single object, but also a single subject. At this point the peoples of the world have been reunited into a single community who know the one God through His one Name: 'YHWH will be king over all the earth, in that day YHWH will be one and his Name one' (Zech.14:9). But one (unstated) implication of Kripke's theory is that there can normally never be just one name: even if the same *sign* is used by every person or group, each different perspective or use makes it a different name because it defines a new relationship.[17] The material signs which are used for names are ultimately unrelated to them because the name can only be the *use* of the sign as a unique relationship between two parties.

Kripke argued that names must refer rather than describe. As we have found, to be able to describe is to have complete access to an object which is open and apparent, with no hidden aspect; a phenomenal concept not yet refined into an idea.[18] Description then reduces to a flat plane – without the depth which nominal reference provides in allowing for transcendence, all is visible. The object as an other is decomposed and articulated into pieces. Its internality, guaranteed by the name which projects an essentiality forever behind its impermeable membrane, disintegrates in plain sight; an autopsy cannot be carried out on a living subject. To perfectly describe is to murder by a process of identification; to reduce, in Adorno's terms, a non-conceptuality to its concept, or in Benjamin's, an *idea* to its *concept*. A concept which is nothing but an aggregate, constituted of parts and nothing more. To be a unity is to have an internality of some kind, a transcendent aspect which is not stateable and not merely that which materially exists in the world; in Wittgenstein's terms, that which cannot be said clearly, in perfect language. The flat world of perfect description is without play of meanings or alternative interpretation. As Derrida points out, several voices are necessary to speak – multiplicity is essential, even or especially for God, who must be approached from multiple perspectives.[19] This is not to make God multiple (as R Abuya does in understanding Metatron as a second god) but to accept the multiplicity of human understanding, which itself can never reach the oneness *behind* the names.

Likewise then, the ideal of a single name is a kind of death, a dis-integration: both of the object and of language itself. Of language, because all speech which intends to describe is not translation but transliteration, of fact into word; the single name commands a single immediate understanding, without perspective because it claims itself as the only perspective. The word and the fact then are equated in description: there is no difference whatsoever between object, concept, and description. The single name in fact desires (the impossible, contradictory) communication *without* language, or knowledge *without* name. This immediacy is a flatness, absolute knowledge without any play or interaction. The desire for identity and the flatness which comes with identicality, the object being identical to itself and thus knowable in its entirety: without any transcendent element, subsumed in the subject and dis-integrated. Without the name, everything and yet nothing is known; nothing of *that* object which could be named. This single name which is the absence of name thus leads inexorably toward a destruction of other-hood via absolute knowledge. The nameless other is dead and inert, surfaceless and therefore open to view; broken into pieces; lacking integrity. This idolatry of objects, of parts, kills the multivalent truths of relation, reducing all expression to a flat voice of facts: a place of absolute consistency where everything is apparent and nothing hidden.

This is exactly how Abulafia envisions the Messianic goal: God and humanity meet like lovers, in an embrace which becomes a oneness. The Zohar too, in Lachter's reading (2004), posits a unity of human and God through the identity of their essences, one which ultimately, I would argue, is only possible in going *through* the Name; in destroying it, the barrier which segments *Ein Sof* from itself. The image of the Temple curtain torn in two, a curtain cut from the fabric of the garment of creation which bears God's Name.

I have posited herein a formlessness at the heart of objects. The *tohu va-vohu* which God formed into discrete entities by the magical process of naming remains, the prima materia which still constitutes objects remains but is now concealed within order, hidden behind a name. This formlessness in fact is that which guarantees irreducibility: Because there is a concealed element not sub-sumable under any description, which can only be referred to and never totalised by rational language, it is formlessness which is at the heart of all identity. The essence refuses form and is thus inarticulable; the name being both the articu-lation or calling into particularity, and paradoxically that which provides the possibility of inexpressible essence. With identity, chaos is locked away and concealed behind the name. It is confined within named existence and articulated/ divided into multiple relations. Chaos remains but is safe and invisible, for it has become essence.

Then, is the internal essence of God also chaos, *tohu va-vohu*? I am com-pelled to agree with Scholem who calls God 'ultimate formlessness' (1996, 8). If any internal essence is precisely that without form, that which admits a single name because it is knowable only to itself, then what we call God would be that which lacks metaphysics, raw material – that which refers to itself as matter. That which is, the unconditioned.[20]

Conversely, to know the single name at the heart of an object is to flatten that object, to reduce it to identity, in other words *to become it* because it is no longer othered. To know God's secret name then, is apotheosis: exactly as happened with Enoch, who became the little Yahweh and thus an aspect of God,[21] and as Abraham Abulafia claimed is the ultimate goal of the kabbalistic mystic: to become Metatron, sharing the Name of God.

Of course, all this is implied in the initial revelation of the Name to Moses. When God reveals that his Name is AHYH, 'I Am', Moses stealthily transposes into YHWH, 'He Is.' But 'I Am' is the name that all of us have for ourselves. Thus all identity is identical at the core; the core of selfhood is identical within every self. This dimensionless point of I, a qualityless unity, an internality shorn of attributes because it is shorn of relations, I = I *whoever* that I is; A = A for any value of A. But note that this name *is* a description; albeit a qualityless one. It is identical with the described (hence how what it describes is identical in every case); it is the only name which posits not namer and named, but posits the identity of namer, named, name and naming. To be I Am is to exist. Or rather, to exist is to have the name I Am; the self as self-existent *is* open and apparent to itself, and so is susceptible to description. It is perhaps through this that we can understand the interesting fact that *ain*, the primal kabbalistic nothingness which takes the name of AHYH, is also an anagram of *ani*, I. Or as Jeremiah 14:9 puts it: 'You are in our midst, O YHWH; we are called by Your Name!'

So when humanity recognises God in his Name – YHWH – and when we understand it in stating Him as other to us, this is the point where we dissolve into the Name (Metatron), which is the immersion into God, thus understanding God not only as YHWH but in His internal Name of AHYH, overcoming the otherhood of God and recognising that otherness is always also identity, it is because of otherness that identity is possible at all.

And likewise it is the thing in itself, outside of the playful distortions created by the distance of relation (free of the epistemic gap between subject and object), which we know through the single language, which is a logic void of information content, wherein it is described.

The epistemic gap in fact then is the name – the name is the veil between subject and object. In closing the gap, both become the name. They meet in the middle, and become the name that describes – and therefore is – them: AHYH. The unity of subject and object, in the word 'I'.

So, as objects are realised by their names – and the names then are the final element of their identity, that which merely seals together the diverse elements into a unity, so the Name of God is the final element of Creation – once all objects find reality in the names, the names are united into the Name of God which seals all of reality as a unity. The initial oneness of God and His Name then means that it is only via the articulation of creation that God's Name leaves Him, and becomes separate. Until the end of creation, until the Messianic age the Name is hidden, concealed *in potentia*. The history of reality is that of the construction of the Name from the names of objects. History finds meaning in the Name but not because the Name came before and provided for reality, but because it comes after and seals reality – it functions as the end of the world. Paradoxically, it is through this final articulation of the Name that reality will then become concealed – projected behind the Name as an irreducible essence.[22]

Notes

1 Idel remarks: 'Thus, language is not only a result of revelation but is the true expression of the essence of phenomena' – at least, in the material world. Abulafia makes very similar remarks a number of times, many of which are collected by Idel, e.g.: 'Know that for anything in existence, its form corresponds to the name that nature bestowed upon it; for the form, name, and remembrance are identical' (*Sefer Hayyei ha-Nefesh*, Idel, 1989, 147); 'The noun is the root indicating (its) substance and

essence' (*Sefer Or ha-Sekhel*, ibid.). However it is only group nouns, not proper names which Abulafia is considering, at least not proper names given by other than God:

> And the noun informs us as to the true substance and essence when it is the name of a species or a genus. But the [proper] noun does not inform us as to its essence, because it is not specifically designated for him and is not within him.
>
> (*Sefer Mafteach ha-Sefirot*, Idel, 1989, 148)

> Know that these names, that Scripture states were given by God, contain wondrous secrets, and are not all limited to the plain meaning, but rather, they inform us as to the veracity of the hidden meaning of language and its secrets; that God gave them names not out of convention, but in accordance with their nature.
>
> (*Sefer ha-Melammed*, Idel, 1989, 149)

2 Handelman (1991, 71–78) offers a different analysis, placing both Scholem and Benjamin under the aegis of a German Romantic view of language, ultimately descending from the seventeenth century debates about Adamic language; which itself apparently drew upon kabbalistic ideas which had filtered into Christendom during the Enlightenment.

3 Jewish interpretation of this passage has usually focussed on the correctness of the names Adam provides – they are not neologisms, and are not frivolity on Adam's part, but rather are the actual (metaphysically correct) names of the animals in question, and which Adam has somehow accessed. This is supported by rabbinic discussion of the passage, where in Ber.Rab.17:4 the angels manage to *fail* at the task of giving names; this sugya subsequently relates Adam naming not only himself but also God: 'It is fitting for Thee to be called Adonai, since Thou art Lord over all Thy creatures'. The absence of the Tetragrammaton here is interesting (a fact which could indicate the different nature of naming which is taking place in this tradition: one of the name not as designator but as description). Adam does name God 'YHWH' in Pes.Rab.14:9: ' "That is my name" – by which the first man called me.' Also here the angels fail to name the creatures, for they 'did not know' the names. Jacobs (1969) refers to a further rabbinic tradition that Adam competed with the angels and the devil in naming things – God helped Adam with an acrostic containing the first letter of each animal's name. (Unfortunately the source is not specified, and I have been unable to locate such a tradition myself).

4 The objection of Speculative Realism (see Chapter 3) to correlationism is based on the assumption that knowledge or thought is subjective; the theological interpretation, rather, depends on the strong assertion that correct knowledge is in fact something which participates in a trans-subjective and trans-human realm, the noumenal which is part of, or designed by, God.

5 We read in b.Ber.7b that 'the name [of a person] has an effect [upon his life]' (Cf. *Midr. Tanh.*, ha'azinu, 7). A similar motif, of 'the radical effect of the name on its bearer' in the work of S.Y. Agnon has recently been investigated in Hadad (2012, 5). Hadad concludes that in Agnon's Hebrew fiction: 'Names can change lives – for better or worse.... And so, names can destroy lives, names can kill. In Agnon's literary world, they are ultimately a site of catastrophe' (Hadad, 2012, 241). Agnon, who himself changed his name, swapping his given one for a Hebraic neologism descended from *aguna* would appear to be particularly sensitive to that 'link between man and name that determines his fate' (ibid., 242) because 'names do not simply fit or fail to fit their bearers but also make their bearers, mold and affect them' (ibid., 243). *Aguna* itself means a deserted, though not divorced, wife who is still bound to her vanished husband; and standing symbolically for the desertion of creation by God.

6 This opinion is shared by Scholem, who writes that 'The original paradisiac language of man still had this character of the sacred: language was still immediate and authentically bound to the essence of the things it sought to express' (Judaica III:55, Jacobson, 2003, 146).

7 Abulafia's assertion that a key component of the Messiah's mission was the revelation of the 'Hidden Name of God,' along with his knowledge of the nature of this name as AHWY, indicates his belief in his own messianic nature; see Idel (1988, 140 and 95–96). Similarly, R Abraham ibn Ezra cites R Joshua the Karaite as claiming 'there was a tradition in Israel from their fathers that the redeemer of Israel discovered a new name that was not heard' (*Commentary to the Torah, Exod.3:13*, Idel, 1988, 140). On the hidden name see Chapter 2, Note 8.

8 Idel writes:

> However, the revelation of the divine name is only one aspect of the relationship between name and redemption. According to other writings of the ecstatic Kabbalist, the redemptive experience of the messiah is related to his becoming unified with God or the Agent Intellect, a state understood as a deep spiritual transformation, described also as the change of the name of the messiah to a theophoric one. God's theophany at the end of time, described in terms of changes of both names and attributes, is related to the messiah's apotheosis as part of his individual transformation. Given that the process of apotheosis is explicitly described as triggered by a technical use of the divine name, we may conceive the topic of the divine name as comprising the mode of theophany, the goal of apotheosis and the technique to reach it. Or, to express it in other terms: the revelation of the divine names, which is identical with the future reign of the attribute of mercy, is an objective event, namely a theophany, which is to be accompanied by personal redemptions and apotheoses, which consist in a transformation of individuals into spiritual beings, designated by the theophoric names, by means of reciting letters of the divine name.
>
> (2011, 83)

9 On the heavenly book motif, see esp. Baynes (2012).

10 Or another interpretation which we may care to read into the doctrine: all personal names will be one, all having returned into the fold of either YHWH or AHYH, humanity having become Metatron/the Active Intellect, or all having been reabsorbed into God, respectively.

11 As Herman Cohen puts it: ''A day shall come when I will transform the language of all peoples into a clearer language, so that they will invoke the name of God all together' (Zeph.3:9). This is the original Messianic meaning of the divine name' (*Judische Schriften* I, 1924, 63, Scholem, 1972, 67).

12 *Chashmal* (lightning) is a common kabbalistic euphemism for Metatron.

13 Compare the versions in *OTP* 1 (1985, 314).

14 See Chapter 1, Note 24.

15 Cf. *Alphabet of R Akiva*, where each word has seventy meanings.

16 The roots of this myth have been examined in Handelman (1991, 71–78, see Chapter 7, Note 2). Just two modern texts which presume and play on this motif are Adrienne Rich, *The Dream of A Common Language* (1978) and Umberto Eco, *The Search for the Perfect Language* (1995).

17 An idea also suggested by Derrida's *Des Tour de Babel*, wherein he argues that multilingualism is essential; writing that: 'The "tower of Babel" does not merely figure the irreducible multiplicity of tongues; it exhibits an incompletion, the impossibility of finishing, of totalizing, of saturating, of completing something' (1985, 165).

18 Levinas develops a similar theory in *Meaning and Sense* where he writes: 'For God, capable of an unlimited perception, there would be no meaning distinct from the reality perceived; understanding would be equivalent to perceiving' (1996, 35). Perfect perception then does not indulge in the epistemic gap which makes meaning possible, and reality is diaphanous.

19 '[I]t is always necessary to be more than one in order to speak … exemplarily, when it's a matter of God' (1995, 35).

20 Janowitz (1989) claims that the Hekhalot literature presents an alternative creation where God speaks His own Name, as opposed to Genesis where he speaks the names of the world – but here we find that these two are in fact the same.
21 The angelification of Enoch *et al.*, is in fact a divinisation of those who come face to face with God; likewise, the bearing of the Name is the divinisation of those who come close enough to understand the single Name: 'the vision of the Glory entailed the transformation of the visionary into an angelic likeness of that Divine Image' (Rowland and Morray-Jones, 2009, 334).
22 Abulafia wrote that:

> The entire Torah constitutes the names of the Holy One, blessed be He, and in this there is neither addition nor diminution and every letter is a world in itself. Our sages O.B.M. have already stated that had the Torah been given to us in its proper order, man would be able to resurrect the dead [Midr.Tehillim 3:2]. And God obscured the order (so that it not be misused by the degenerates of the generation), and revealed it to those who are worthy of being able to resurrect the dead by its means.
>
> (*Sefer Mafteach ha-Tokhachot*, Idel, 1989, 80–81)

This relates to the effective reconstruction of the correct order, via meditation on the Name. This meditation, in leading to the Messianic Age, where everything again 'bears its correct name', may be a metaphor for the resumption of identity, everything has the same name – AHYH – so there is no externality, only the internality of identity.

Bibliography

The Babylonian Talmud (32 vols). 1990. Edited by Rabbi Dr. I. Epstein. London: The Soncino Press.

Bet ha-Midrash (3 volumes). 1855. Edited by A. Jellinek. Leipzig.

Midrash Rabbah (10 vols). 1939. Translated by R Dr. H. Freedman and Maurice Simon. London: The Soncino Press.

Old Testament Pseudepigrapha (2 vols). 1985. Edited by James Charlesworth. New York/London: Doubleday.

Asher ben David, R. 1996. *Complete Works and Studies in his Kabbalistic Thought.* (Hebrew). Edited by Daniel Abrams. Los Angeles: Cherub Press.

Baynes, Leslie. 2012. *The Heavenly Book Motif in Judeo-Christian Apocalypses 200 B.C.E.–200 C.E.* Leiden: Brill.

Benjamin, Walter. 1969. *Illuminations.* Edited by Hannah Arendt, translated by Harry Zohn. New York: Schocken.

Benjamin, Walter. 1977. *The Origin of German Tragic Drama.* Translated by John Oliver. London: NLB.

Benjamin, Walter. 1978. *Reflections.* Translated by Edmund Jephcott. London: Harcourt Brace Jovanovich.

Benjamin, Walter. 1996. *Selected Writings v1: 1913–1926.* Edited by Marcus Bullock and Michael V Jennings. London: Harvard University Press.

Benjamin, Walter. 1999. *Selected Writings v2: 1931–1934.* Edited by Michael W. Jennings, Howard Eiland, Gary Smith. London: Harvard University Press.

Dan, Joseph. 1986. *The Early Kabbalah.* Mahwah: Paulist Press.

Derrida, Jacques. 1985. Des Tours de Babel. In: Joseph F. Graham. ed. *Difference in Translation.* Translated by Joseph F. Graham. London: Cornell University Press, 165–207.

Derrida, Jacques. 1995. *On the Name.* Edited by Thomas Dutoit, translated by David Wood, John P. Leavey Jr., and Ian McLeod. Stanford: Stanford University Press.

Eco, Umberto. 1995. *The Search for the Perfect Language: Making of Europe.* Translated by James Fentress. Oxford: Blackwell.

Gikatilla, Rabbi Joseph. 1994. *Sha'are Orah: Gates of Light.* Translated by Avi Weinstein. London: Harper Collins.

Goldberg, Joel R. 2001. *Mystical Union, Individuality and Individuation in Provencal and Catalonian Kabbalah.* PhD diss., New York University.

Hadad, Shira. 2012. *'A Thousand Names They Called Him': Naming and Proper Names in the Work of S.Y. Agnon.* PhD diss., Columbia University.

Hall, Robert G. 2011. Pre-existence, Naming, and Investiture in the *Similitudes of Enoch* and in Hebrews. *Religion & Theology* 18, 311–333.

Handelman, Susan A. 1991. *Fragments of Redemption: Jewish Thought and Literary Theory in Benjamin, Scholem & Levinas.* Bloomington: Indiana University Press.

Hanssen, Beatrice. 2004. Language and Mimesis in Walter Benjamin's Work. In: Davis S. Ferris. ed. *The Cambridge Companion to Walter Benjamin.* New York: Cambridge University Press, 54–72.

Idel, Moshe. 1988. *The Mystical Experience in Abraham Abulafia.* Albany: State University of New York Press.

Idel, Moshe. 1989. *Language, Torah, and Hermeneutics in Abraham Abulafia.* Albany: State University of New York Press.

Idel, Moshe. 1998. *Messianic Mystics.* London: Yale University Press.

Idel, Moshe. 2010. *Old Worlds, New Mirrors: On Jewish Mysticism and Twentieth-Century Thought.* Philadelphia: University of Pennsylvania Press.

Idel, Moshe. 2011. *Kabbalah in Italy 1280–1510: A Survey.* New Haven: Yale University Press.

Jacobs, Noah Jonathan. 1969. *Naming Day in Eden: The Creation and Recreation of Language.* Revised edition. London: The Macmillan Company.

Jacobson, Eric. 2003. *Metaphysics of the Profane: The Political Theology of Walter Benjamin and Gershom Scholem.* New York: Columbia University Press.

Janowitz, Naomi. 1989. *The Poetics of Ascent: Theories of Language in a Rabbinic Ascent Text.* Albany: State University of New York Press.

Kripke, Saul A. 1980. *Naming and Necessity.* Oxford: Blackwell.

Lachter, Hartley. 2004. *Paradox and Mystical Union in the Zohar.* PhD diss., New York University.

Levinas, Emmanuel. 1996. *Basic Philosophical Writings.* Edited by Adriaan T. Peperzak, Simon Critchley and Robert Bernasconi. Bloomington: Indiana University Press.

Rich, Adrienne. 1978. *The Dream of A Common Language: Poems 1974–1977.* New York: W.W. Norton & Co.

Rowland, Christopher and Christopher R.A. Morray-Jones. 2009. *The Mystery of God: Early Jewish Mysticism and the New Testament.* Leiden: Brill.

Scholem, Gershom. 1966 [1965]. *On the Kabbalah and its Symbolism.* New York: Schocken.

Scholem, Gershom. 1972. The Name of God and the Linguistic Theory of the Kabbalah. *Diogenes* 79, 59–80.

Scholem, Gershom. 1973. The Name of God and the Linguistic Theory of the Kabbalah. *Diogenes* 80, 164–194.

Wolfson, Elliot R. 2000. *Abraham Abulafia – Kabbalist and Prophet: Hermeneutics, Theosophy, and Theurgy.* Los Angeles: Cherub Press.

Wolin, Richard. 1994 [1982]. *Walter Benjamin: An Aesthetic of Redemption.* Second edition. London: University of California Press.

8 Conclusion

The metaphysical meaning of the Name

Some historical conclusions and avenues for further research

As the frontispiece to this study, I cited Rosenzweig's statement,

> For what is it with the name? An ethic of the name would still be conceivable – (one's given name). Even a logic of the name – (name of a thing). But a theology of the name? Even when otherwise a name is not sound and smoke, yet with God surely it is?
>
> (Rosenzweig, 1998, 43)

The study contained within has attempted an answer to this question, and I concur with Rosenzweig, who straight away answers himself: 'We shall see: precisely not with God'. The Name of God has herein been demonstrated to have a profound and lasting meaning in Jewish thought; one that persisted from biblical times, through the Second Temple Period, into rabbinic and later kabbalistic Judaism. Finally this doctrine emerged once again, albeit transformed anew, in the secular Jewish philosophy of the twentieth century.

Scholem claimed that for the Jewish mystic, the Name of God could be conceived as the metaphysical origin of the universe, the universe being constituted linguistically, and language being an outgrowth from the Name. This study has demonstrated that, while this is unquestionably the case within the realm of Kabbalah, the earlier sources which fed the kabbalists' imaginations present a far more complex picture. The identity of the Name with the Word spoken at creation is a much more convoluted matter than has previously been believed – one tied to the early rabbis' search for doctrinal identity in the chaotic milieu of Late Antique monotheism. The Name, despite Fossum's claims, was not a creative tool for the rabbis, although it formed a seal on creation, constraining into identity. Neither was it, as the hypostatic-nominal tradition suggested, a second-god or in any way ontologically distinct from God – in fact the rabbinic writings on Metatron make clear that the Name – as also expressed in the Prologue to John – is the phenomenal aspect of God, God-for-Human.

While I can conclusively agree with Scholem and Dan that the Name rejects semantic interpretation, having no formal meaning, and their claim that the

Name sits at the heart of language, I must reject Dan's claim that the divine Name(s) 'are the essence of God' (1996, 237). This study has shown that there is a thoroughgoing distinction between God in essence and His Name, although this was articulated in a complex and misleading way by Gikatilla, to name one. Yet the Name, just like the object it represents, can only function as a unity – when broken into its components it is no longer Name.

One reading which the structure of this study allows is the demonstration of how certain trends nascent in Second Temple Judaism, and evicted from the rabbinic movement during Late Antiquity, exercised influence on the – nominally rabbinic – Jewish mysticism of Medieval times. The first four chapters established that, while ancient biblical traditions regarding the Name-Angel fed and contributed to certain hypostatic and binitarian trends in Late Antiquity, eventually culminating in Christianity, such a blunt ontological reading was rejected by the rabbinate, along with the associated tradition of the Name's role in creation. Thus the Name-Angel, whose implied associations with both creation and messianism were within easy reach during the later centuries of the commonwealth, came under scrutiny during the rabbinic reformation (due, I believe, to their use in explicitly Christian circles as well as for simple theological reasons); yet these traditions were preserved in the subterranean passageway created by the Hekhalot literature.[1] These texts themselves made innovative theological leaps, while also absorbing new interpretations and formulations of ancient material from the emerging Christian communities (semi-Christian, Jewish-Christian, or however we may choose to label the large grey areas between rabbinate and Church). The rabbis found themselves arguing against not only the new Christian *conversos*, Gentiles who sought to appropriate the scriptures into their own theological paradigm, but also against Jews who were imbibing these developments into their world-view in new and unusual ways. The name Metatron became a byword for a specific variety of hypostatic entity, one including certain Christian as well as Gnostic ideas, and one which the rabbis sought to redefine in their own way. This redefinition drew on extant traditions such as those of the Memra in order to refine the binitarian implications which were growing in influence, and to present the Name-Angel as an aspect of God, as it appears to have been in biblical times. While the Merkavah mystics drew on the developments in rabbinic thought, their unsystematic approach led to a proliferation of angelic names and terms, all of which however still basically represented the same concept: an angelic 'servant' who is God's vicegerent, shares in His Name, and carries out His will in the world.

The Medieval mystics thus inherited a wealth of material which was complicated, unsystematic, unorthodox *and yet*, intellectually striking and curiously well-aligned with certain implications extant in the biblical and rabbinic literature so as to provoke the conception of a mystical substrata to the teachings of the Talmud.[2] Thus, the mystics – who were themselves, of course, also rabbis – adopted a group of traditions which the early rabbis had actively sought to evict from their Judaism, all the while reading these traditions as implicit within and complementary to the rabbinic texts.

Metatron's reappearance in a messianic role in the later chapters may seem provocative, especially given the prior emphasis on the 'correction' to which rabbinic Judaism subjected the nascent Name-Messiah doctrine. To an extent this is a result of certain contemporary trends within scholarship which is pursuing such topics with great fervour, although with an agenda which is in no way unitary. My own conclusions regarding this are that the hypostatic developments during the Second Temple period are linked inextricably to the Israelite Name-Theology, which was nascent in the Name-Angel of Exodus and *shem* of Deuteronomy (among others). The Second Temple period generated a host of intermediary figures, all of which draw on and develop the inchoate principles present in the biblical text. During the extrication of Judaism and Christianity from one another, these doctrines were tugged into new shapes and elements of them dropped entirely. Metatron, while displaying undeniable similarity to Christ, should in no way be thought of as a Jewish answer to him, but rather as a uniquely rabbinic attempt to interpret the traditions which had emerged within the broad field of Judaism in accordance with their own theological principles. In my reading the rabbinic Metatron is not a binitarian power, but an aspect of God; an epistemological function made necessary by the very unknowability of God's essence.

As a postscript to these comments, I should note that although the tradition is buried deep within Christian theology, it is still there to be found by some inquisitive thinkers. I am referring here to Aquinas,[3] and of course to Paul Tillich who wrote that: 'A name is never an empty sound; it is a bearer of power; it gives Spiritual Presence to the unseen', and 'within the name, that which bears the name is present' (1963, 77). In particular there has been an on-going debate since the beginning of the last century, when the Russian Orthodox monk Ilarion, formerly of Athos, wrote his treatise *In the Mountains of the Caucasus* (1907) – a text which helped found a sect calling themselves the Imyaslavie, or *name-glorifiers*, claiming that the name of Jesus had special powers when 'clung to' in prayer, that 'in the name of God there is present God Himself – with all His essence and with (all) His infinite properties' (1907; Tchantouridzé, 2012, 222), and finally that 'the name of God is God (Himself)'.[4] There is an urgent need for more research on both the historical and theoretical relationship between kabbalistic and Imyaslavie thought.

More broadly, much work remains to be done on the influence of the Kabbalah on modern intellectual movements generally. Allison Coudert has provided several studies demonstrating the influence of the Kabbalah on Leibniz, and the on-going project of translation and publication of Pico Della Mirandola's kabbalistic library will enable scholars to study the texts which were being made available from the fifteenth century onwards.[5] However, the ways in which Leibniz's absorption and restatement of these ideas have gone on to influence the work of twentieth century philosophers – surely not only Wittgenstein and Benjamin – requires much deeper investigation.

These two areas are not unconnected: While the Imyaslavie have effectively redeveloped some important ideas of the Kabbalah, many of the notable Imyaslavie theologians (by whom I mean Pavel Florensky, Alexey Losev, and Sergey Bulgakov) were polymaths who displayed an intense interest in the kabbalistic writings of Mirandola (Burmistrov, 2007). These influences deeply affected the aforementioned thinkers' mathematical work, much of which was based on the application of naming to set theory (Graham, 2011); itself an interesting development from a Jewish mathematician with notably mystical leanings, Georg Cantor (the basis of Horwitz's aforementioned study *Reality in the Name of God* [2012], who may have drawn on some kabbalistic influences in his doctrine of infinity – although at this stage we can only speculate). Research connecting the dots from the kabbalistic doctrines which, along with the Cappodocian Fathers, helped to form Imyaslavie theology and practice, is, I believe, an important avenue for further study which will help to demonstrate the lasting influence of kabbalistic thought on the modern world.

Analysis

> It is as if the nothing said *I am nothing* and one were to ask then whether anything had come to pass.
>
> (Derrida, 2002, 217)

I will now highlight some philosophical themes emerging from the foregoing study, which require tying together. It is worth at this point restating a notion to which I have referred throughout this study: while I have been principally examining the Name of God, the conclusions reached have much broader implications for naming generally. The Jewish mystical theology has been examining the nature of essence; the philosophical speculation on the nature of God, the rejection of attributes in search of simplicity and unity, and the attempt to discover how then humans can interact or relate to God, these are all part of a project which maps with surprising ease onto entirely a-theistic and a-theological philosophical concerns. Because: 'The name of God is only a special case of the problem of names in general', (Rosenzweig, 1999, 89) theology itself can be seen as a meditation on questions of existence, essence and relation. The conclusions found regarding God can then be expanded to all issues of subject and object or internality and externality.

Bielik-Robson (2012; 2014) presented the Jewish nominal tradition as a rejection of Greek metaphysics, a conclusion supported by this study: in the name, static being is replaced with being-with; it is the presence of the object. 'To be' is an abstract statement, one to which could be attached only a limited order of truths. Language and names are always partially performative rather than information bearing: to name is to call into presence, thus forming a point of contact between subject and object. It designates relation not essence, rupturing the staticity of both Kantian phenomenal subjectivity, and Platonic eternal being. What Bielik-Robson calls 'Jewish Nominalism' stands in contrast to the Greek philosophical tradition, which, 'more or less begins with the insight that a word is only a name, i.e. that it does not represent true being' (Gadamer, 2004, 366).

This *negative nominalism*, the belief that a name stands somewhere on a scale of correctness based on the success of its correlation with an object, defines the Greek-dominated western philosophical approach ever since – at least until the explosion of secular Jewish philosophy in the twentieth century. For those philosophers, a name either describes or fails to describe – an approach which seems likely to be based on a particular inherited metaphysics which enthrones Being as a static form: a Nature set in stone, a substance which exists truly only in isolation from everything else. There is a tradition in Jewish thought which sees Being temporally, as something which occurs rather than being located; being is presence and as such is always related to that to-which the thing is present; being in this sense is always relative, always stated in experience rather than masked by experience.

As Handelman (1982, 7) claims, Greek thought bases truth on the geometric method, which is to say on a spatial brand of mathematics – but as Rosenzweig argued, maths is silence. It does not speak, it communicates nothing other than convoluted tautology – as indeed it must, because if the truth which is sought is that of utter transcendence in a realm outside any subjective knowledge then meaningful, content-bearing statements cannot be made. In refusing to make names informative, we allow the transcendence of that which is not *in* the world, and not merely phenomenal.

So where Greek philosophy tried to make human thought arbitrary in detaching the name from the thing (and ending in the Kantian dualistic divide between the ontological and the phenomenal), Jewish thought rather, according to the arguments advanced herein, perceives a continuum between object and subject, a continuum which is constituted in language. Names, which are equatable with our ideological delineations (where an *idea* is a unified and simple whole, as opposed to a totalising empirical *concept*), are understood both as the subject's ability to identify and relate to an object, and as that particular object's capacity to appear to a subject, that particular subject.

While it appears that kabbalistic thought, drawing on the Neoplatonic tradition which it inherited from Maimonides, suggests an internal nature outside of relation which is articulated as the AHYH, the I Am of an object, it became evident that this nature is *at once*, one of utter emptiness, the Ain which is hidden within the Ein Sof, the unarticulated chaos of *tohu vavohu* which has no nature in its unordered aggregation of base matter; *and* one that is shared by all beings, that chaos of unformedness which is concealed behind the form of the name. While this on the one hand suggests a cosmic unity which is divided only by names, a Nothingness which creates the illusion first of single unity (AHYH, or Keter) and then of difference (YHWH), from which all identities emerge as names separating the Nothing from itself, on the other hand we can find in this doctrine the kernel of a new metaphysics of relation. If internal essence is nothing, then objects find themselves made real only in their relation to one another, and yet this relating always hangs on the suggested transcendental presence of otherhood; while names define and create this otherhood, otherhood is not predicated on a static transcendental nature but rather on the appearance in relation to the subject.[6] Thus nature is both transcendentally and fundamentally relative, articulated in and as name. When Gikatilla argued that AHYH, although being the root of the Tree, is not the true source because that is the Tetragramm-aton which is the trunk, this is how we should read it: It is the Name of other-hood (YHWH), not the name of identity (AHYH), which is truly the statement of God's Being and is irrevocably united with His nature. And in the grander sense, being is found *in* the name: the being of something is identified via its relation, but *without being subsumed* as *this relation.*[7]

Through several chapters of this study I have argued that God's *middot* are sublated in the Name YHWH; the manifest potencies, which have been con-ceived variously as angelic princes, lesser divine names, and the kabbalistic sefirot, are all ultimately suspended in the grander metaphysical entity of the Name, also known as Metatron. The Name, YHWH, then stands as the manifes-tation of God's presence but not as an ontologically independent being. Rather, it is the point of contact between God and Human, and is the formative aspect of both in their dependent independence. The Name is the substrate through which particular qualities and characteristics emerge and in which they are unified. The Name, the unity of phenomenal aspects, itself is neither God nor not-God, but is that principle through which God appears and can be known.

That the Name/Metatron is determined as much by the human, is evident: before the world was created God and His Name were one; i.e. they were ident-ical, they were one thing. But once creation has occurred the Name becomes non-identical with God, because while the Name is known, God is not. Ein Sof/ AHYH becomes differentiated from the phenomenal, *mental being* of God, which is the Name YHWH.

I have argued that names occupy a special place in language – in fact, a place *outside* it. Whereas language can describe, making factual claims (which may or may not be true) about the world and thus existing in a relationship of gradated correlation with it, names do not have meaningful content, and as such are inten-tional: an action directed from a subject towards an object. Proper names occur as the black holes within language, existing on its border; they are non-literal words, words that cannot describe but only refer, and in doing so refer to that which is not describable: identity, the identity of an other.

A name, then, does not speak: it points. And in transmitting no information about the named, the name is silent; as silent as that which is named. As Rosenz-weig (1971) argued, meaning is something which comes only via human lan-guage: the non-scientific, non-absolute talk which exists in the interstices between individuals. Meaningful language is in some sense always a kind of error, because it is founded on the uncertainty of subjective knowledge, admit-ting an epistemic gap between knower and known. In attempting to translate the putatively absolute nature of an object's non-subjective being, we use words and terms that come from relational subjectivity, and so fail the task of approaching the in-itself. The concealed interior of the objective cannot be described by means of folk-language; to attempt statements about this dark realm we could use only the stark languages of maths and logic; languages which admit only, in the last analysis, identity. Logic speaks always of A=A (that same rubric which Rosenzweig used to describe the dark ground of God in his system); while the subject cannot reach this interiority, the name gives some possibility of meaningful reference; it allows the transcendent object into the mental world, rupturing the autistic field of subjectivity; creating a portal to otherhood. It is the name which allows for relation, which in not attempting to describe, provides for contact with the other. This is the insight of Levinas. But there is more to the name than this. In this membrane-like activity, the name provides presence and yet, it asserts a boundary. The name cannot be gone beyond: even when Abulafia approaches the heights of *unio mystica*, he never claims the mystic becomes more than Metatron.[8] What lies beyond the name? It is Nothing; an essential nothing; a nothing which is not a thing, but only the unformed *prima materia*, a base substance which awaits identity, awaits unity, a unity which is conferred by the giving of a name. What constitutes the objects which God speaks into existence, their internal substance, always existed. But in speaking their names He gives them form, giving them identity, solidity and meaningful existence. A name seals a thing into a unity; the indivisibility of the point-like name is directly in concert with the indivisibility of the unified object.

Naming, as an act which the subject commits, is constituted via subjectivity. The subject then is carried into the name as well, as Abulafia (and Benjamin after him) saw: the subject is always moving toward the Name, part of its nature. Humans, in creating other subjects by the process of naming, progress towards *the* Name. They are lifted toward it in the generation of order, of metaphysics, through objects which conceal, defuse, and *seal* the evil of unformed matter.

And what then is subjectivity? The subject who knows itself, knows itself only as I, as I who is: AHYH. The subject is not concealed from itself, but states its own identity in the name which describes, and announces the unformedness of first matter. All identity is Nothing; nothing but identity. As God's hidden ground can be expressed only via terms such as AHYH, Ain, or Ein Sof, so with every subject: the internality which is not *in* the world (although it is identical with it[9]), is pure existence, stuff unformed – formless. This identicality of God and Human, when viewed from the inside, is difficult to fathom, even more difficult to place within the usual platitudes about difference/separation and Jewish religion. And yet it is there.[10]

The essence of God is present as the essence of everything – every object in its internality has the same qualities as God – in fact a qualitylessness which is both unique, unified and total. The inner nature – the essential – is what unites all objects in their difference from each other, an internality which is only possible if projected as transcendent, an internality which at once unites *and divides* all.

This anti-essentialism, the anti-static cloth from which this theory is cut, may best be expressed by Wittgenstein's claim that: 'Words *have meaning only in the stream of life*' (1996, 913). And so objects exist – they are what they are – only in their presence to the subject. Objects are always conditioned by subjects, and without the othering function of a subject to formalise an object into a unity, it remains chaotic and unformed.

One Jewish philosopher who I have referred to only briefly is Baruch Spinoza, who famously wrote that God and nature are interchangeable names for the same single substance, of which everything partakes.[11] God's essence then is the essence of everything: God is all internality. This leads to 'the radical epistemological view according to which the knowledge of God's essence is both trivial (EIIP47) and the sole beginning of knowledge of all things (EIIP10S2)' (Melamed, 2012, 103). Likewise we read in Jeremiah 14:9, 'You are in our midst, O YHWH; we are called by Your Name!' Throughout the kabbalistic tradition we find this concept repeated, that the Name of God applies not just to God. In MMerk§592: 'Everything You created in Your world recites to Your Name.' Moshe de Leon approvingly quotes Isaiah 43:7, 'everyone that is called by my Name, for my glory I created him, I formed him, even I made him' (*Sefer ha-Mishkal*, 4r, Wijnhoven 1964, 166). Wijnhoven comments: 'This verse reveals the mystery of man. He is called by 'the name of the creator', and he is part of the world of creation, of formation, and making' (ibid.). In fact, the ongoing tradition that the Messiah and the Righteous share in the Name of God, likely plays on this motif.[12]

Michael Fagenblat writes that in the Maimonidean system: 'Knowledge of God is a category mistake, for the structure of knowledge – based on definitions, essential attributes, accidental attributes, predicates, and relations – fails when it comes to the absolutely simple, unique, and incomparable unity of God' (2010, 116[13]). But if this is the case then also it fails when it comes to the absolutely simple unity at the heart of all identity; which, we now know, is itself identical with God. Just as it is the Name which presents and conceals the essence of God, so all names present and conceal essence, thus being inextricably tied with the nature of essence and with being which is always being-to, essence being in a way a construct, a projection from the use of names but which takes on its own metaphysical reality; and while this is the case it is also true that names are all that exist, in that they are all that is there to differentiate Ain from itself, to give the appearance of separation; 'in order that the desire beyond being not be an absorption, the desirable (or God) must remain separated within desire: near, yet different – which is, moreover, the very meaning of the word "holy"' (Levinas, 2000, 223).

Because naming (as opposed to describing) infers unity and singularity, God – according to the traditions we have been examining – is in some ways the *only* named rather than described thing; He is the only true unity. But it is the principle of unity which makes for the possibility of any individual substance, and so God – YHWH, unity itself, is written into the existence of every thing that is, because to be named is to be one, to be more than an aggregate, and thus to partake in the unity of YHWH.[14] But most interestingly, the unity itself is empty: just as mathematics can all be reduced to articulations of nothing via the Empty Set, all individual existence is reducible to the tautologous identity of $A = A$ which is also Ain, nothing: to be I Am (AHYH) is to be nothing, which is what is at the heart of named existence (YHWH). As Moshe de Leon put it:

> [S]ince no one can contain God at all, it is called Nothingness, *Ayin* … anything sealed and concealed, totally unknown to anyone, is called *ayin*, meaning that no one knows anything about it. Similarly, no one knows anything about the human soul; she stands in the status of nothingness, *ayin*…
>
> (*Sefer Shekhel ha-Kodesh* 19–20, Fagenblat, 2010, 108)

One important implication of Cantor's set theory is that even within an infinity a part (a subset) can actually be larger than the set itself. Of course any unity is made up of elements, each of which is themselves a unity[15] – the description given herein of the nominal unity is founded on exactly the same precept as Cantor, that a unity (set) is infinitely divisible; there is no base ontological unit, no fundamental atomic level is ever reached, other than unity itself. For Cantor, numbers are themselves sets – beginning with zero as the Empty Set, the set containing nothing, one can progress automatically through the numerical sequence: the set containing the Empty Set has one member, the set containing those sets has two, etc. The numerical sequence then, as divided down reaches only nothingness – the Empty Set, which is identical in this study with the empty name of identity, AHYH. That an infinite set can still be bounded, i.e. given a finite expression and contained within brackets effectively replicates my own argument that the name, while pointing outside of the finite, factual, world, is still entirely within it as the expression of that which *cannot* be contained; the named can be viewed from all angles, it is visible in the world as an entity, as something with finite borders; and yet it cannot be broken down, it is opaque to our sight; the inexpressible within it is like the infinity between two numbers.

For Wittgenstein, logic is the ultimate transcendental,[16] there can be nothing higher than logic or outside it which conditions it; yet there is 'something' not within it, something which is not a thing – the illogical is the unsayable, the unthinkable, that which can only be referred to and not described. To be a thing, to be finite, articulated and describable immediately places one within the world as a fact composed of objects. AHYH, manifest through the Name, is ultimately unsayable (which is why Moses switches it into YHWH). Wittgenstein's division of the world into the sayable and the showable demonstrates an important point: that which is linguistically describable has no use of the name; that named, that suggested, is that which transcends the world.

This means that Wittgenstein's unsayable in fact is internality; the internality of an other who is not in our world.[17] Any object is not susceptible to definition as definition denies it as a thing, making it an aggregate of properties, a mass which can be correlated with words, and totalised within the world. This would be to cut the shoots: not merely the division of the potencies embodied in the sefirot, but the emptying of the divine essence *into* the sefirot, the essence into the phenomenal qualities so that there is no unknown aspect; only in unifying the sefirot into the Name does Ein Sof become projected beyond that Name. It is only through the Name that God can be known because it is only through the Name that God can be unified (as the *shema* may suggest). In naming we create a limit to the finite/sayable, and beyond that can only be the singular – that which is not any thing, and ergo simply 'ehyeh'. I Am is not reducible or fragmentable.[18]

There is an important point here which needs to be extrapolated. Kripke argues that an identity requires no essence 'behind' the manifest properties, to which they might adhere. Identity as a particular incorporates qualities but is not reducible to them, and is not conceivable without them.[19] We can understand this as a rejection of the traditional metaphysics of identity, and a reframing of the question in terms of the flattened phenomenal world-view we are now familiar with: while talk of essence seems to make an ontological assertion, if we consider identity as a pattern or arrangement, it is something which does not exist in-itself but binds together as a whole the elements which constitute it. In this case, there is clearly no *object* in any sense other than metaphorically; there is no *thing* which we can call the essence. Rather, this is apparent only in the fact that these properties are united as an object. Just as Wittgenstein claimed there were no objects corresponding to grammatical terms of relation, rather the relation was the otherwise-indescribable structure demonstrated by the elements' relation to one-another in a *sachverhalte*. So too there is no *substantial* internal identity; such must always be a question of metaphysics, and thus not of what exists in any literal sense. There is an unfortunate tendency to take metaphysical claims as something of a parallel to *physical* ones, only describing a different realm, a merely different *kind* of substance. This depends on the privileging of physical matter as the paradigm of substance, and the idea that all that is in any sense 'real' must exist in a way similar to the peculiar kind of objective existence which we ascribe to matter.[20]

If all truths are identical and empty, A = A, the statement of content then falls to either the untrue or the nominal. Since the untrue makes claims which do not reflect reality, we are left with the nominal which makes a non-factual claim, that of relation – a relative and non-absolute truth is thus the model of a meaningful statement, a word which points but does not depict, which has reference but no meaning, yet can still be used truthfully or not. Because: names make for knowledge; a knowledge of relation ... of the spaces between that separate identities, whereas the untrue does not give knowledge and the true gives knowledge only of the emptiness of identity.

Now we can reread the formula A = A, where A is AHYH (Nothing) and = is the Name that stands between. Without the Name =, there would be only A, which is not even a statement but only the beginning of an alphabet.

In the end then, all that exists are names; it is only names which exist as points of division within the single universal essence, Ein Sof, which is itself nothing – the mere flatness of unordered matter. As Elliot Wolfson writes of the kabbalistic hermeneutic, they:

> [P]ortrayed the goal of the linear process as coming full circle; when one reaches the core at the end and returns thereby to the surface from the beginning, one realizes that where one ended up was where one had begun, and

consequently one comes to see that the innermost secret was folded within the initial allusion.

(Wolfson, 1999, 1981)

By going to the name the human can discover our essential unity with the essence that *appears* to be on the other side. Absence is unknowable except in and as presence – the absence which constitutes divine selfhood, the lack of all property or complexity which is the nature of internality, cannot by its nature be known by another but only as self – which is to say as radically immanent presence unmediated by the differential complexity of otherhood. AHYH can be stated only in presence *as* (as oneself) rather than presence *to* (to one, as another). Notably, if the name is presence, then by removing or rending it, we find not mystical union with what was concealed behind it; we find nothing.

This is perhaps the most curious implication of this study: if God and self are both the same substance, and this substance is in fact nothing, an emptiness constituted only of absent *prima materia*, the formless evil of *tohu vavohu*, then the Name is the only thing which has being. The Name not only *allows* for otherhood as has previously been suggested, but *is itself* otherhood, because it is the only other-than-Nothing; it is the only holiness apart from the evil of matter which pervades all selfhood, even the divine self. This is why it is only through the process of naming, of generating names, that redemption is possible: names redeem substance from itself. It is only via naming – in Cantorian terms, by the creation of sets[21] – that nothingness progresses into somethings, and can repeat the process infinitely, thereby generating the meta-substance of divinity; *the* Name.

When everything is made clear, transparency overrides meaning; sense is lost in the mechanism of facts. In a picture reduced to its elements, the relationship between those elements is made diaphanous, so that not only the viewed (the object) becomes a mere aggregate but the viewer (subject) also is lost through its integration into that whole; in going through the name rather than stopping at it and respecting it as a boundary, the subject dissolves into an only apparent complexity which is as flat and meaningless as the projected heat-death which stands at the end of the universe. Entropy is usually termed as complete order, but it also is the absence of complexity – everything laid flat, disconnected, the depiction of a cosmology which denies cause and effect: all things separate and unrelated; *without metaphysics*. This would be the end-point of the progression *through* the Name: a disorder in extension. Only by going back to the Name but stopping at that point can the relationship to unity be glimpsed, and thus the unity of each organism be withheld, reminding us that in being one we participate in the One, the One of the Name which is the Name of the One. The Name which exists as a suspension of all names, in both senses of the term: suspending in abeyance, but also a pensile permanence in which all are preserved. It is also here that we realise internality is the only true universal, and that which transcends individuality threatens always to override us as particulars, to tear and rend the protective confines which singular names provide; the threat is both within and without, waters above and below.

It is curious that in this reading, Metatron straddles the divide, being the human which meets God and the God which meets the human, and thereby evidencing the symmetry of the Name. As the membrane between finite and infinite Metatron represents the role of the name in communication, and the fact that a name always states not just the object but also the subject – in Graham Harman's rereading of Husserl, the third 'intentional object' which comes into being as two distinct beings form a system.[22] That God's name for humanity is the same as humanity's Name for God demonstrates, this symmetry has been established; the implication is that in any act of relation, my name for another is identical with the other's name for me, a name which states the relationship of us both, in the state of relating with the other.

Finally it must be said: because name exists only as relation, and as without name all is chaos, it is then only in relation, in relating to others, that identity is found, and that creation is guaranteed; as God and Human find themselves through each other, so all humans find themselves only in relation to other humans, through naming each other. This is the secret of human identity and nature – Benjamin claimed that the human expresses his essence in naming other things, but our essence as individuals is found only in the process of naming each other, which is to say, of forming bonds with others.

Notes

1 It may be especially pertinent to note that more than once, Christian interpretation seems to associate the 'servant' of God with the 'Name' of God – on this see Hurtado (2007).

2 While much has been written about the problematic anachronism of asserting a rabbinic 'orthodoxy' in Late Antiquity, the time may be ripe for more research to focus on the nature of such a presumed orthodoxy even into the thirteenth century; the medieval mystics in Europe certainly do not appear to regard the esoteric material in any different light to the legal material and it is my view that their inheritance of a large body of tradition was without the striations of normativity which we now apply.

3 His claim that: 'Were we able to understand the divine essence itself as it is and give to it the name that belongs to it, we would express it by only one name' (*Summa Contra Gentiles* 1.31) clearly draws directly on his reading of Maimonides.

4 For an in-depth analysis of the Name theology of the Imyaslavie in relation to Deconstruction – though sadly without any reference to the Jewish aspects of either – see Gourko (2009).

5 This joint project by the Institut für Judaistik of the Freie Universität Berlin (Germany) and the Istituto Nazionale di Studi sul Rinascimento (Firenze, Italy) has so far seen five publications including manuscripts of Gikatilla, Recanati, and the Bahir, as well as previously unpublished texts.

6 The people of Babel said: 'Come, let us build ourselves a city, and a tower with its top in the heavens, and let us make a name for ourselves; otherwise we shall be scattered abroad upon the face of the whole earth' (Gen.11:4). Of course, the people were scattered; their attempted name was shattered into seventy fragments, demonstrating that we cannot make names for ourselves; naming is a process dependent upon otherhood.

7 Judith Butler has pointed in this direction in arguing that the political (that is, the socially-constructed metaphysical) reality of some sexual minority groups is impossible if 'there is no frame and no story and no name for such a life' (2004, 25). This

refusal or inability to comprehend then is a kind of violence which should most correctly be countered by the immediately social nature of the body; and it is this socially integrated ('porous') nature which for Butler defines the possibility of identity; not from within but from without, by the network within which it exists.

8   By contemplating the Supernal Name the mystic becomes identified with it, emptied and filled with the Name; but as such is not absorbed into the formal identity of AHYH, remaining on the very edge, the zero dimensional point of the Name YHWH as the point at which God and human meet.

9   'I am my world' (Wittgenstein, 1974, 5.63).

10 It is worth noting the findings of Lachter, that 'the human person and the divine person … are both embodied as manifestation of the limitlessness of *ein sof*' (2004, 86); 'according to the Zohar, the core of the human self is the core of the divine self. It is the infinite non-being that is the grounding for all being, expressed as that which is beyond all linguistic demarcation' (ibid., 129); 'The kabbalist is capable of mystical union with God because he is, in the end, already one with God' (ibid., 137).

11 *Deus sive natura*, a concept which may well descend itself from kabbalistic speculation; Abraham ibn Ezra made the gematrial equation of *elohim* and *ha-teva* (86), which was also picked up by Abulafia and later Abraham Herrera.

12 In the Zohar we read that Adam 'is the form that includes all forms … the name that includes all names' (*Greater Holy Assembly*, 3:135a). Rosenberg comments that here, the Zohar 'regards "Adam" as one of the names of God' (1973, 8). In another passage the Zohar claims Adam is a divine name (1:34a). On Gikatilla's use of the spelled-out version of the Tetragrammaton, יוד הא ואו הא, which gematrially equals *Adam* (45), see Blickstein (1983, 157–161). In some Late Antique texts Adam's name was converted into a four-letter variant, perhaps reflecting the four-letter Name of God: Syb. Or.3:24–6 and 2En.30:13–14 – the latter making even stranger the fact that *2 Enoch*, although now dated convincingly to pre-70CE (Böttrich 2012; Orlov 2012, though see the criticisms offered by Navtanovich 2012 and Suter 2012), contains no indication of importance for the Name of God at all. This suggests that the text comes from a Jewish community disinterested in the nominal theology and, although drawing upon much of the earlier Enochic speculation, perhaps not even aware of *Similitudes*. In contrast, witness the Samaritan fascination with the Name – detailed in Chapter 1 – the Samaritans being a community who privilege Moses but demonstrate no interest in Enoch whatsoever (and of course, the relationship between Moses and the Name are obvious). What is most interesting given the tradition's ostentatious absence from much of the Enoch literature is that subsequently Enoch-Metatron should have come to be identified as the Name itself.

13 Cf. Maimonides 1956, I.50–52, 58.

14 This notion of the universal participation in the One as a guarantor of individual identity was an integral part of Neoplatonic thought, and likely known to the early Kabbalists from there. However, it is worth reiterating the striking fact that the *aleph*, representing the number one and therefore unity, functions as the initial letter of AHYH, and also graphically symbolises the value twenty-six. The creative word YHY, is twenty-five, one less than the YVY of aleph; and thus intimating *aleph* (1) in itself.

15 This counter-intuitive precept which has been a formative aspect of this study, that the unity, the one of subjective identity, is constructed metaphysically over and above the no-less-valid notion of any one's perpetual divisibility, has also been argued for recently by Katerina Kolozova in *Cut of the Real: Subjectivity in Poststructuralist Philosophy* (2014).

16 A=A is transcendental in Wittgenstein; but not transcendent. It is necessarily immanent in the world.

17 This question of internality relates to the philosophical problem of other minds. The problem is that their internality posits an alternative to one's own, a perspective and

world-view which challenges the immediate validity of ours, and in this sense they are non-reconcilable. An alternative internality then threatens to overwhelm, to annihilate one's own. The boundary must be established which can prevent this from occurring; according to the arguments herein, this boundary is the name. To be face to face with another and not feel the threat or risk of being subsumed, consumed by them.

18 It could be argued that I Am is indeed fragmentable into I and existence. I reject this along lines which I believe Wittgenstein would have approved: To state 'I' already demands existence of it; the fact that the word has sense means that its referent being unreal is illogical. In this way, even the English I Am is effectively a tautology, a redundant statement, although this is not as grammatically clear in the Hebrew, which is what we should adhere to in this discussion. *Ehyeh* is a single word representing a single concept.

19 'What I do deny is that a particular is nothing but a 'bundle of qualities' whatever that may mean ... [philosophers] have asked, are these objects *behind* the bundle of qualities, or is the object *nothing but* the bundle?' (Kripke, 1980, 52). But it is neither: the particular object cannot be reduced any further.

20 'Real' is of course nothing but a term of attack: it is used to promote the aspects of reality which we believe are important, and to denigrate those we do not. It is nothing but polemical, and in philosophical terms is as meaningless as saying 'the world exists'.

21 'By a manifold or a set I understand in general every Many that can be thought of as a One' (letter to Richard Dedekind 1883, in Graham and Kantor, 2009, 26).

22 Harman argues that not ethics but aesthetics is first philosophy, claiming that 'ethics unjustly divides the world between full-fledged humans and robotic causal pawns, in a manner little different from Descartes' (2012). While acutely aware of the danger of subsuming ethics to any other philosophical approach, I am sympathetic to the call for a pre-ethical foundation for the ethical, conceivable as the possibility of a non-sentient subjectivity of which aesthetics and ethics are a development. The unfortunate apparent attack upon ethics then would be only of an ethics that privileges the human subject, and the basis for human-human relations in the structure of consciousness would be found in the structure of object-object relations in themselves.

Bibliography

Old Testament Pseudepigrapha (2 vols). 1985. Edited by James Charlesworth. New York/London: Doubleday.

The Zohar (12 vols). 2003–2014. Translated by Daniel C. Matt. Stanford: Stanford University Press.

Aquinas, Thomas. 1955. *Summa Contra Gentiles, Book One: God.* Edited by Joseph Kenny, O.P., translated by Anton C. Pegis. New York: Hanover House.

Bielik-Robson, Agata. 2012. 'The Promise of the Name: 'Jewish Nominalism' as the Critique of Idealist Tradition.' *Bamidbar* 19(3), 11–35.

Bielik-Robson, Agata. 2014. *Jewish Crypto-Theologies in Late Modernity: Philosophical Marranos.* London: Routledge.

Blickstein, Shlomo. 1983. *Between Philosophy and Mysticism: A Study of the Philosophical-Qabbalistic Writings of Joseph Giqatila (1248–c.1322).* PhD diss., Jewish Theological Seminary of America.

Böttrich, Christfried. 2012. The 'Book of the Secrets of Enoch' (2 En): Between Jewish Origin and Christian Transmission. An Overview. In: Andrei A. Orlov and Gabriele Boccaccini. eds. *New Perspectives on 2 Enoch: No Longer Slavonic Only.* Leiden: Brill, 37–67.

Burmistrov, Konstantin. 2007. The Interpretation of Kabbalah in Early 20th Century Russian Philosophy. *East European Jewish Affairs* 37(2), 157–187.

Butler, Judith. 2004. *Undoing Gender.* London: Routledge.

Coudert, Allison P. 1995. *Leibniz and the Kabbalah.* London: Kluwer Academic Press.

Dan, Joseph. 1996. The Name of God, the Name of the Rose, and the Concept of Language in Jewish Mysticism. *Medieval Encounters* 2(3), 228–248.

Derrida, Jacques. 2002. *Acts of Religion.* Translated by Gil Anidjar. New York: Routledge.

Fagenblat, Michael. 2010. *A Covenant of Creatures: Levinas' Philosophy of Judaism.* Stanford: Stanford University Press.

Gadamer, Hans Georg. 2004. *Truth and Method.* London: Continuum.

Graham, Loren. 2011. The Power of Names. *Theology and Science* 9(1), 157–164.

Graham, Loren and Jean Michel Kantor. 2009. *Naming Infinity: A True Story of Religious Mysticism and Mathematical Creativity.* London: Belknap Press of Harvard University Press.

Gourko, Helena. 2009. *Divine Onomatology: Name of God in Imyaslavie, Symbolism, and Deconstruction.* Saarbrücken: Vdm Verlag Dr. Müller.

Handelman, Susan A. 1982. *The Slayers of Moses: The Emergence of Rabbinic Interpretation in Modern Literary Theory.* Albany: State University of New York Press.

Harman, Graham. 2012. Aesthetics as First Philosophy: Levinas and the Non-Human. *Naked Punch.* Last modified 21 June. Accessed 9 April 2015. www.nakedpunch.com/articles/147.

Horwitz, Noah. 2012. *Reality in the Name of God, or, Divine Insistence: An Essay on Creation, Infinity, and the Ontological Implications of Kabbalah.* Brooklyn: Punctum Books.

Hurtado, Larry W. 2007. 'Jesus' as God's Name, and Jesus as God's Embodied Name in Justin Martyr. In: Sara Purvis and Paul Foster. eds. *Justin Martyr and His Worlds.* Minneapolis: Fortress Press, 128–136.

Ilarion, Schemamonk. 1907. *In the Mountains of the Caucasus.* (Russian). Batalpashinsk.

Kolozova, Katerina. 2014. *Cut of the Real: Subjectivity in Poststructuralist Philosophy.* New York: Columbia University Press.

Kripke, Saul A. 1980. *Naming and Necessity.* Oxford: Blackwell.

Lachter, Hartley. 2004. *Paradox and Mystical Union in the Zohar.* PhD diss., New York University.

Levinas, Emmanuel. 2000. *God, Death and Time.* Translated by Bettina Bergo. Stanford: Stanford University Press.

Maimonides, Moses. 1956. *The Guide for the Perplexed.* Translated by M. Friedlander. New York: Dover.

Melamed, Yitzhak. 2012. Spinoza's Deification of Existence. *Oxford Studies in Early Modern Philosophy* 6, 75–104.

Navtanovich, Liudmila. 2012. The Provenance of 2 Enoch: A Philological Perspective. A Response to C. Böttrich's Paper 'The Book of the Secrets of Enoch (2 En): Between Jewish Origin and Christian Transmission. An Overview'. In: Andrei A. Orlov and Gabriele Boccaccini. eds. *New Perspectives on 2 Enoch: No Longer Slavonic Only.* Leiden: Brill, 69–82.

Orlov, Andrei A. 2012. The Sacerdotal Traditions of 2 Enoch and the Date of the Text. In: Andrei A. Orlov and Gabriele Boccaccini. eds. *New Perspectives on 2 Enoch: No Longer Slavonic Only.* Leiden: Brill, 103–116.

Rosenberg, Roy A. 1973. *The Anatomy of God: The Book of Concealment, The Greater Holy Assembly and The Lesser Holy Assembly of the Zohar with The Assembly of the Tabernacle.* New York: Ktav.

Rosenzweig, Franz. 1971. *The Star of Redemption.* Translated by William W. Hallo. London: Routledge & Kegan Paul.

Rosenzweig, Franz. 1998. *God, Man, and the World: Lectures and Essays.* Edited and translated by Barbara E. Galli. Syracuse: Syracuse University Press.

Rosenzweig, Franz. 1999. *The New Thinking.* Translated by Alan Udoff and Barbara E. Galli. Syracuse: Syracuse University Press.

Suter, David W. 2012. Excavating 2 Enoch: The Question of Dating and the Sacerdotal Traditions. In: Andrei A. Orlov and Gabriele Boccaccini. eds. *New Perspectives on 2 Enoch: No Longer Slavonic Only.* Leiden: Brill, 117–124.

Tchantouridzé, Deacon Lasha. 2012. In the Name of God: 100 Years of the *Imiaslavie* Movement in the Church of Russia. *The Canadian Journal of Orthodox Christianity* 7(3), 216–228.

Tillich, Paul. 1963. *The Eternal Now.* New York: Charles Scribner's Sons.

Wijnhoven, Jochanan H.A. 1964. *Sefer ha-Mishkal: Text and Study.* PhD diss., Brandeis University.

Wittgenstein, Ludwig. 1974. *Tractatus Logico-Philosophicus.* Translated by D.F. Pears and B.F. McGuinness. London: Routledge.

Wittgenstein, Ludwig. 1996. *Last Writings on the Philosophy of Psychology, Vol. I.* Chicago: University of Chicago Press.

Wolfson, Elliot R. 1999. 'The Glorious Name and the Incarnate Torah.' In *The Jewish Study Bible*, edited by Ade Berlin and Marc Zvi Brettler, 1979–1990. Oxford: Oxford University Press.

Appendix

Hagiga 15a manuscript variations

The various manuscript versions of the list of proscribed heavenly activities from b. Hagiga 15a

לא עמידה ולא ישיבה לא קנאה ולא תחרות לא עורף ולא עיפוי	Munich 95
לא עמידה ולא ישיבה ולא קנאה ולא תחרות ולא עורף ולא עיפוי	Goettingen 3
לא ישיבה ולא קנאה ולא תחרות ולא עורף ולא עיפוי	London BL Harl. 5508 (400)
לא עמידה ולא ישיבה לא קנאה ולא תחרות ולא עורף ולא עיפוי	Munich 6
לא עמידה ולא ישיבה ולא קנאה ולא תחרות ולא עורף ולא עיפוי	Oxford Opp. Add. Fol. 23
לא ישיבה ולא קנאה ולא תחרות לא עורף ולא עפוי	Vatican 171
לא עמידה ולא ישיבה ולא קנאה ולא תחרות ולא עורף ולא עפוי	Spanish Print (c.1480)
לא ישיבה ולא תחרות ולא עורף ולא עיפוי	Pesaro 1514
לא ישיבה ולא תחרות ולא עורף ולא עיפוי	Vilna/Bomberg
(לא עמידה לא) ישיבה לא ערף ולא ייפוי ולא קנאה ולא תחרות	Oxford – Bodl. heb. d. 63 (2826) 32
לא ישיבה ולא תחרות ולא עורף ולא עיפוי	Venice Print (1521)

Index